The
Eleventh
Wing

The Eleventh Wing

An Exposition of the Dynamics of I Ching for Now

Khigh Alx Dhiegh

Nash Publishing, Los Angeles

Title page art by Walter Boye, Prior of Taoist Sanctuary

Library of Congress Catalog Card Number: 70-186928
International Standard Book Number: 0- 8402-1252-6

Published simultaneously in the United States and Canada
by Nash Publishing Corporation, 9255 Sunset Boulevard,
Los Angeles, California 90069.

Printed in the United States of America.

First Printing.

To Mary Kathleen, Mary Adelaide and Capitola —who have effected the most significant changes in my life.

Foreword

It is said that Confucius once remarked, "If additional years were added to my life, I would give fifty to the study of the *I*, and might then escape falling into great errors." In any event, he wore out the leather thongs that bound his copy of this Chinese classic three times. Confucius approached the consultation of *I Ching* as a ritual; for him, the ceremony included unfastening the leather thongs which held the text together.

Khigh Dhiegh has his students approach the *I* in a similar ritualized fashion. Indeed, there is no way that *The Eleventh Wing* can pay justice to Dr. Dhiegh's keen abilities as a teacher. His students learn to use *I Ching* as part of a ceremony preceded by meditation. Thus, each consultation of *I Ching* becomes an exercise in attaining an altered state of consciousness, an experience in abandoning one's traditional time-space boundaries and entering non-ordinary reality. Approached in this manner, *I Ching* is far more likely to provide a useful direction than if one merely opens its pages at random and points blindly to a kua.

For several centuries, ten classical commentaries on *I Ching*, the Ten Wings, have been used by students of this celebrated text. Dr. Dhiegh's "Eleventh Wing" adds a new dimension to the understanding of this document. The first two wings concern themselves with the structure of the kua. The third and fourth interpret the symbolism of the kua. Numbers five and six deal with the kua in terms of their cultural implications. The seventh wing discusses the concepts of yin and yang while the eighth deals with *I Ching*'s system and content. The ninth and tenth wings stress the continuity of the kua and define each symbol. What we have in *The Eleventh Wing*, therefore, is a discussion of the *I*'s relevance to the contemporary world.

Chinese sages were using *I Ching* while the forebears of the Athenians were living a semicivilized nomadic life in the hills of Greece. *I Ching*, the *Book of Changes*, stands with four other texts (the *Book of History*, the *Book of Odes*, the *Book of Rituals*, and the *Annals of Spring and Autumn*) as the ancient classics which represent the earliest Chinese written cultural heritage. How is it, then, that the *I* is considered relevant to modern people and their concerns? The *I*, for centuries, has assisted people to trace their paths wisely in a complex world. Never has life seemed more complex than it does to the twentieth-century individual. As a variety of institutions, social codes, and religious dogmas lose their relevance and fall into disrepute, *I Ching* remains useful because it represents an open system. The *I* does not impose itself on the universe but follows each day's course of events, allowing for a swerve here and a turn there. It is process-oriented rather than doctrine-oriented, thus always remaining in tune with the times.

There is no doubt that *I Ching* can lend itself to misuse, just as other potentially powerful procedures can be abused. For example, the peyote ceremony devised by members of the Native American Church appears to assist the spiritual development of many American Indians who ingest this hallucinogenic plant under the structured conditions provided by adherence to their ritual. However, peyote has been known to precipitate panic, confusion, and anxiety among some individuals who take the substance in a casual, nonritualistic manner.

Indeed, sexual intercourse is capable of providing the human being with some of his most ecstatic and meaningful moments, especially if performed within a structure which adds to the esthetic development, the sensual experience, and/or the love relationship of the partners. However, sex can be abused if the episode is connected with force, violence, trickery, manipulation, or motives exterior to the mutual growth and satisfaction of those involved. Nature's most treasured gifts can be used positively or negatively; anything capable of transporting an individual into the realms of bliss, joy, and understanding, can also—if misused—perpetuate his ignorance.

As with all potentially powerful processes, *I Ching* should not be utilized too often. Most of life's decisions can be made by reflecting upon one's alternatives, thinking about what one has learned from past experience, and combining these thoughts with one's subjective "feeling" about the course to follow. *I Ching* is best utilized when there is a conflict between "thinking" and "feeling," or when none of one's alternatives appear to be workable. When a person has reached the limits of his personal resources, both rational and emotional, it may be time to turn to *I Ching*. The ritual of manipulating the sticks or tossing the coins, the meditative approach to the task, and the symbolic nature of the designated kua may well give a direction that was missing before. As a person's consciousness becomes transformed through *I Ching*, memories, possibilities, and insights which were previously unavailable may open up, thus providing an unanticipated direction and plan of action.

One of *The Eleventh Wing*'s chief virtues is its discussion of causality and acausality. It is tempting to proclaim that everything is the result of cause and effect, or to dogmatically assert that all events are synchronous. However, an individual's freedom would disappear under both circumstances. If everything dates back to a 'first cause', fatalism would be the most reasonable attitude to adopt. Yet, if everything is completely random, one's actions would never produce results and a person could not participate in the complexities of change. Only a universe which holds the potential for both causal and acausal events provides intelligent entities, such as mankind, with opportunities to fully participate in the flow of events. The student of *I Ching* knows when to drift in his canoe down the primordial stream, when to steer his canoe gently so as to take advantage of the current, and when to row his craft energetically to avoid a mishap. Those who do not row at all find themselves beset with misfortune as often as those who refuse to adapt to the underlying current and attempt to row continuously.

In my experience, I have found *I Ching* to be of special interest to many young people. Because they live in a quickly changing world, those who survive and prosper have learned to be flexible and open-minded. Hence, they are often aware of the several viable ways one may approach cause and effect, as well as space and time. The most perceptive of these young people also see the necessity for structure in their lives; a willow tree may bend with the wind but it will blow away if it is not firmly rooted. *I Ching,* and the wisdom it contains, can help provide this structure. Like a gem of great value which has been polished for thousands of years, it reflects a beauty and a durability that enables its students to avoid the hazards of both future shock and the stress which accompanies our contemporary world of pollution, violence, and chaos. How delightful it would be if the younger generation of the Western world found this ancient Eastern text to be the twentieth century's best survival manual! *The Eleventh Wing* will facilitate this possible turn of events, thus contributing to both the survival and enhancement of human consciousness.

STANLEY KRIPPNER, PH.D.

Director of the Dream Laboratory
of the Department of Psychiatry
Maimonides Medical Center
Brooklyn, New York

Contents

Introduction

The present neo-technological period of global development is characterized by widespread 'ego-strife'—man warring against man—and an equally widespread 'eco-strife'—man warring against nature. In a time of contention and universal conflict only the principles of the highest and most simplifying laws can be effectual and pervasive. Conflict is resolved through union of opposites: this is the evolutive law of harmony. This law applies to the world of the senses and forms the basis of aesthetic pleasure, and it also applies to the world of mind and spirit where it forms the basis of a universal system of psychology. What we commonly call history forms one of the subbranches of this system of psychology, which itself is but an aspect of celestial harmonics. In fact, the acceleration of conflict is what defines history from the harmonic point of view. When conflict reaches a maximum, there is a resolution of tension through a transformative union of opposing forces.

This is precisely what is described by Dr. Khigh Dhiegh when he speaks of a worldwide process of intertransference now taking place, exemplified by the "acceptance of *I Ching* by Westerners at the very time it appears that most Chinese are turning away from it." Dr. Dhiegh continues: "The 'mystical' East is divesting itself of saffron robes, gilded shrines and temples filled with choking incense. The 'materialistic' West, stunned by the mutilation of its land and natural resources, the ethical decline of its society and the moral and psychological bankruptcy of individuals—all of which has evolved in the name of progress by its pragmatic technocracy—now turns to experience the psychological warmth of a saffron robe, the aesthetic pleasures of a gilded shrine and the spiritual excitation of temples filled with choking incense."

In the terminology of *I Ching,* the yang of the West is now transforming itself into yin. The most ancient is becoming accepted as the most modern; the vestiges of the neolithic suddenly remanifested in the heart of the neo-technological. In the world of modern Western art, the post-modern era has already begun, and side by side with examples of precision and computer-tooled artifacts are ritualistic objects and environments. The rusted gear shafts of the machine sprout the feathers of the near-extinct eagle. There are children of the more advanced technocracies who prefer to go barefoot, wearing the overalls of their farmer grandfathers, or the buckskin of a race that is now scarcely with us. The misapprehensive scorn these customs as regressive atavisms, the put-on of a generation of children who no longer care about the progress of a society that bores them. Others claim that a widespread anti-intellectualism is spreading and that the most cherished ideals of the present civilization are slowly dying.

Whether it is dying or not, it is certainly clear that the West is undergoing a profound transformation of values and life-styles. The consequences are worldwide, since it is the West, and most specifically the United States, that has dominated the world in ideas and technological innovations since the inception of the brief period known as the Industrial Age. Born with the machine was a disquietude, felt from the beginning by such thinkers as Rousseau and the poets and artists of the Romantic period early in the nineteenth century. By the 1890s Paul Gauguin had fled civilization for the climate and culture of the "noble savage" in the South Seas only to find the missionary and the bureaucrat stalking his shadow. Early in the twentieth century, D. H. Lawrence left the coalfields and smokestacks of England for the remnants of the native American cultures in Mexico and the American Southwest, prophesying the return of the plumed serpent to avenge the brutal deracination of the race of Quetzalcoatl. Other Western writers and thinkers such as Herman Hesse and Dr. Carl G. Jung explored the symbolisms of the outer precincts of non-rational modes of thought. By the middle of the twentieth century, it became utterly clear for the Western non-rationalists that there was physically no place left to go. The cultural conclusion of this fact was that the Westerner had to transform himself where he was, in his very own home.

By the 1950s, Zen Buddhism was being practiced and investigated by an influential circle of artists and writers. Though some were still traveling to and spending time in the East to absorb the disciplines and spiritual techniques, most returned for a further synthesis. By the late 1960s, aided by the novel Western innovation of lysergic acid diethylamide, and a vogue for hallucinogenics, in general, an unprecedented interest in Oriental cultures and religious forms had become a distinguishing feature of the avant-garde. FM radio stations incorporated daily readings from the *Book of Changes* into their regular programming. In addition to Karate and Judo, Aikido, Kung Fu, T'ai Chi Ch'uan and Hatha Yoga were becoming disciplines to be pursued at the local YMCA. If the turmoil and social unrest of the 1960s had achieved anything, it was firmly to implant in the mainstream of Western culture outposts of more ancient forms of thought and life. Simplicity, an increasing spirituality, and a tendency to turn away from the great complications of contemporary life for one more directly rooted in nature—these are the characteristics developing in the midst of the most advanced technologies. A dialectical process of a surprising nature has manifested itself; in direct contrast to the materialism of recent Western civilization, a counterpoise of mysticism and a correspondingly simplified, though synthesized, life-style has resurfaced. William Irwin Thompson has stated:

A new ideology is being created in advance of its social need; what particular institutional form this ideology will take no one can say ... Perhaps it will take no institutional form at all, for it seems that social institutions are no longer adequate vehicles of cultural evolution ... Now only mysticism seems well-suited to the post-institutional anarchism of technetronic culture on the one hand, and the infinite, post-human universe on the other ... Mystics think that they are solitary visionaries of God, but actually, in the transition from civilization to what Teilhard de Chardin called the "planetization of mankind," they have become the true political scientists. Mysticism seems impractical in technological culture because it is the Marxist negation of that culture and the affirmation of the next culture ... The mechanist and the mystic may be opposites in content, but they are not opposites in structure, because cultures progress dialectically.

It is against this background of synthesis and metamorphosis that *I Ching* emerges in the New World. It offers itself as one of the *Easy Handbooks* by which post-technological man can enter into a new relationship with the universe. Careful study of the *Book of Changes,* as foreseen by Master Knecht in Hesse's *Magister Ludi,* is one of the aids in training the mystic as the political scientist of the future. But transitions from one phase of cultural dialectic to another are never simple or easy, at least from the point of view of the previous cultural attitudes which, based in long-established tradition, are deeply rooted in the mind. As evidenced by the example of Richard Alpert/Baba Ram Das, not even 300 or more "acid trips" could effect a permanent change of mind. What the Buddhists call a "turning in the deepest seat of consciousness" is ultimately what is required. Ivan Illich clearly intends this idea in appending to his concept of "deschooling" the further notion of "deconditioning." Unless a thorough and concerted effort is fearlessly pursued, the change of the current cultural revolutionary or reformist will only be superficial, and even worse, ineffectual. Or, put in the words of the *I* in the Judgment to kua 48, Ching, (the Well):

The Well: The town may be changed, but
the well cannot be changed.
It neither decreases nor increases.
They come and go and draw from the well.
If one gets down almost to the water
and the rope does not go all the way,
or the jug breaks, it brings misfortune.

As Dr. Dhiegh has perceived—and here lies the preeminent value of *The Eleventh Wing*—as long as Westerners approach *I Ching* with a fundamentally intellectual or rationalist mind, it is as if "one gets down almost to the water and the rope does not go all the way." The result is misfortune, for the rope is the rope of intuitive consciousness without which *I Ching* has little effective value. The *Book of Changes* is bound to no one form, and the Wings are the records of its growth, much like the rings of a tree. As each phase of growth of a tree is in accordance with the nature of the particular season, thus accounting for the variegated appearance of every tree, so the Wings of *I Ching* reflect the changing needs of the times through which the *idea* of change has passed. Change is adaptability, and it is adaptability which makes change unchanging. *The Eleventh Wing* is, then, the eleventh strand of the rope that reaches into the well—Ching—of divine inspiration that has always been the source of the sages of change.

In the present instance the primordial idea of change as originally developed by the Chinese is not only confronted with a new time, but a new geographical region as well. The situation of *I Ching* passing from China to this country is reminiscent of the Sufic tale of the stream running into the sands of the desert. The stream is cautioned by the sands not to hurl itself in its accustomed manner through the desert lest it totally dissipate its energy, but rather to let itself be absorbed by the wind which will carry it across the desert and release it on the other side in the form of its natural element water, whence it may once more become a stream. If the current popularity of the various translations of *I Ching* may be compared to the wind of the Sufic tale, then *The Eleventh Wing* of Khigh Dhiegh is the channel whereby the rain of the *Book of Changes* upon our spiritually destitute times may flow once again as a stream of refreshing vitality. The lesson of *I Ching*, survival through change and maintenance through a continual adaptability, is one that may be applied to our own situation. Adaptability is the clue to further evolution. In evolution it is not really the species that is ultimately furthered, but the very impulse for life. *The Eleventh Wing* emphasizes what is crucial to survival, and hence to further evolutionary possibilities: adaptation to a new mode of consciousness—the consciousness of symbolic awareness, of renewed intuition. In contrast to the rationalist one-at-a-time approach, it is multiple, synchronistic, many-leveled and wholly absorbing. To a literalist it is a wilderness recalling Baudelaire's "Correspondences":

> . . . a temple whose living colonnades
> Breathe forth a mystic speech in fitful sighs;
> Man wanders among symbols in those glades
> Where all things watch him with familiar eyes.

The Eleventh Wing brings home the message time and time again: to understand the *I* one must enter that temple of living colonnades, divesting oneself of the intellectualist mannerisms of the present civilization, and try to appreciate the symbols—the pa kua—of the *Book of Changes* as directly as possible, to see the world innocently and without names, to breathe its air and smell its perfumes without the dictionary of encumbrances that we call mind or intelligence. To the rationalist, the realm of symbolic awareness, the world of intuition, *is* a wilderness—but as the Sierra Club motto cautions, "In wilderness is our survival."

As I write this introduction, I look out through my window at a forest of pines and a sky of moving clouds overhead. My friends, who have been here longer than myself and who are more aware of the overall ecological pattern of North America, assure me that this area of the northwest coast of this vast continent is one of the last remaining areas of wilderness. The races of Europeans who came here before me have all but exhausted themselves in these forests and on these shores. The spirits of a decimated race still move with the wind through the pines, and from far in the West, beyond the farthest of the Pacific shores, other spirits are moving continually east toward the sun. All this meets here on the western coast of the North American continent, resulting in a speeding up of life processes: evolution in action. The last frontier is the first; where the visible ends, the invisible begins. Knowing having been atomized into a billion discrete packets of knowledge, quantified and microfilmed, finally evaporates, leaving in its wake a great void, the void of 'knowing'.

For the disinherited race of Western intellectualism, the great sea of 'knowing' cannot really be apprehended through words, only through symbols, for symbols alone hint at the vision of wholeness. In many different ways Khigh Dhiegh presents this truth, which is the essence of *The Eleventh Wing*: a philosophical psychology and a psychological philosophy presented through the deceptively simple forms of broken and unbroken lines. As Dr. Dhiegh points out, "Knowledge results from a restriction of our 'knowing'," To return then to 'knowing', the path of words must be eschewed.

Comparing what Khigh Dhiegh calls the state of 'knowing' to what the rationalist and present-day civilized person would call "wilderness," recalls the words of the Sioux Indian, Chief Luther Standing Bear:

> We did not think of the great open plains, the beautiful rolling hills, and the winding streams with tangled growth, as a "wild." Only to the white man was nature a "wilderness" and only to him was the land "infested" with "wild" animals and "savage" people. To us it was tame. Earth was bountiful and we were surrounded with the blessings of the Great Mystery. Not until the hairy man from the east came upon us and the families we loved was it "wild" for us. When the very animals of the forest began fleeing from his approach, then it was that for us the "Wild West" began.

'Knowing', too, is defined only by the advent of knowledge. As the earth has slowly become civilized (literally, citified), so the mind has become 'knowledgized' and confined within various reasonable categories. Beyond the limits of the categories lies the wilderness of 'knowing' with its wild beast, the repressed and hunted creatures of the unconscious, or the spirits and entities of a consciousness not yet arrived at by any except the few enlightened ones, those who have been able to penetrate to the realm of the Great Mystery, Wu Ch'i.

So, we have come full circle and are faced with the problem of entering a wilderness of our own creation, and which is essentially our original state: 'knowing'. What is difficult is relinquishing the deep-seated conditioning factors of an essentially materialist outlook. Buckminster Fuller refers to this process simply as one of passing from the physical to the metaphysical:

> This is the essence of human evolution upon Spaceship Earth. If the present planting of humanity upon Spaceship Earth cannot comprehend this inexorable process and discipline itself to serve exclusively that function of metaphysical mastering of the physical it will be discontinued, and its potential mission in universe will be carried by the metaphysically endowed capabilities of other beings on other spaceship planets of the universe.

The direness of the metaphysical imperative at this time more than anything else has called for the *The Eleventh Wing*. The actual capabilities of *I Ching* can only be comprehended and put to work from a nonmaterial or metaphysical point of view. Only from this point of view can the unique capabilities of the human organism be unleashed. The kernel of this nonmaterial understanding is the very essence of *I Ching*—symbolic awareness. In drawing our attention to the pa kua, the eight basic symbols of *I Ching*, Dr. Dhiegh has performed an invaluable service. Like all tools, *I Ching* must be appropriately approached and handled to yield the right results—nothing less than a transformation from the present limited state of consciousness to an all-embracing intuitive understanding. This is the state in which man knows himself in all things and all things within himself. The approach to this new cosmological viewpoint can only be through symbols which are the bridge between the lodestone of the physical body, drawing upon itself our sensations and psychic consciousness, and that immeasurable realm which is the ground of all experience—the source-realm Wu Ch'i, the Great Mystery, called by the Buddhists *Alaya Vijnana*, "stored consciousness." But, as Khigh Dhiegh comments, "Not many Westerners approach the *I* at a level of image representation and archetypal significance." This fact, once again, underlines the importance of *The Eleventh Wing* which does exactly that: it brings the eight emblems of change into what may be considered their proper role as universal world symbols, capable of transcending cultural barriers precisely because of their nonlinguistic nature. This is the teaching of *The Eleventh Wing:* to go beyond the literal meaning, to tune into the symbols themselves. "Kua is that part of *I Ching* that enables us to grasp, handle and/or manipulate something." If, through the use of symbol, an 'at-one-ment' is attained, Khigh Dhiegh cautions that even the symbol itself must be transcended: "When you become one with things, how could there be a symbol?"

Until this state is reached, however, Khigh Dhiegh presents, through *The Eleventh Wing*, a number of brilliant symbolic devices, aids and ideas. In this respect *The Eleventh Wing* serves another purpose. It demonstrates that the *I* is a multileveled system; it is "a discipline that can effectively succeed in subjectively bringing us into an objective self-relation." It is a system for acquiring self-knowledge that is a complete cosmological, psychological and sociological conception capable of being adapted to all situations. And this is so because of its profoundly symbolic character, the ceaselessly changing yin-yang process that determines the temporal appearance of the kua—each one of which contains within itself the possibility of every other kua.

At this point I feel that words no longer suffice for this introduction, especially since the main import of *The Eleventh*

Wing is the necessity of going beyond words and intellection, in general, for a proper comprehension of *I Ching*. For this reason I am prompted to continue my own dialogue with *I Ching* by asking it for its view about introducing *The Eleventh Wing*. After all, it is quite an event for a tradition like *I Ching* to be so generously and vitally explicated as it is in *The Eleventh Wing* in a land and culture far from its seeming origins.

The kua I received was Sui, ☰☰ , the lower image being Chen, "The Arousing," ☰☰ , and the upper Tui, "The Joyous," ☰☰ , translated by Wilhelm/Baynes as "Following," by Siu as "Acquiring Followers," by Blofeld as "Following, According With," and by Legge, "Sui symbolizes the idea of following." What is indicated is the idea of acquiring followers by according with or adapting to the nature of the time. Chen is the eldest son; Tui, the eldest daughter; Chen places itself beneath Tui, the male acquiesces to the female and in this way is able to arouse the female. Chen also symbolizes the foot—that which incites movement—and is the thunder that comes out of the earth, here depicted as resting within the lake. Significantly, Chen is also the dragon, symbol of celestial power, an age-old emblem of Chinese culture. In the "Inner World" arrangement of the pa kua, the position of Chen is the east, and signifies the early morning. Tui is opposite Chen and symbolizes the west and evening. Chen is that which moves, and Tui is that which distributes.

Chen is the power of the dragon from the East whose teachings are contained in *I Ching*, which in this case may be symbolized by Chen readying itself for arousal at the bottom of the lake of the West. Chen also signifies daybreak, the time in which this dragon appears, and may further symbolize the dawn of a new time resting and preparing itself in the waters of the West. The West, in turn, as symbolized by Tui whose position is evening, is in a state of decline, at the end of its day. Its energy will be aroused and renewed by the dragon which is now within. Further indicating the nature of the West is the fact that Tui symbolizes the mouth—speech, intellection, verbal discourse— and metal—the element in which the West has excelled technologically. Perhaps the West may be characterized as a "metal-mouth" culture. Tui also signifies the sheep, that creature which follows. In its negative aspect, it characterizes the West as a "nation of sheep"; positively, it indicates that there is a potential for following the "new" force of the dragon Chen. This clearly states the position of the *I* within the present cultural context. The function of *The Eleventh Wing* is to aid in adapting the *I* to this situation, and to adapt ourselves, the West, to the *I,* which is already within our cultural confines. It should be further noted that the dragon, as a celestial symbol lying within the lake, symbolizes the potential religious awakening of the West—and of the world—an awakening in which the *I* may be very instrumental.

The changing lines were the second and third places, transforming the dragon into the symbol of heaven itself, Ch'ien, ☰ also symbolized by a dragon. This suggests that the force presented by the dragon within the lake will grow in strength and appear in the heavens, and that "following" shall be obtained through *The Eleventh Wing.* The commentaries on the changing lines read:

> Six in the second place means:
> If one clings to the little boy,
> One loses the strong man.

and six in the third place means:

> If one clings to the strong man,
> One loses the little boy.
> Through following one finds what one seeks.
> It furthers one to remain persevering.

This is essentially evolutionary advice. In the context of *The Eleventh Wing,* the "little boy" is our limiting and almost exclusive dependence upon reason or intellect to solve all problems. By clinging to intellect, the "strong man" of deepening insight and all-embracing consciousness will be lost. This is emphasized again in the third line, though put in a reverse order—the yin and the yang of it indicating the simple necessity of transformation. No matter; what is important is being able to give up a dependence upon intellect and what it brings us—civilization—and turn instead to the "strong man"—the divine within—while perseveringly following the admonitions of the intuitive realm, for in this way we shall find what we seek.

The transformed kua is Kuai, ☰, translated by Wilhelm/Baynes as "Breakthrough (Resoluteness)," by Blofeld as "Resolution," and by Siu as "Removing Corruption." The ideas begun in our reflections on the second and third lines of Sui, "following," receive a reinforcement with this kua. Its structure is that of five light lines topped by a yin line, and since the movement goes from the bottom up, the yin line is in the process of being pushed out. This indicates that the movement begun by *I Ching*'s introduction into our present cultural circumstances must be resolutely pursued. In this image heaven is beneath the lake, which means that the lake of the West is in the process of evaporating, thus giving rise to the possibility of a breakthrough—a cloudburst through the power of heaven. There is an even more intimate connection here between the dissolution and/or transformation of the West and its "metal-mouth" culture, and the rising influence of the dragon, symbolic both of the East and, in this case, of the primal strength of the celestial and divine light of intuitive consciousness. Nothing can stop the movement of this force—Ch'ien—or the force of this movement—*I Ching*.

The Judgment of Kuai speaks of the function of *The Eleventh Wing:*

> Breakthrough: One must resolutely make the matter known at the court of the king.
> It must be announced truthfully, danger.
> It is necessary to notify one's own city.
> It does not further to resort to arms.
> It furthers one to undertake something.

The position of *I* in the West is one of "breakthrough" at this time. However if it is to succeed, the "matter" of its nature must be resolutely known at the court of the king; i.e., the proper way of comprehending the *I Ching* for our time must be revealed in a resolute manner, and it must be announced truthfully. This is the purpose of *The Eleventh Wing*. There is danger of misconstruing; there is danger in our total, global situation due to the fact that there is still one yin line at the very top of the kua, which still holds all of the power of the light in check. *The Eleventh Wing* is the notification of one's own city—the call to turn inward to our own inherent powers of mind, in Khigh Dhiegh's definition of religion, "to tie back to the one." For this reason it is not necessary "to resort to arms"; the process is a natural one of returning to home base. "It furthers one to undertake something" suggests simply that there is no point or place for self-satisfaction in this process, but that our own introspection will yield further to be developed.

Khigh Dhiegh offers some of the examples of how this furthering process can be developed through the discipline of *I Ching* in the various "study aids"—including the marvelous "Catechism"—which are contained in *The Eleventh Wing*. Many of these study aids, such as the *I Ching* mandala as put together by Dr. Dhiegh, are yantric devices for reflecting upon the associative flow generated by the different orders of the kua and the various qualities which they embrace. These devices may be described as mnemonic maps—keys to self-remembrance—and the *Book of Changes* itself as a blueprint for an accelerating self-remembrance program.

From alpha to omega, from yin to yang; from yang to omega, from yin to alpha—the changes distribute themselves as water pouring down from heaven, which is why, in the words of the image of "breakthrough,"

> . . . the superior man
> dispenses riches downward
> and refrains from resting on his virtue.

Likewise *The Eleventh Wing* is a further dispensing downward of the riches of *I Ching*, an act which the sages of change have always emulated. The serious student of *I Ching* dispenses his own riches by adding his input to the symbols and recasting them according to the uniqueness of his own experience. This is an act of total renewal—which is the purpose of *The Eleventh Wing* itself: to renew the *I,* and to help others be renewed through *I Ching.* No other words seem necessary, except perhaps a tribute to the man, Khigh Dhiegh, about whom it may one day be said that in a strange land and in a time of confusion and despair he helped to renew the people by renewing *I Ching,* for as it is written in one of the Commentaries to the kua, I, "The Corners of the Mouth (Providing Nourishment)": ". . . The great man fosters and takes care of superior men, in order to take care of all men through them."

José A. Argüelles, Ph.D.
The Evergreen State College
Olympia, Washington

The
Eleventh
Wing

Preface

Among the many achievements of ancient Chinese culture none has been more enduring and meaningful to persons on every rung of the societal ladder and in all areas of human pursuit than the philosophical system of *I Ching*. Upon first examination it appears to represent a distinctly self-complete and isolated cultural heritage. This initial impression is so emphatic that for some few hundreds of years since its introduction to the Western world by the Jesuit missionaries, it has been treated by Occidentals as merely another interesting Oriental curio. This attitude of very questionable fairness has prevailed until just recently. Now it is beginning to dawn upon more and more Western thinkers that a single volume, surviving for thousands of years, whose content has been the inspiration for an enormous quantity of specific commentary literature and that has influenced almost every walk of life (religion, agriculture, medicine, politics, science, physical education, martial arts, warfare, healing, philosophy, nutrition, arts, navigation, etc.), must be of important significance.

To think that *I Ching* is a kind of quackery and nonsense is to advertise a biased ignorance of both its history and its wisely defined principles. It was a Chinese physician-sage, Pien Ch'iao, who lived during the fifth and fourth centuries B.C., who expressed the thought: "Belief in quackery does not help anyone."

I Ching is several thousands of years old. As the text comes to us, it is a literary composition that sets down what the ancient sages held to be fundamental processes of life. It perceives the existence of 'mutual oppositions', 'mutual dependence', and 'mutual causation', between all phenomena of nature. *I Ching* conceives man as a cosmos in miniature, fashioned after and similar to the universe, acting and reacting within the influence of the same forces and laws which prevail in nature.

The Chinese identified these influential forces as Tao, yin and yang, and the five primary elements.

Today many people are attracted to *I Ching*. There is a growing curiosity about it. Is it a philosophy, a kind of Oriental magic, an oracle, or what? In this book it will be presented as a compendium of formulas for effecting sociological, physiological, psychological and spiritual changes in the human experience. Its purpose is to help the reader master the intellectual, mechanical and meditative techniques which, when combined with the wisdom of *I Ching*, will quicken within the individual a consciousness responsive to one's unique intuitive 'knowing'.

This is not a book on how to use *I Ching* to see into the future. *I Ching* is not primarily a system of fortune-telling. An aim of this book is to counteract the popular occult conception that limits the definition and significance of *I Ching* to the constraining diameter of hocus-pocus, fortune-telling and soothsaying. Yet, it would disavow all historical evidence to say that *I Ching* cannot and has not been used for such purposes. Indeed it has been and is still being so used. Here we will focus upon *I Ching* as a philosophical psychology and psychological philosophy.

It is part of the historical and literary records that King Wen, Duke of Chou, Wang Pi, Tung Chung-shu, Han Yu, Hsiung Shih-li, Gottfried von Leibniz, Hegel, Legge, Richard Wilhelm, Carl Jung, Aldous Huxley, Hermann Hesse, R. G. H. Siu, Kuo Mo-jo (the late cultural official of the People's Republic of China), John Cage and others, have all devoted considerable time and study to *I Ching*. A roster of such distinguished persons surely indicates that this timeless wisdom must be something more than a means to foretell the future.

At the present time there is a great proliferation of books, pamphlets and articles dealing with *I Ching*. These many efforts represent varying degrees of competency, sincerity and clarity. The only justification for adding another volume to the present bibliography of *I Ching* is that there is something fresh to say, something more than merely marveling anew at the divinatory abilities of the oracle. Indeed, there is a growing recognition that we can no longer alienate ourselves from articulated and written ideas which express the intuitive 'knowing' of man. This book will present the concept of continuing change as a vital modern experience, pregnant with meaning, confirmation and application now! As the author, I am not so much concerned with how the ancients saw these ideas, but rather, how I may use them now to help me understand and cope with the world of scientific technology in which I am living.

Dr. Shafica Karagulla, from whom I shall borrow certain terminology, notes in the preface to her book, *Breakthrough to Creativity:*

> Today, man is pacing the outer perimeter of his five senses with an increasing awareness of limitations. Are there things to be sensed which his five senses do not encompass? Is a breakthrough occurring in the field of human perception? Is man breaking through his five senses' barriers into the realm of Higher Sense Perception? The human being is a living, evolving instrumentation. It is logical to suppose that a development such as the ability of Higher Sense Perception is a part of the evolutionary process.[1]

This observation partly explains the facts that have en-
couraged a growing popular and deeply sincere curiosity about
I Ching. We want to know why this, man's oldest continuously
used wisdom, functions with such amazing effectiveness and
meaningfulness in activating the otherwise dormant mind-
energy (or subconscious 'knowing') into a dynamic force which
enables us to deal with an endless multiplicity of human
situations.

The number of Western persons who are turning to the *Book
of Changes* as a source of inspiration, divination, guidance,
wisdom and enlightenment is increasing. The question comes to
mind immediately—is it merely a passing fad? When we come to
study the *I* and begin to understand its philosophical principles
and psychological structuring, we will realize that we are witnessing a phenomenon of widening human consciousness.
I Ching is an instrument of wisdom that functions as a catalyst
awakening the conscious mind to the content of the 'ever-
conscious.'* To experience the potential of its nature, we must
recognize it as being a prescription for action, to be taken or
not taken, in order to realize a desired result.

The devotion to, confidence in and common usage of this
ancient text are not without precedent. China is one of the
world's oldest continuous civilizations. All of its historical records testify that the wisdom of *I Ching* predates its written
history. It has been an important instrument in shaping China's
tens of centuries of existence. As Dr. Siu notes in the preface to
his book, *The Man of Many Qualities:*

> For centuries, the *I Ching* has served as a principal guide in
> China on how to govern a country, organize an enterprise,
> deal with people, conduct oneself under difficult con-
> ditions, and contemplate the future.[2]

---

*'Ever-conscious' is my equivalent for 'subconscious' and 'unconscious'. I
am indebted to Mr. Paul King, a long-time devotee of the *I*, for this
distinction. Neither 'subconscious' nor 'unconscious' convey the meaning
of what we are talking about. The conscious mind has its waking and
sleeping states, its aware and unaware states. The thing we are talking
about is that part that is forever, eternally aware, conscious and active—the
'ever-conscious'.

To enable one to apply the *I* to these aspects of living is the raison d'être of this endeavor. The timeliness of this effort is supported by the following statistic:

In 1965 there were only two English-language editions of *I Ching* available in the United States which were of any merit. Now, some seven years later, there are seventeen or more different editions of *I Ching* available in English, an exciting testimony to the growing interest of Westerners in this ageless Chinese wisdom, which has survived the rise and fall of fifteen dynasties covering a period of over four thousand years.

Many of these current editions of the *I* are primarily reiterations of either the James Legge translation or of the Wilhelm Baynes translation. The only other original and scholarly translations of merit available are those by A. Terrien de Lacouperie (1892), John Blofeld (1965) and R. G. H. Siu (1968). These five English translations, each in its manner, are the only truly skillful and creative translations attempting to express the essence of the original Chinese text.

But for all the skill displayed by these profound students in interpreting the Chinese text, the average Western reader often finds himself holding before his eyes a volume of enigmatic and perplexing arcana. Such cryptic phrases as: "Treading on the tail of a tiger, which does not bite him," and "Good fortune, evil fortune, occasion for repentance, and reason for regret all arise from activity," or "Hidden dragon, do not act" tend to confound him. The following pages are, in essence, an attempt to make the *I* meaningful, comprehendible and attractive so that one can make practical use of its wisdom, even though he be unfamiliar with the background of Chinese folklore, cosmology, philosophy and cultural and ethical values.

This eleventh commentary offers *I Ching*, a wisdom once endemic to China, as a prescription of guidance and inspiration pregnant with meaning and use that can be related to all time and proven valid on a worldwide basis. When one seeks to use *I Ching,* he must visualize himself as approaching, not the ancient sages, but the sage of eternal enduringness who, like a Chinese physician, softly asks: "For how long a time have you lost your peace of mind?" And you must answer the question.

In this way you will gain a perspective on its importance. The next question asked will be: "What exactly disturbs the centering of your being?" After carefully thinking about this question phrased in eight words, construct your reply in precisely eight words. The reason for this will be gone into within the text of this book. This technique, ritual or procedure, whatever you may wish to call it, sets up communication between the 'ever-conscious' and conscious forces of mind.

This commentary will suggest to the student reader methods which, when applied, will help in the development of heightened awareness, in awakened consciousness to the intuitive nature, and in attaining a release from the restrictions of words, images and symbols. Man does not exist apart from the universe. *I Ching* teaches that the total cosmos is affected by every event of intention and accident, and it offers a key whereby the individual man can greatly direct the manner and degree to which he may choose to be affected.

For the past thirty-five years, many hours of my study time have been devoted to the *I*. I have long felt a need for reexpressing and explaining the fundamentally universal principles which are at the core of the *I*. When the Westerner recognizes the point of his tradition's departure from that of China's tradition, he will discover that his existence in the realm and authority of his pragmatic and idealistic philosophies is the same as the Chinese 'beingness' in the cosmogony of Tao. As creatures of self-will and intelligence we are all destined to pursue the same goal, aiming, as it were, at the one universal target, but from the individualized spot of each from his own footing. In this way, each can gain a sense of what is valuable in *I Ching* and learn how to use its wisdom to achieve one's own expansion of consciousness.

It has been my privilege to serve as director of the International *I Ching* Studies Institute for the past six years. In this capacity I have been afforded opportunities to lecture on the *Book of Changes* from coast to coast in the United States. Also, I have instructed many *I Ching* seminars, both elementary and advanced. In pursuing these activities I have had many avenues of communication opened to me: radio, television, universities, colleges and various organizations. These experiences have brought me into touch with many levels of interest in *I Ching* which are not touched upon in any of the regularly available translations. A few volumes purport to explain *I Ching* as a mystical source of divination. These certainly have their value and their audience. Here, however, our primary concern will be with the philosophy of *I Ching*, and the psychological applications of its wisdom. How a philosophy can be actually used in everyday living is much more important than the poetry of its ideas, the eloquence of its phrasing or the intricateness of its expression.

I shall feel fully rewarded if this effort has some success in achieving its aim. That is to demonstrate the phenomenology of *I Ching* so as to awaken in each reader a consciousness enabling him or her to use this wisdom both for spiritual growth and as an expression of individual potential.

Here, then, is what I most humbly offer as *The Eleventh Wing* to *I Ching*. Throughout this book, by various means and new perspectives, I hope to present some serviceable instruction concerning the *Book of Changes*. By moving from target to target, some stationary and some moving, I hope to excite my reader in such a way that he or she can identify with this inspiring and highly practical wisdom.

To accomplish this I shall have to call upon the teachings and writings of many persons, ancient and modern. Yet, in the final analysis the reader will discover that the meaningfulness of *I Ching* is not a thing that can be transmitted from one person to another. The revelation of another's excitement about *I Ching*, and accounts of the truth they find in it, can only serve as a stimulant to encourage each to discover in *I Ching* his own meaning and his own truth. Long ago, it was wisely written:

The Masters of the secret teachings say that the truth learned from another is of no value, and that the only truth which is living and effective, which is of value, is the truth which we ourselves discover.[3]

Elsewhere I have listed words of gratitude to only a small number of the persons to whom I am deeply indebted for the teaching, learning and help I have acquired from them, and without which this book could not be. But I must here express an especial word to my very dear friend and associate Ch'ao-Li Chi. His distinguished scholarly research and years of counsel have been responsible for keeping me apprised of many profound and meaningful refinements of translation and evolutionary interpretation of Chinese characters, thereby opening to me insights of *I Ching*'s relevancy to contemporary Western concepts in philosophy, psychology and the sciences. In a sense, what may prove to be the most important content of this book will be the fruits of his unselfish genius. So, on behalf of my readers and myself, I express deep gratitude to Ch'ao-Li Chi.

The real merit of this book will not be found in the words which follow, but rather in their awakening in the individual the ability to discover the uniqueness of himself and the means of fulfilling his potential.

K. A. D.
Los Angeles,
February, 1972

One
An I Ching
Catechism

Perhaps while we're in the opening chapter, it will help set a foundation of confidence to present a sort of catechism of *I Ching*. However, let it be clear that this is not the usual dogmatic type of catechism of directed questions followed by doctrinaire answers which must be accepted as final. To the contrary, the questions here are frequently those that have been asked by students of the Institute's study courses and by persons in the audiences at the many open lectures. Such answers as are given are intended to be the expression of only one way of seeing the matter posed. It is hoped that the final result of these interrogatory exercises will be to stimulate the reader's own mental processes into discovering the most productive cycle for creatively "tuning in" to the frequency patterns of his surrounding universe.

Initial Questions

1. *What is "Eye Ching?"*
   Let us commence by pointing out that the majority of scholars prefer to pronounce *I Ching* as though its English spelling was "Ee Jing."

2. *Okay! What is "Ee Jing?"*
   I Ching is primarily a philosophical psychology and a psychological philosophy.

3. *What is meant by "a philosophical psychology and a psychological philosophy?"*
   The phrasing is meant to express the fact that the ancient sages saw man as inseparable from the cosmic phenomenological process. We can understand more about man when we recognize that he is a microcosm perfectly replicating the macrocosm. Man is conscious of his being through his awareness of response to the experiences of soma and psyche.

   The functioning of soma and psyche is connected to the roles played by philosophy and psychology:

   Philosophy is the concern of man's thinking with problems of value.

   Psychology as defined in popular dictionaries is "that branch of science studying the processes, motives, reactions and nature of consciousness, especially of the human mind, mental processes, motives, etc.; character, especially as interpreted by modern psychologists." This is only a part of what is meant by psychology when the term is used in connection with *I Ching*. Psychology is a phenomenon of mental, physical, emotional, psychical and intuitional intelligence and energy, or any manifestation of two or more of these. They should be traceable and explainable by the analytically structured systematization of knowledge from which conclusions are drawn from observation, and the study of which may be projected as anticipation of human, animal and elemental behavior. *These anticipations may precede or follow the event to which they are pertinent.*

When I say that *I Ching* is a philosophical psychology and a psychological philosophy, it is to emphasize that this ancient wisdom is an expression of man's concern with the application of values and how they affect his behavior as experiences of pleasure and pain. The *I* is a record expressing the knowledge gained by the sages as the result of their having observed nature. The manner in which they recorded this knowledge enables us to anticipate the consequences of specific action in any given specific circumstance or situation.

The *I* is a structuring of ritual and of language which together, constitute an instrument that may be used to successfully probe into the 'ever-conscious,' and awaken to a conscious level one's capabilities of maximum creativeness. Thus, *I Ching* functions as a process of interaction in man as a thinking creature and man as a behavioral creature.

4. *Who are the sages mentioned in the previous explanation?*
   "The sages" is a reference that encompasses some of China's greatest thinkers, many of whom lived hundreds of years before the Western Christian era. Most of the important Chinese philosophers have written commentaries on *I Ching*. To name a few: King Wen and his son, Tau, known as the Duke of Chou (circa 1120 B.C.), Confucius, Mencius, Chuang Tzu, Wang Fu-Chih, Shao Yung, etc. During the entire course of China's history, we are told that her greatest reformers, almost without exception, drew their inspiration from this great book.

Intellectuals of present-day China have also made important contributions to the voluminous literature that attends *I Ching*. For example, see Hellmut Wilhelm's introduction to the third English edition of Richard Wilhelm's translation of the *Book of Changes,* page xvii.

5. *How old is* I Ching?

The exact age of *I Ching* is unknown. Scholars are at wide variance with one another on dates, as well as differing in their definitions of exactly what constitutes the formal structure of *I Ching*.

It had its origins in the remote prehistory era of China's existence. The most popularly known account is one that attributes the *I* to the mythological semidivine Emperor Fu-hsi. He, it is reputed, was the first to devise the linear images of the *I*. This would place its beginning somewhere close to three thousand B.C.

6. *When did* I Ching *become known to the Western world?*

It first became known to the Western world through the writings and travels of Jesuit missionaries who pioneered the message of Christianity to China in the seventeenth and eighteenth centuries.

Hellmut Wilhelm writes: "It is no accident, that of the early Jesuit scholars who were pioneers in making China's culture known in Europe, those who concerned themselves with the *Book of Changes* were all later declared to be insane or heretic."[1]

7. *Who were the first important Westerners involved with* I Ching?

The great German philosopher Hegel gave lectures on *I Ching*. Gottfried von Leibniz came upon Shao Yung's diagram of the *I* through his acquaintance with certain of the Jesuit missionaries. After studying the diagram, Leibniz recognized his own system of binary mathematics in it. This excited him to open up correspondence with the emperor of China. Frequent mentions of this period are recorded by Leibniz in his *Novissima Sinica*.[2]

James Legge, the distinguished Protestant scholar who had translated the four great books of Confucius, also rendered *I Ching* into English. This was in the mid-eighteen hundreds.

In the late eighteen hundreds and early nineteen hundreds, the Swiss psychiatrist, Carl Gustav Jung, was attracted to a study of the *Book of Changes.* In it he recognized a phenomenal factor at play for which he coined the term, "synchronicity."

Richard Wilhelm and his son, Hellmut Wilhelm, individually have made important contributions to Western knowledge; through the definitive translation by the former, and the valuable explanatory eight lectures by the latter.

Arthur Waley, the widely read scholar on China's history, literature and thought, wrote many articles on *I Ching* for various academic journals.

A most valuable work, *The Oldest Book of the Chinese— The Yh-King and Its Authors* by A. Terrien de Lacouperie, while difficult to obtain is certainly worth the search.

R. G. H. Siu, a scientist specializing in the field of biochemistry, has given us the most exciting contemporary translation of the original text, to which he has appended a wealth of quotations from world literature covering some thousands of years, thereby demonstrating the universality of the wisdom of *I Ching.*

8. *Isn't* I Ching *really fortune-telling?*
This question will be asked many times in many different ways. It must be answered each time in a slightly different way. *I Ching* is not fortune-telling. When one goes to a fortune-teller, he or she is told such and such a thing is

going to happen. One then has only to return home, and sit and wait for the foretold event to occur. If it does, the fortune-teller gains in reputation. If it doesn't, the fortune-teller falls into disrepute.

In contrast to this, *I Ching* prescribes a type of action, and defines what the results of that action will be. One cannot go home and wait—just the contrary. After consulting the *Book of Changes,* one has to become mentally and physically active, carrying out the *I*'s prescription of action, in order to realize and experience the kua.

9. *Is* I Ching *a religion?*

You would probably be surprised at how many people have asked me this question. The answer to it must be determined by what one means when using the word "religion." Since there are as many definitions for the word as there are people who use it, the question shall have to be answered by first defining the word "religion." Then we can proceed to answer.

Back in 1920, the late Bertrand Russell expressed a meaning of the word "religion," in *The Practice and Theory of Bolshevism.* He wrote: "By a religion, I mean a set of beliefs held as dogmas, dominating the conduct of life, going beyond or contrary to evidence, and inculcated by methods which are emotional or authoritarian, not intellectual."[3]

If we use this as a reference, *I Ching* is decidedly not a religion. There is nothing expressed in it that goes "beyond or contrary to evidence," and one would be hard-pressed to find an emotional line in its text, with the possible exception of: "Then follow laughing words—ha, ha!"[4]

As a younger man, in 1912, Russell expounded on "The Essence of Religion." He held that: "The three elements of religion, namely worship, acquiescence, and love, are intimately interconnected; each helps to produce the others, and all three together form a unity in which it is impossible to say which comes first, which last. All three can exist without dogma, in a form which is capable of dominating life and of giving infinity to action and thought and feeling; and life in the infinite, which is the combination of the three, contains all that is essential to religion, in spite of its absence of dogmatic beliefs."[5]

In this sense, *I Ching* may be regarded as a religion. It is a wisdom expressing through images and metaphor a description of nature and the sequential ordering of its manifestations as they occur according to the laws of 'change'.

When one becomes conscious of the deep significance of *I Ching,* one experiences a transcendent wonder that Carlyle called worship. With this consciousness one acquiesces, like Confucius, to the inspirational directives of the *I,* and thereby participates with his fellows in love. It is to move knowingly within Tao.

10. *Was* I Ching *influenced by the Buddhist or Taoist religions?*
    I Ching predates both religions. Scholars are unanimous in agreeing that the *I* exercised a very strong influence upon both Taoism and Buddhism, at the time when they were first developing as influences in China's cultural life. As the centuries rolled along, the phenomenon of interaction came into play. Today, one who is studying *I Ching* and either or both of the aforementioned religions will find abundant evidence that there is an undeniable reciprocal influence that is exercising within them.

11. *In what area of human experience can* I Ching *be used?*
    Hellmut Wilhelm has written: "The *Book of Changes* represented the gate to the whole man and to the whole world . . . the Chinese turned to the *Book or Changes* whenever problems arose in the conduct of life."[6]

The wisdom of *I Ching* is expressed through images which represent:
1. The primary needs of man
2. The evolution of personality
3. Situations found in societal life
4. Individual character traits
5. Phenomena of suprapersonal significance

12. *Since* I Ching *originated in China, how can it apply to situations and problems of Western people?*

As stated in the *I,* there is one universal law for all life. Whether one be native to the East or the West, all living things have primary needs, such as the need for nourishment. All living things experience the evolution of personality, such as passing from innocence to knowledge. All living things are constituted by conditions and situations of a form of societal life—such as mating, wooing, following, etc. All living things display individual traits, such as modesty, bigness, softness, smallness, hardness, etc. All living things, from the pantheistic view, experience or display manifestations of suprapersonal significance. There is the consciousness of the god-being and of the devil-being—feelings of confidence and despair. There is movement or quiescence. There is projection and reception.

13. *What is meant by "consulting* I Ching?*"*

There are several answers to this question. However, none of them conform to Bierce's definition: "Consult, v.t.—To seek another's approval of a course already decided on."[7]

For the moment, let "consulting *I Ching*" be descriptive of the motivation, the ritual action, and the resulting kua referred to that terminates the procedure. To explain it differently: If a person, through study and inner conviction, or because of trust in another's assurance or recommendation, holds within himself a sense of recognition and expectation (which is a quality of belief) that the *I* can be of help, he then needs only to be disturbed by a particular anxiety (a question, problem or difficulty of some character or another) to be motivated to approach the *I*. This motivation may be fulfilled in many different ways. The two oldest known and traditionally recommended techniques of fulfilling this motivation is either through the ritualistic manipulation of the yarrow stalks, or the simpler rite of tossing three coins a prescribed number of times. By means of an established association of numbers with each procedure, one is keyed to turn to particular passages in the *Book of Changes*. Upon reading these specific passages one has then completed the business of "consulting *I Ching*."

14. *Does that mean that the problem or question has been solved or answered?*

No! If one did not know how to accomplish a particular thing, but had a strong desire to do so, what would one do? He would go to someone who could teach him how to do that which he strongly desired to do. The teacher would instruct. However, if the person seeking merely sat before the teacher, and did not listen to the instruction nor try to exercise the technique or principles being propounded, he would leave the teacher in the same condition of incapability as he was in when he approached the teacher. So it is with *I Ching*. If one lacks the insight, the awareness and responsive sensitivity to translate or transform the particular passages into action, he is no better off than before. Like all things in life, unless you use the *I* and do something with it, it will not do anything for you. All life is the phenomenon of going outward from within.

15. *Isn't manipulating yarrow stalks or tossing coins the selecting of advice by mere chance?*

We must take into account the fact that modern psychology has shown us many substructures of the human psyche which are the source of our strivings to see meaning and order in what is apparently coincidental. Out of this grows our conscious attempt to fit ourselves into the content of this order, so that in the parallelism between what is without and what is within us, the position and course of the one may also be meaningful for the other. This attitude is old; indeed, it is inherent in human nature.

Also, we should bear in mind that events which happen by chance are no less real in their nature than so-called causal events nor is there less significance to whatever meaning we may discover in them. This is an aspect of life that has been deeply characterized by St. Thomas Aquinas.

16. *Would you call* I Ching *scientific?*
Yes. It deals with the predictability of 'change'.

17. *But isn't it referred to as divination?*
Yes.

18. *If it is divination, how can it be scientific?*
The word science means "to know." We are born into a state of 'knowing'. Our 'knowing' diminishes as we grow and mature. We develop, through the experiences of our senses, a consciousness of knowledge. Divination—the practice of divining—is finding out; in a word, getting into a state of 'knowing'. The answer to both questions is not contradictory.

19. *What is the difference between 'knowing' and knowledge?*
Everything that exists is composed of intelligence-energy; that is to say, everything has intelligence and energy. For this reason it is said that we are born into a state of 'knowing'. It is 'knowing' that perpetuates us, and knowledge that changes us. Consider the fact that there seems to be an intelligence and energy that continually

replaces dead and dying cells with living new cells. There is
an intelligence and energy that manifests itself through the
activity of collection of cells, such as the blinking process
of the eyelids, or the pulsation of the heart, etc. The
metabolic process is that part of our beingness that results
from 'knowing'.

That we hear and understand only those words or ideas
which another either speaks or writes to us, is a condition
of limitation we undergo when we accept the false proposition that sound and sight are indispensable requisites
for human communication. Yet a great many of us have
experienced, sometime in our life, the indescribable thrill
of total communication with a loved one without a word
having been spoken or written.

Knowledge results from a restriction of our 'knowing'.
That is, we separate our consciousness from our beingness
by limiting our awareness to the definitions of our physiological senses only. But when a man is awakened to divine
essence—to Tao—he will hear the song of the flower, smell
the beauty of a song, feel the texture of nothingness, savor
the taste of the rainbow and see the formlessness of form.
This is something akin to the difference between knowledge and 'knowing'.

20. *Wouldn't it be more logical to read this so-called book of
wisdom cover to cover, then select that section which had a
logical relevance to the issue that one might be consulting*
I Ching *about?*

If you hold that reason is the only medium for understanding, then the method you outline is as good as any.
But if you want to be "more logical," why consult
I Ching? Logic is the art of correct reasoning. However, to
reason correctly does not guarantee that you will arrive at
the meaning. To explain things in terms of cause and effect

will not necessarily reveal the intended significance of the thing explained. In studying the *I*, students are frequently cautioned not to mistake the explanation for the reality!

The question posed arises because there is a mental and emotional block that locks out any knowledge that is not rational. Dr. R. G. H. Siu has impressively wrestled with this issue. He points out (in reference to what I would call empirical science) that, "reason is the only medium for understanding. There may be other wellsprings of enlightenment. But priding himself on his rational mind, many a scientist is reluctant to rely on these less obvious avenues. At best, he may attempt to rationalize whether or not these alternate approaches to knowledge and truth are possible. But to judge something that lies *beyond* reason by means of reason itself does not appear reasonable. . . . After all, scientists are a mite superstitious themselves, if we care to put the proposition thus. They do believe in baffling unknowns; they do have faith in the existence of things beyond the compass of their current knowledge. Otherwise where do their research problems originate and why is the unknown pursued so vigorously?"[8]

Yes, it could possibly be more logical to read the *I* cover to cover, and select that passage that seemed to have the greatest relevance to the situation involved. But this would be an exclusion of the insight and understanding that may possibly be furnished by intuitive knowledge and no-knowledge, as philosophically explained in many books and treatises dealing with oriental thought. Briefly, we may think of it as that knowledge which surpasses all understanding.

Dr. Siu reveals a key to enlightenment when he suggests that successful living is the use of our rational knowledge, intuitive knowledge, and no-knowledge, integrated with the applicable techniques of the positive and the negative, the yin and yang of *I Ching*. "Each of the forms of knowledge is especially effective for certain games in life. Since we are called upon to play the entire series . . . we should be equipped with the complete spectrum of understanding."[9]

21. Isn't a scientific fact a repeatable thing? That is, given the same conditions one will get the same result?
Yes.

22. Then if I Ching *is scientific, shouldn't I get the same answer each time I ask the same question?*
Yes.

23. Aha! Then I Ching *isn't scientific. I've asked the same question and I have always gotten a different answer.*
That is because you've always asked a different question.

24. Oh, no! Not at all. I've asked the same question, using the identical words!
Do you imagine that the words can be separated from the totality? You may have thought that it was the same question, but actually it wasn't. In nature (and this is a universally accepted fact) there is no duplication.

With the example you have presented, whatever it may be, the time-space aspects have changed. The information foundation is now different. It is akin to an artist falling heir to a large chunk of moon rock. He wonders if it can be carved into a form of his creation. He carves it. Then, as he looks at the finished work, he wonders if the stone would always respond to his chisel strokes in exactly the same way. So he decides, as an experiment, that he will carve the same statue. But there's the rub. He can neither carve nor recarve the same statue again. He can only carve another very similar—but not the same one.

Once an answer is given there is a new factor added to our experience. You imagine because you use the same words that they *are* the same words, and that they articulate the same question. They are not the same words, and it is not the same question. The question you ask the second time is really a new question. What it expresses, in effect, is a condition of doubt and/or challenge. "Is what was said before the true answer to my question?" That is closer to what "the same words" mean in the new time-space relationship.

To understand the so-called second answer to the "same" question, one must comprehend it in the sense of what really is being asked.

25. *How did* I Ching *begin and when?*

Scholars are agreed that the root origins of *I Ching* are lost in the preliterate past of China's antiquity. For the purpose of general information, the following synoptic history should prove to be informative.

CIRCA 3000 B.C.

Folklore, custom and cultural practice established the groundwork for pointing to its originating principles being set by the mythical Emperor Fu-hsi.

1150 B.C.

King Wen records the wisdom and his commentaries, while his son, the duke of Chou, defined the lines and codified the literature.

460 B.C.

The Commentaries are enlarged upon by the sage K'ung Fu Tzu, known to the Western world as Confucius.

213 B.C.

I Ching escapes the great book burning under the Emperor Ch'in Shih Huang Ti, who decreed that all wisdom should be historically recorded as beginning with his reign.

140 B.C.

The *Book of Changes* is given a preeminent distinction by being the only non-Confucian classic to remain in the Imperial Academy.

Between this period and the seventeenth century of our present era, there were many exceptionally distinguished men who expounded on *I Ching* and used it as a source of inspiration, guidance and instruction for conducting their lives, professions, social and political responsibilities. In the late A.D. 1600s, Jesuit missionaries in China became deeply absorbed in the *I*. Many turned to its study with great dedication. In time, however, its study and reading were discouraged by orders from the Vatican.

A.D. 1700s

Gottfried von Leibniz recognized that the underlying principle of his system of binary mathematics preexisted in the yin-and-yang concept of *I Ching*. This was demonstrated to him when he examined the diagram of Shao Yung's sequence, depicting the evolution of the linear images.

A.D. 1800s

The great philosopher Hegel lectures on the significance of the thought contained in *I Ching*.

A.D. 1876

The first English-language translation of the *I* is published in Shanghai, authored by the Reverend Canon McClatchie, M.A., the Secretary of C.M.S. Missions in China.

A.D. 1882

James Legge, the highly respected scholar of Chinese literature, publishes the English-language translation, which was originally completed in 1854-55.

A.D. 1924

The now-famous Richard Wilhelm translation was published in Germany and in the national language of the country. It attracted the attention and interest of sinophiles throughout the world.

A.D. 1950

Cary F. Baynes translates Wilhelm's German translation into English. It was first published by Pantheon for the Bollingen Foundation. Carl Gustav Jung wrote his very provocative foreword for this edition.

A.D. 1965

John Blofeld, an Englishman who had donned the saffron robe of Buddhism in Thailand, presented a new English translation, giving particular emphasis to the divinatory aspects of *I Ching*.

A.D. 1968

Dr. R. G. H. Siu, a Chinese-American scholar, presented a brilliant new English-language translation of *I Ching*. To each portion of the text he appended a thesaurus of corresponding wisdom, gleaned from the literature of the nations of the world and covering a period of some six thousand years.

There are other translations and arrangements of *I Ching* in English, of varying quality and importance. The prospect at present would indicate that even more names will be added to the roster that now includes, in alphabetical order: E. Albertson, V. P. Boyle, L. T. Culling, Alfred Douglas, Gia-Fu Feng, Jerome Kirk, Jung Young Lee, Chin

Lee, Frank J. MacHovec, J. Murphy, Charles Ponce, C. F. Russell, J. Shimanl, Z. D. Sung, Raymond Van Over, Clae Waltham and Kay Wong. The newly stimulated interest of the Western world in this ancient Chinese wisdom has inspired a great surge of new texts, and will continue to do so for quite some time to come. This particular volume is not a translation of the text, but rather an attempt to make understandable, in modern terminology, the philosophical principles contained in the *I,* so that no matter what translation one may be involved with, he will be more sensitive about making a correct psychological application of these philosophical principles.

26. *What does* I Ching *mean?*
The second part, *ching,* may be translated as an equivalent to book, classic, tome, canon, etc. The Chinese character for Ching looks like this: 經

The first part, *I* (pronounced "Ee" or "Yi"), is the more important. A better understanding is possible if we make a brief study of the character: 易 This character is a composite. If we break it down into its parts, we find the following ideas being expressed and/or suggested. There is 月 , expressing the idea of the sun moving daily through the heavens. Here is the idea of cyclicity and movement. It is the same thing that is ever changing. This lower part of the character, 勿 , can be read as banners which are waving in the wind. This is easy movement, facile change, and never recognizable as repeating itself. In other words, the image here is one of sequential, non-recurring change. It is said also to represent a chameleon.

Some of the possible translations into English are: the *Logic of Changes,* the *Laws of Permutations,* the *Book Chameleon,* the *Book of Changes,* the *Canon of Change,* the *Classic of Motion,* the *Easy Handbook,* etc., etc.

27. *What is meant by "the law of changes"?*
Things in the universe are ever changing according to an
endless cycle. All existent things are composed of intelligence and energy. Intelligence is forever influencing and
energy is forever actively reacting. This produces development and transformation. All things in the universe follow
a clearly defined order according to which they move
everlastingly in a scheme of becoming and 'begoning'.

Somewhere in the literature of the *I* it is written: "Because
of this principle, everything that reaches a certain peak
must then revert to its opposite. 'When the sun has reached
its meridian height, it declines, and when the moon has
become full, it wanes.' Thus in Ch'ien, the first linear
image (kua), the dragon, described in the first or lowest
line as lying hidden, reaches its highest peak in the fifth
line when it is flying in the sky, but in the sixth or
topmost line, "the dragon exceeds the proper limits and
there will be occasion for repentance." Confucius reported
on this thusly:

"This phrase, 'exceeds the proper limits,' indicates that he
knows to advance, but not to retire; he knows preservation
but not destruction; obtaining but not losing. He only is
the Sage, who knows to advance and to retire, to preserve
and to destroy, without ever acting improperly. . . ."

28. *How is this "law of change" connected to the linear
images?*
Every law expresses a force of authority that either by
nature or relationship or by the strength of dominance of
will or power, be it intellectual or physical, is intended to
define and explain through language, written or spoken,
that which is indefinable, invisible, intangible and inactive.
Once established by custom or in writing, the law may be
used to justify its enforcement by any means determined

as requisite and necessary. Law is wisely explained by the sage Lao Tzu, where he writes: "Tao does nothing, yet through it all things are done."

The *I,* as recorded by the sages of old, is a magnificently beautiful attempt to spell out in images of metaphorical archetypes the unmoving force that eternally moves the universe of spirit and matter, of intelligence and energy. They did this by establishing yin (a broken line − −), to represent the passive, receptive force; and yang (an unbroken line ──), to indicate the active and projective force of that ultimate cosmos-chaos from whence all things originate.

By building upon this dyadic principle, the ancients multiplied the broken and unbroken lines until they had constructed sixty-four images of six parallel lines each. They interpreted these linear images as an arrangement of nature's dyadic forces (yin and yang), that, symbolically, enabled one to see into, or understand, the course of cosmic designs—whether they be of macrocosmic or microcosmic proportions.

The lines, broken and unbroken, which compose the sixty-four linear images of *I Ching* have been assigned particular identifications representing natural phenomena, familial relationships, anatomical parts of the body, specific animals, certain colors, societal functions, etc., etc. All of these serve as symbolic keys that open our understanding to the various forces at play within both the microcosm and the macrocosm. All these cosmic aspects are experienceable by each individual being.

As one develops a subjective sensitivity and intuitive recognition of the significance of the endless movement of these lines, one will gradually come to comprehend the workings of the law of 'change'. All that happens in nature is symbolically represented by the ever-changing interplay of the lines composing the kua.

With this we conclude the elementary catechism of *I Ching*.

Two
Images
of Wisdom

Attributes of the Pa Kua

I Ching is the most significant of China's ancient writings. It is the product of an intense restructuring, performed in the twelfth century B.C., of a much older work composed of ancient dated documents and vocabularies. It therefore has a legitimate claim to being the oldest literature of the Chinese civilization. Indeed, some feel it to be the oldest living literature in the world. Ideas provoked by the concepts and principles expressed in this work have been recognized as most reliable counsel in handling the situations of living through life.

What is distinctively unique about *I Ching* is that it has had an equally strong appeal to people of widely differing intelligences, occupations and sensitivities. *I Ching* has been the inspiration for right action and purposeful direction to simple naive peasants and to beneficent or tyrannical rulers. It has influenced the thinking of philosophers, and helped to define the strategy of generals. It has given a systemization to medicine, and a tonal range to music. It furnished a guiding method to agriculture, and supplemented the insights of astrology. It is reputed to have inspired the invention of things for use on land and water and supplied cues to heighten the divinatory perceptions of palmistry, body divination and religion. It was used to prescribe the movements of T'ai Chi Ch'uan and Kung Fu, and it describes the nature and processes of universal change. It has depicted the primal order of these changes; and, in another arrangement of its pa kua, it pictures the variations of the changes we experience as actuated sequences of phenomena in our lives.

Let us, then, examine this marvelous wisdom and see if we can come to understand the thoughts and the thinking process that has enabled it to survive through these tens upon tens of centuries. This phenomenal work captured the imagination of Western travelers a number of centuries ago. They brought it back with them and so, today, in the societies of Western civilization, interest in and involvement with *I Ching* is impressively active. It is recognized as an aid in reaching sageness.

R. G. H. Siu has written:

> As a person matures to sageness, the explicit knowledge of the formal pronouncements of the hexagrams disappears into his deeper subconscious. Eventually, he becomes oblivious of the very preachings themselves, and the spirit of the *I Ching* merges with his very being. From then on, his actions are no longer heralded by his own learning but evoked by the universal harmony. Being one with nature, he apprehends the all—totally, instantaneously, ineffably. This is the ultimate lesson of the *I Ching*.[1]

To attain the sage experience we must first try to understand the ancient Chinese concepts of the origin of all that is, and be able to translate these concepts into modern equative language and imagery.

The Chinese have always resorted to graphic means to express ideas. We shall study and analyze one of the most ancient diagrams used to depict the evolution of the fundamental principles of natural forces with which *I Ching* is concerned. With the recent plethora of books translating and/or explaining *I Ching*, this diagram has been burdened with many names and titles. In one work it is labeled: "Fu-hsi's Diagram of the Derivation of the Sixty-four Hexagrams." Responsible scholarship suggests that the diagram, in all probability, may be properly attributed to the genius of Shao Yung, who lived in the eleventh century. Dr. Fung, in his highly reputable *History of Chinese Philosophy*, describes it as the "Diagram of Cosmic Evolution in Terms of the Sixty-four Hexagrams."[2]

This graphic representation of 'cosmic evolution' is structured as a rectangle divided horizontally into seven areas. Each of these areas (save one) is then divided into smaller parts. Altogether, the rectangle contains 127 parts. In terms of Western numerology, this adds to ten. Ten symbolizes completeness, totality. In modern computer language, it contains the basic components—one and zero—of the binary system of mathematics elemental to computer science. Also, the number ten relates to *I Ching* as yin (0) and yang (1), negative and positive. Thus we commence by observing that it is possible to read into this diagram a variety of meaningful and significant indications.

Of course, the very possibility of being able to read meanings into the diagram will stimulate, in some quarters, reactions ranging from mild skepticism about the merit of *I Ching* to emphatic denunciation of it as an incredulous nonsense, fit only to be part and parcel of a mountebank's wares.

But do we not read meaning into nearly everything? What meaning is there to a word other than what is given to it through mutual consent? What is the difference in meaning between 我忙了 and its Latinized form "wo mangle"? Both mean the same thing. But unless you speak or read Chinese, the above graphic patterns will hold little meaning for you. Someone may be ambitious and try to rationalize an interpretation of the Latinized writing to mean "Whoa! A mess," or "Stop! You'll mangle everything!" In Chinese it means "I'm busy now," which implies that I wasn't busy before.

To observe that meaning is being imposed upon a thing is not a logical justification for rejecting or condemning that thing.

The important thing to look for is some clue that will demonstrate that the meaning being imposed upon a thing serves a constructive and productive purpose. It matters not whether the meaning imposed is an individual meaning or one of collective consent. With this in mind, let us now turn our attention to the "Diagram of Cosmic Evolution."

```
┌──────────────────────────────────────────────┐
│                                                │
│                   WU CH'I                      │
│                                                │
└──────────────────────────────────────────────┘
```

The first area we are concerned with is the bottom of the "Diagram of Cosmic Evolution." It is a narrow rectangle stretching across the lowest portion of the diagram. Often it is a blank space. At other times it may have one of any number of identifying labels: "The Great Ultimate Ultimatelessness," "The Supreme Ultimate," "The Ultimate Form Because It Has No Form," "Wu Ch'i—the 'Before-the-beginning,' " etc., etc. The concept being represented here is a declaration of the realized and acknowledged limitation of human intelligence and consciousness.

At times I've remarked to students that, due to our preoccupation with answers, many Westerners find it either difficult or embarrassing to admit not knowing something. How many times have we not all experienced the inconvenience this has caused? You go to a new town, or an unfamiliar area in your own city, looking for a particular address. You wander about searching, but you are unsuccessful in finding the street or the building number. Hoping to locate the place, you ask someone for directions. Almost always you will receive rather explicit directions, which you later discover are almost always wrong! You seldom find people who will simply excuse themselves from helping you by admitting that they really don't know.

We have a strong compulsion to appear knowledgeable about all things. The scriptures of the Judeo-Christian-Islamic traditions open stories of the Creation with phrases which confirm this observation. "In the beginning, God created the heavens and the earth." The Gospel according to John, in the New Testament, reads: "In the beginning was the Word. . . ." And we also note that stories for our very young children often open with: "Once upon a time. . . ." We *have* to know, or so it would seem. We have to speak from some locatable time or place. We speak and write as though we were an infinitely knowledgeable people. And, sad to say, most of us believe we are.

You will remember I warned earlier that in order to develop an understanding of *I Ching,* we may have to change some of our ways of thinking. I mean that we shall have to adopt the Chinese way of happily recognizing that there is a limitation upon our ability to know. It is openly expressed when the Chinese speak of Wu Ch'i. "Wu" expresses the idea of 'non-being.' "Ch'i" is a mystical ether and fluid of heaven and earth. Together they stand for the concept of 'Before-the-beginning.' It is a thought that admits of a limitation to our spiritual, physical, intellectual and emotional beingness.

As far back as the first century B.C., the Chinese were giving thought to matters of cosmological valuations. Prince Huai-nan's writings illustrate this quite clearly. In the second chapter of *The Cosmology of the Huai Nan Tzu,* we read the following:

> (1) There was a beginning. (2) There was a beginning of an anteriority to this beginning. (3) There was a beginning of an anteriority even before the beginning of this anteriority. (4) There was being. (5) There was non-being. (6) There was 'not yet a beginning of the non-being'. (7) There was 'not yet a beginning of the not yet beginning of non-being'.[3]

These somewhat cryptic phrases become understandable when we read the explanations which follow:

> (1) The meaning of "there was a beginning" is that there was a complex energy which had not yet pullulated into germinal form, nor into any visible shape of root and seed and rudiment. Even then, in this vast and impalpable con-

dition, the desire to spring into life was apparent; but, as yet, the genera ot things had not yet formed.[4]

(2) At the "beginning of an anteriority to this beginning," the fluid (Ch'i) of heaven first descended, and the fluid of earth first ascended. The yin and the yang united with one another, prompting and striving amidst the cosmos. They wandered hither and thither, pursuing, competing, interpenetrating. Clothed with energy and containing harmony, they moved, sifted and impregnated, each wishing to ally itself with other things, even when, as yet, there was no appearance of any created form.[5]

(3) At the stage, "there was a beginning of an anteriority even before the beginning of anteriority," heaven contained the quality of harmony, but had not, as yet, descended; earth cherished the vivifying fluid (Ch'i), but had not, as yet, ascended. There was a void, still, desolate, vapory, without similitude. The vitalizing fluid floated about without destination.[6]

(4) "There was being" speaks of the coming of creation. The nuclei and embryos, generic forms such as roots, stems, tissues, twigs and leaves of variegated hues, appeared. Butterflies and insects flew hither and thither; insects crawled about. This was a stage of movement with the breath of life everywhere. At this stage things could be felt, grasped, seen, followed, counted and distinguished.[7]

(5) The state of 'non-being' was so called because when it was gazed on, no form was seen; when the ear listened, there was no sound; when the hand grasped, there was nothing tangible; when gazed at afar, it was illimitable. It was limitless space, profound and a vast void, a quiescent subtle mass of immeasurable translucency.[8]

(6) The state of "there was not yet a beginning of non-being" wrapped up heaven and earth, shaping and forging the myriad things of creation. There was an all-penetrating impalpable complexity, profoundly vast and all-extending. Nothing extended beyond it, yet even the minutest hair and sharpest point could not be within it. It was a space uncompassed by any wall, and it produced the basis of being and non-being.[9]

(7) In the period of "there was not yet a beginning of the not yet beginning of non-being," heaven and earth had not

yet split apart, the yin and the yang had not yet become differentiated, the four seasons were not yet separated, and the myriad things had not yet come to birth. Vast-like, even and quiet; still-like, clear and limpid; forms were not yet visible. It was like light in the midst of non-being which retreats and is lost sight of. [10]

The above, quoted from the *Huai Nan Tzu,* [10] is taken directly from Dr. Fung's brilliant *History of Chinese Philosophy.* These seven statements, each describing a singularly different phase of cosmic and precosmic phenomena, serve to define the concept symbolized by the lowest rectangle in the "Diagram of Cosmic Evolution." It is the abode of cosmos and chaos—each in a state of beingness that is beyond our ability to comprehend, yet crammed with the potential of infinite expression!

This area of Wu Ch'i, symbolizing the source and origin of things, images the actual bafflements in our own personal experiences which we cannot fingerpoint as a tangible, explicitly identifiable beginning—puzzling wonderments like: "Why am I?" "Why am I white—or black—or yellow?" "How is it that I am male or female?" "What is the reason for my being tall or short?" These are the faces of Wu Ch'i in our individualized beingness. These are results of phenomena that precede essence: 'before-the-beginning' of energy and intelligence, therefore beyond the possibility of our 'knowing'.

Our 'knowing' commences with the 'coming-into-beingness' of energy and intelligence. In the "Diagram of Cosmic Evolution" this stratum is identified as an area of polarization of forces. Polarization is not opposition but complementariness—

the dark and the light, the negative and the positive, the female and the male, the cold and the hot, the receptive and the projective, the soft and the hard, the empty and the full, the manifestation and the idea; in short, the yin and the yang.

This divided area presents to us an image of the nature of all that is, and all that can be experienced within this known and yet-to-be-known universe wherein we exist. It graphically displays the 'being' and 'non-being' of everything that will be humanly experienceable.

This concept is not singularly peculiar to oriental mysticism, as some may think. We find recognition of this thought in the writings of various Western philosophers. A case in point may be found in the writings of the distinguished American educator and philosopher John Dewey. In one of his books, *Experience and Nature,* he observed Lao Tzu-like:

> The visible is set in the invisible; and in the end what is unseen decides what happens in the seen; the tangible rests precariously upon the untouched and ungrasped.[11]

Indeed, our 'being' is determined by our 'non-being'. It is the limitation imposed by 'non-being' upon the processes of our becoming that gives us definition. This is part of the significance of the 61st kua, "Inner Truth". In the Sequences it is written of "Inner Truth": *"Through being limited, things are made dependable . . . Inner Truth means dependability."* [12] The yin and yang become a graphic expression of the unification of polarized forces which are not antagonistic to each other, but rather which are complementary. Yin and yang is a portrait of the two forces of phenomena which are necessary to express our 'beingness'. They are like the positive and negative charges of electricity, without which there is no way to give evidence of the potential power of expressiveness that is electricity.

We inhale and the lungs are inflated. Breathing in air is indispensable to the living process as it is known to our consciousness. But we cannot inhale only. In order to live we must release each breath of life-giving air. This process of exhaling in turn deflates the lungs. Life is function, happening 'polaritously'. It is expressed within a polarity of dynamic immanence. Life is inseparable from Wu Ch'i, yet it has no conscious concern with it.

These may be difficult concepts to grasp immediately. Our Western languages are not grammatically equipped to express such ideas, except as unique innovations in our thinking process. The Chinese language, on the other hand, has the concept of ultimate unity and that of eternally enduring change built into its grammar. In consequence, such ideas do not appear as unique innovations of thought, but rather as natural conceptualizations reflecting the actualities of life about us. More will be said about this later.

So far, the "Diagram of Cosmic Evolution" (see page 37) reminds us that there are aspects of our nature that we experience with no hope of ever knowing how, when, or where they began. It informs us that there are deep realities within our experiences, and superficial realities, both of which fall into this category of untraceable things that go back into the 'Before-the-beginning'. It is a simple and direct way of saying: "Wake up and recognize what you can understand and control, and recognize what is beyond your understanding and control. In a word, come to know what you can bend, and what you must bend to!"

This second stratum of the diagram, pictures the underlying principle of individualized beingness. This principle is called yin and yang—in mechanical terms, cause and effect. But yin-yang as a principle symbolizes something far greater than just cause and effect. The more significant thing symbolized is made quite clear by John Dewey.

A 'cause' is not merely an antecedent; it is that antecedent which if manipulated regulates the occurrence of the consequent. That is why the sun rather than night is the causal condition of day.[13]

I Ching is a method of causal manipulation. Yin and yang awaken us to the binary requisites for successful and productive living. It pictures the systole and diastole action for all of the organic involvements of life. By organic involvements, I mean all the vital manifestations which persons experience as mental, physical, intellectual, emotional and psychic functions which impinge upon, or issue from, a state of awareness.

In Chinese literature there are numerous writings which describe, explain, define and example the concept of yin and yang. There are many theoretical projections as to what the principle is, and its usefulness in helping us to comprehend the universe about us and the life force within us.

Yang indicates a forward movement, and yin is the movement of drawing back. They serve as polarized terminals of force which are forever engaged in an exchange of influence one upon the other. The product of this interaction is called 'change'. 'Change' is without limit as to the variety of things it becomes through the processes of decay and growth. 'Change' is that which transforms itself. 'Change' is a sequence of becoming and 'begoning'. This is a meaning of yin and yang. To try to hold what is passing is painful. To grasp at what has not yet arrived is foolish. As we release what is passing, we center into the 'now' and avoid the pain of attachments. By being involved with the 'now', wherein we are centered, we avoid the frustrating anxieties of anticipation. Thus we master the meaning of yin and yang.

The third stratum of the "Diagram of Cosmic Evolution" is divided into four sections. Each section symbolizes an element: water, wind/wood, metal, fire; and a fifth element, earth, which is understood to contain, and to enable the expression of, the other four. Another symbolic meaning identified with the four sections is that of the seasons of the year, winter, spring, summer, and autumn, as contained within and following each other consecutively throughout the year.

It is important to understand that the five elements do not refer to organic substances. They are, instead, representative of forces—forces which, in terms of human experience, may be expressed in attitudes, behavior, feelings or intellectual manifestations. We hear of someone who romanced with a fiery passion. Of another it was said, he had a will of iron and nerves

WATER	WIND/WOOD	METAL	FIRE
WINTER	SPRING	AUTUMN	SUMMER

of steel. Another will be referred to as a "milktoast" with a backbone of water. And we may caution someone not to try to advise such-and-such a person, for it is useless to talk to him—he has a wooden ear. We may recommend that a friend going on a trip visit another friend, as he is a very enjoyable and "earthy" person. And we understand, in each instance, that these elements represent degrees of intensity of the interrelationship of the forces symbolized by yin and yang. The content is not the substance represented by the word, but the force or faculty symbolized by it.

Students sometimes ask: "Why do the Chinese not regard air as one of the basic elements?" The ancient Greek and Roman philosophers held the four elements to be fire, air, water and earth. To the Chinese, air is an etherlike thing. It is closely akin to, if not symbolically identical with, Chi and Ch'i. Dr. Wing-Tsit Chan, writing on the difficulties of translating a number of Chinese philosophical terms, endorses the point I shall try to make.

No two translators of Chinese terms will ever agree entirely on their translations. Since each Chinese character has several meanings, different emphases by different translators are inevitable. Some terms are so complicated in their meanings, like yin . . . and its opposite, yang, that they have to be transliterated. Others call for interpretation rather than a literal translation. [14]

In order to develop an understanding that will equip us with the means whereby we can successfully apply the wisdom of *I Ching* in the course of our everyday lives, I shall draw upon the meanings of both Chi and Ch'i. If justification is needed, let me rest my right to do so upon Dr. Chan's observation that, "In a number of cases, the translation is difficult and controversial. While personal choice is in order, there should be adequate reasons behind it." [15] My reason is set forth in the desire to develop an understanding that will help us to fuse *I Ching* intelligently into our lives.

I've stated that air is closely akin to, if not symbolically identical with Chi and Ch'i. I mean by this that air is like a finger pointing at "The moving power, the bond, the commensurate incipient force, the already, the vital force, etc., but it must never be mistaken for being any one or all of these." [16] These are some of the meanings of Chi and Ch'i. We have only to look at Dr. Chan's appendix to get a sense of the breadth of ideas possible when different people translate and interpret Chinese characters. Dr. Chan writes about Chi and Ch'i:

> Chi, "subtle, incipient, activating force." Graham expresses the sense of the term most correctly in the phrases "inward spring of movement" and "incipient movement not yet visible outside." Both Bodde's "motive force" and Carsun Chang's "state of subtley" are correct but incomplete. [17]

> Ch'i, "concrete thing." This is a technical philosophical term that should not be understood in its popular meanings of an instrument, an implement, or a vessel, or be distorted to mean matter, substance, or material entity. Philosophically it means a concrete or definite object in contrast to Tao which has neither spatial restriction nor physical form. It also includes systems and institutions, or any thing or affair that has a concrete form. [18]

> Ch'i, "material force." Every student of Chinese thought knows that Ch'i as opposed to Li (principle) means both energy and matter, a distinction not made in Chinese philosophy. Both "matter" and "ether" are inadequate.

Dubs' "matter-energy" is essentially sound but awkward
and lacks an adjective form. Unless one prefers trans-
literation, "material force" seems to be the best. In many
cases, especially before the neo-Confucian doctrine of Li
developed, Ch'i denotes the psychophysiological power
associated with blood and breath. As such it is translated
as "vital force" or "vital power," and in the case of hao-jen
chih ch'i as "strong, moving power." Such are the cases in
Mencius, 2A:2.[19]

To explain it as simply as possible, Chi and Ch'i permeate all
things. We conceive of all things as being composed of molecules moving about at different degrees of compactness in
space. There is air in water, in wood, in metal, in fire and in the
earth. Therefore air is not a basic element, but an all-
encompassing dynamic entity, with, in, and about the five
elements. It is apparent that air, ether and spirit frequently have
a very similar value in Chinese thought. As in many non-Western
and also in unsophisticated Western cultures, the Chinese speak
of wood-spirits, water-spirits, fire-spirits, etc., etc. From a
Chinese view, air is not one of the basic elements. Later I shall
enlarge upon the scope and definition of what is symbolized by
these archetypes: yin and yang, the four complexions of its
nature, and the five elements, sometimes called the five agents
or five stages of 'change.'

These five elements (五行 wu Hsing), water, fire, wind/
wood, metal and earth are archetypes which correspond to and
express various human activities. The ancient sages furnished
these metaphors whereby a man could examine himself. It is
written in the *Book of History*—one of the Confucian classics—
" 'the nature of water is to moisten and descend. The nature of
fire is to burn and ascend. The nature of wood is to be crooked
and straight. The nature of metal is to yield and be modified.
The nature of earth is to provide for sowing and reaping.' Of
these it is said, 'that which moistens and descends produces
saltiness; that which burns and ascends produces bitterness; that
which is crooked and straight produces sourness; that which
yields and is modified produces acridity; that which provides
for sowing and reaping produces sweetness.' "[20]

While each element alludes to a human activity, only two, water and earth, are explored in any depth as to archetypal significance. Since it will further our understanding of *I Ching* and enhance our ability to meaningfully interpret its wisdom, we shall acquaint ourselves with the rationale of Chinese thought in this area. Perhaps the most difficult idea for non-Chinese thinkers to accustom themselves to is that of a nearly limitless succession of influences that can be initiated by a single source, element or metaphor. As we develop this kind of elasticity in our thinking, the practicality of *I Ching* will become clearer. So, let us study what Dr. Fung refers to as "a very curious idea expounded in the *Kuan-Tzu* (Ch.39)." [21] The following excerpts are from the fourteenth Chuan, pp. 1-3, as quoted by Dr. Fung:

> The earth is the origin of all things and the root of the living. It is the producer of the beautiful and the ugly, worthy and unworthy, stupid and eminent. Water is the blood of the earth, and flows through its muscles and veins. Therefore it is said that water is something that has complete faculties. . . . It is accumulated in heaven and earth, and stored up in the various things (of the world). It comes forth in metal and stone, and is concentrated in living creatures. Therefore it is said that water is something spiritual.[22]

> Man is water, and when the producing elements of male and female unite, liquid flows into forms. . . . Thus water becomes accumulated in jade, and the nine virtues appear. It congeals to form man, and his nine openings and five viscera appear. This is its refined essence. . . . What is it, then, that has complete faculties? It is water. There is not one of the various things which is not produced through it. It is only he who knows how to rely (on its principles) who can act correctly. . . . [23]

> Hence the solution for the sage who would transform the world lies in water. Therefore when water is uncontaminated, men's hearts are upright. When water is pure, the people's hearts are at ease. Men's hearts being upright, their desires do not become dissolute. The people's hearts being upright, their conduct is without evil. Hence the sage when he rules the world, does not teach men one by one, or house by house, but takes water as his key. [24]

Dr. Fung sums up the content of this portion with the following words: "In this passage water is made the origin of all things, so that the regulation of water becomes the means for the ruling of men. If one wishes to reform the world one must reform men's hearts, which can be done by changing the quality of the water."

Throughout the ten upon tens of centuries of Chinese civilization, there have been great fluxes in the philosophical, religious and social customs, values, mores and ideas of her people. From China's earliest recorded times the concepts of yin and yang, along with the principles of 'change' as indicated in *I Ching*, have exercised a great influence in shaping the expressions of its culture. To grasp any worthy degree of understanding of *I Ching*, it is important to consider all the philosophies which have experienced prominence during the era of *I Ching* influence. To be sure, many of these philosophies were at great variance with one another, as well as being in strong competition. This wisdom is the oldest continuing influence in Chinese life. It preceded the two dominant forces of Taoism and Confucianism by many centuries. The present influence of communism (especially as conceptualized by Chairman Mao) is not wholly alien to the fundamental basic propositions of *I Ching*. Indeed, the philosophical tenets of Mao are in many respects updated modern affirmations of ideological concepts which are basic to the Chinese psyche. There is no unbridgeable gap between the Marxist dialectic of 'negation of the negation,' and the symbolism of each thing having seeded within it its opposite, as imaged in the T'ai Chi Tu. More will be said about this later. For the moment let us return our attention to studying the third stratum of the "Diagram of Cosmic Evolution."

WATER	WIND/WOOD	METAL	FIRE	
	WINTER	SPRING	AUTUMN	SUMMER

We have already noted that its four sections are offered as a graphic representation of the five elements of agents of the life experience. The stratum itself is the symbol of earth which both holds the other four elements (water, wind/wood, metal and fire), and simultaneously is composed of them. These five agents, it should be remembered, are not physical substances, but are archetypal symbols of forces and modes which dominate or strongly influence particular periods of time, such as the seasons which cycle annually in a succession that is preestablished.

If we give serious study to the identification of the five elements with a selection of nineteen correspondences, we will become more proficient in comprehending the principles of the phenomenon of 'change'. The following "Table Of Correspondences for the Five-Agents System" is taken from *Sources Of Chinese Tradition,* a valuable reference for acquainting oneself with the history of Chinese philosophy.

The traditional assignments can be seen in the above chart. Wood corresponds to the spring season, which is associated with the color green and the direction east. Fire is placed with summer; its color is red and south is its location. The element of metal is assigned to autumn; its color is white, its direction in west. Water is paired with winter; its color is black and it is located in the north. Earth holds the yearly cycle symbolized by the insertion of the twelve animals of time (the zodiac); yellow is its color and it is located in the center of all directions.

The "Table of Correspondences" contains sufficient material for writing an entire new volume just to expand upon the symbolic implications of the various correspondences cited. For now, we need only accept the tradition that holds that they proceed in an order by which they generate each other. Water nourishes seed and produces wood; wood furnishes the fuel for fire; fire, creating ashes, establishes earth; earth cooling and hardening produces metal; metal sweating creates water, and here the cycle recommences.

Before moving on to the fourth stratum of the "Diagram of Cosmic Evolution," it should be mentioned that the idea of the

The Five Agents [25]

CORRESPONDENCE	WOOD	FIRE	EARTH	METAL	WATER
Seasons	Spring	Summer	Zodiac*	Autumn	Winter
Divine Rulers	T'ai Hao	Yen Ti	Yellow Emperor	Shao Hao	Chuan Hsu
Attendant Spirits	Kou Mang	Chu Yung	Hou T'u	Ju Shou	Hsuan Ming
Sacrifices	Inner door	Hearth	Inner Court	Outer Court	Well
Animals	Sheep	Fowl	Ox	Dog	Pig
Grains	Wheat	Beans	Panicled millet	Hemp	Millet
Organs	Spleen	Lungs	Heart	Liver	Kidneys
Numbers	Eight	Seven	Five	Nine	Six
Stems	Chia/i	Ping/ting	Mou/chi	Keng/hsin	Jen/kuei
Colors	Green	Red	Yellos	White	Black
Notes	Chueh	Chih	Kung	Shang	Yu
Tastes	Sour	Bitter	Sweet	Acrid	Salty
Smells	Goatish	Burning	Fragrant	Rank	Rotten
Directions	East	South	Center	West	North
Creatures	Scaly	Feathered	Naked	Hairy	Shell-covered
Beasts of the Directions	Green Dragon	Scarlet Bird	Yellow Dragon	White Tiger	Black Tortoise
Virtues	Benevolence	Wisdom	Faith	Righteousness	Decorum
Planets	Jupiter	Mars	Saturn	Venus	Mercury
Officers	Minister of Agriculture	Minister of War	Minister of Works	Minister of Interior	Minister of Justice

*This space is blank in the original chart. I have inserted the word "Zodiac" here for the purpose of rounding out the chart by emphasizing that the annual cycle of the four seasons constitutes the total year. In the Chinese "zodiac," the signs consist of twelve animals. Each is taken to exercise an influence over a year. In Chinese astrology the signs are figured on the basis of annual influences which recur every twelve years in a sexagenary cycle.

cyclicity of phenomena is thought to characterize all 'changes'. However, there are two interpretations of this cyclical process, each having played the leading role at one time or other in Chinese history. One theory promotes the idea that one force *overcomes* another. The other theory postulates the view that one force *produces* another. In time, the Chinese concept came to accept the thesis that all forces are harmonized, each supporting one other and negating another.

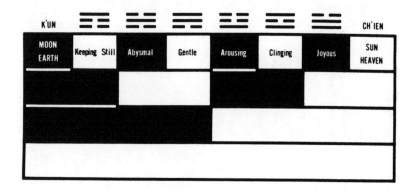

The fourth stratum of the "Diagram of Cosmic Evolution" is a composite of eight subdivisions. This pictures the particularizations of force and form which result by extending the phenomenal processes of 'change'. It is said Confucius remarked: *"Ch'ien and K'un are indeed the gate of change."* This diagram pictures heaven and earth (the two long-enduring things), enclosing "Standstill," "The Abysmal," "The Gentle," "The Arousing," "The Clinging," and "The Joyous" (the six short-enduring things). These concepts can be interpreted in various ways. Another view: firmness, stability = mountains; softness, encompassment = water; form, structure = wood; vibration, sound, space = thunder; heat, light = fire; placidity, calm = lake —all phenomenal forces evolving within the night and day of time or what may be thought of as the consciousness and unconsciousness of experience. To recognize a reflection of the cosmic thing in the man-thing is what enriches *I Ching* with meaning. When this is learned, one can then use *I Ching* in meeting and coping with everyday experiences.

The Chinese express many relationships by reference to these images. For example: heaven is high, ☰, and earth, ☷, is low. This clearly indicates that there are distinctions between the high and the low; it thus enables the honorable and the humble to locate their places. Activity and tranquillity have endurance, thus we can distinguish between the strong and the weak. It is said, "In the heavens, forms (heavenly bodies) appear and on earth, shapes (creatures) occur. In them 'change' and transformation can be seen." [27]

The fourth stratum of eight subdivisions is of basic importance. It is at this stratum that all the fundamental principles, which are contained in each of the basic pa kua (the eight trigrams), are symbolically or otherwise represented. Here we will discover the pictorial inspiration for the ancient sages who "determined the Tao of heaven and called it the dark and the light. They determined the Tao of the earth and called it the yielding and the firm. They determined the Tao of man and called it love and rectitude." [28]

The wisdom of *I Ching* embraces the timeless concept of yin and yang. It holds that their interaction created the four forms: major yang, minor yang, major yin and minor yin. To each of these are assigned one of the five elements (water, wind/wood, metal and fire). The fifth element, earth, taken as the repository containing the other four elements, is likewise here assigned to the idea symbolized by the T'ai Chi Tu, which encompasses the total action-interaction of yin and yang.

T'ai Chi Tu

The evolution of the four forms into eight images is partially explained in chapter two of the Eighth Wing (Shuo Kua 說卦). [29] "Heaven and earth determine the direction." The meaning becomes clear when you look at the diagram. Heaven and earth each occupy an extreme outer division of the stratum's eight subdivisions. "Direction" here refers to something more than the points of a compass. It connotes, among other ideas: aggressive action and degressive action, projective and receptive energy, systolic contraction and diastolic expansion, outward and inward perception, forward movement and backward movement; in short, the orientation of the yin and yang propensities as they are experienced through conscious awareness on whatever plane.

The next sentence reads: "The forces of mountain and lake are united." Here the idea of union is indicated by the mountain that is lifted up by the earth, and the lake in the mountain's crest that is held down by heaven. Union becomes the consequence of a properly proportioned relationship of yin and yang.

The focus and direction now changes from the outside of the diagram moving inward, to the center of the diagram from where it will begin the outward movement. This is an important switch. It graphically illustrates the forward and backward movements described in the subsequent paragraph of this part of the Shuo Kua. Hence, the third statement reads: "Thunder and wind arouse each other." The principle being expounded is that of giving equal consideration to the appropriateness of gentle and quiet influences as well as to harsh and forceful ordering. It is only by examining both sides of issues that we come to an adequate understanding whereupon we may determine the most effective goal-reaching action.

The last statement made in this part of the Shuo Kua is "Water and fire do not combat each other." Again the yin and yang aspects of life are reemphasized. It is only in the phenomenal world that water and fire appear to be irreconcilables. In the cosmic universe there is no conflict between water and fire. Their relationship is of a complementary nature; together they are the means of effecting the germination of all life forms. The reality displayed here is one designed to awaken us to a realization of the fact that all phenomena in a polarized universe of manifested things are the result of a proper use of the positive and negative terminal forces of that polarity. It is stated in the *Tao Te Ching* of Lao Tzu in the following words:

> Thirty spokes converge upon a single hub;
> It is on the hole in the center that the use of the cart hinges.
>
> We make a vessel from a lump of clay;
> It is the empty space within the vessel that makes it useful.
>
> We make doors and windows for a room;
> But it is these empty spaces that make the room livable.
>
> Thus, while the tangible has advantages,
> It is the intangible that makes it useful. [30]

This principle of 'complementarity' is treated in Western thought by Hegel, and was developed in Marxian dialectics. It was poetically stated by the author of the biblical book Ecclesiastes in the third chapter (3:1-8).

> To every thing there is a season, and a time to every purpose under the heaven: a time to be born, and a time to die; a time to plant, and a time to pluck up that which is planted; a time to kill, and a time to heal; a time to break down, and a time to build up; a time to weep, and a time to laugh; a time to mourn, and a time to dance; a time to cast away stones, and a time to gather stones together; a time to embrace, and a time to refrain from embracing; a time to get, and a time to lose; a time to keep, and a time to cast away; a time to rend, and a time to sew; a time to keep silence, and a time to speak; a time to love, and a time to hate; a time of war, and a time of peace. [31]

We have examined separately each of the eight subdivisions of the fourth stratum of the "Diagram of Cosmic Evolution." We see that four of the divisions are used to symbolize natural phenomena (thunder, wind, rain and sun). The remaining four areas are used to represent conditions man experiences in life, such as "Keeping Still" (contemplativeness), "The Joyous" (pleasure pursuits), "The Originating" (biological, artistic, intellectual and constructural creativity), and "The Receptive" (docility, empathy, understanding, obedience and serving). Each of these eight subdivisions is characterized by a kua. A kua is a trilinear construct composed of whole or broken lines, or combinations of whole and broken lines. These eight linear constructs of three lines are known as the pa kua (the eight images). They constitute the basic elements of the sixty-four kua (linear images of six lines each), to which are appended the expressed wisdom and the philosophy of 'change'. By squaring the eight three-line kua, you get the sixty-four six-line images.

By restructuring the "Diagram of Cosmic Evolution" in eight vertical segments we shall see how the linear image is a logical picture of the interrelationship of the forces of yin and yang as depicted in the full diagram under examination. (*I Ching* deals with the forces which are operative in life as we experience them on a manifested plane.) Therefore, the eight basic linear images reflect the interplay of energy and intelligence from the yin-yang strata of the diagram. This is the plane of 'being' and 'non-being,' the plane that is known to and experienceable by man as a living creature.

STAGES 8 and 1

By picturing the black areas of the "Diagram of Cosmic Evolution" as yin (--), and the white areas as yang (—), you can see how each segment in the tier of the diagram contributes to the structure of each kua. Thus in stage 1 the segment of each tier is white (yang), giving the emblem for Ch'ien as three unbroken lines. At the opposite end of the diagram, stage 8, the segment of each tier is black (yin), giving the emblem for K'un as three broken lines. These two emblems constitute the two long-enduring things: heaven and earth; positive and negative; systole and diastole action, etc., etc.

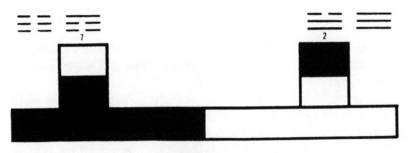

STAGES 1 and 2

Stage 2 shows the segment of the bottom two tiers as white (yang), and the segment of the third (top) tier as black (yin), giving the emblem for Tui. The opposite corresponding section of the diagram, stage 7, shows the segments of the bottom two tiers as black (yin), and the segment of the third (top) tier as white (yang), giving the emblem for Kên. These are the first two of six emblems representing the short-enduring things. They symbolize mountain and lake; "Keeping Still" and "The Joyous"; the high dry land and the low marsh land, etc., etc.

Stage 3 of the diagram is one of pictorial balance. The segments of the bottom and top tier are white (yang), and the center tier segment is black (yin), giving the emblem for Li. The corresponding area in the opposite section of the diagram, stage 6, has the segment of the bottom and top tiers as black

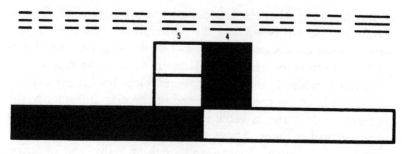

STAGES 5 and 4

(yin), and the center tier segment is white (yang), giving the emblem for K'an. These kua symbolize fire and water; hot and cold; darkness and light, etc., etc.

Stage 4, where the segment of the bottom tier is white (yang), and the segments of tiers two and three are black (yin), gives the emblem for Chên. Adjoining it, on the opposite side of the center of the diagram, is stage 5. The segment of the bottom tier is black (yin), while the segments of tiers two and three above are white (yang), giving the emblem for Sun. These symbolize "The Arousing" and "The Gentle"; thunder and wind; blatancy and subtlety, etc., etc.

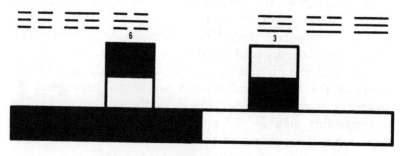

STAGES 6 and 3

These eight emblems constitute the foundation for every phrase, idea and prognostication of *I Ching*. De Lacouperie was not sympathetic to the occultism attached to *I Ching* by both the Chinese and many of the European scholars of the eighteenth and nineteenth centuries. Yet he was always seeking information that could be added as confirmation of a possible connection of the pa kua with the knotted cords or Quippos, and with the eight arrows of Marduk, as treated in his *Early History of Chinese Civilization*. Many of the very early European scholars felt that there was a bearing between *I Ching* and belomancy (divination with arrows). This was especially true of such men as J. P. Schumacher of Wolfenbuttel (1763), Dr. O. Piper (1849-53), Adolf Helfferich (1868), P. A. Zottoli, who was with the Nankinese Mission (1880), and P. Regis, the brilliant Jesuit scholar who authored the entire *I Ching* text and the commentaries in a Latin translation. I mention these old interests in the hope that they will be reexamined as sources which may yet enlarge our understanding of this most challenging and perplexing literature.

I propose that any serious study of these diagrams will develop a deeper understanding of the indications intended by the interplay of the forces symbolized. Once the dynamic of the phenomena of 'change' becomes deeply rooted in one's consciousness, one will meet and successfully cope with any unusual or unexpected situation with which one may be confronted. Let us begin by reviewing a partial list of the basic forces symbolized by yin and yang as they are used in *I Ching*.

Yin is dark, yielding, receptive, beneath, female, negative, the derived principle, serving, the cow with a calf, the mother, cloth, square, frugality, a kettle, level, large wagon, form, the multitude, a shaft, and among soils, it is the black. Yin is low, cold, weak, moon, following, limited, 'being'.

Yang is light, firm, projective, above, male, positive, the effecting principle, commanding, the dragon, the father, jade, round, prolific, high, formless, the one, a horse with power, a horse of endurance, a horse of firmness, a horse of strength, fruit. Yang is that which endures through 'change,' limitless, 'non-being'.

The "Diagram of Cosmic Evolution" should be viewed as a communicator reporting in code the activities and processes of 'change.' Each stratum informs us that there is a development in the equivalence of the forces known as yin and yang. We may think of these forces as complements of many different things; such as energy and intelligence, form and formlessness, being and non-being, ideas and things, etc., etc. Whatever our thought may be, the "Diagram of Cosmic Evolution" expresses an alteration of equivalence between the polarities with which we are operating.

The portion of the diagram representing the "Before-the-beginning," (Wu Ch'i), is here omitted. We will commence our inquiry by going back to the second stratum that images yin and yang. In passing, I would comment that yin and yang are closely akin to the 'being' and 'non-being' concept of existentialism. In the T'ai Chi Tu (see page 49) we can observe how yin and yang picture the union of beingness with non-beingness. It graphically reveals how we can differentiate because of the interrelationship of consciousness with non-consciousness. Yin-yang symbolizes how form is determined by formlessness, and how the formless is dependent upon form. Yin presents an accomplished fact of being that stands as testimony for the unexpressed potential hidden in the non-being of yang.

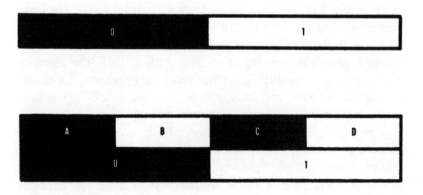

Once the process of manifestation commences, each terminal of polarity continues to express itself in subsequent polarity. By this means, the hidden potential of Wu Ch'i individuates on more and more numerous planes. Hence, the third stratum of the diagram is subdivided into four areas.

Area A is called the great or major yin, while area D is the great or major yang. Area B is called the lesser or minor yang, and area C is known as the lesser or minor yin. How does this develop? Out of the "Great Ultimatelessness" (Wu Ch'i), there came the darkness (yin) and the light (yang). If we were to describe it differently—out of the potential of 'non-being' there emerged 'being' (yin, the dark, the form), and the residue that did not become, remained as 'non-being' (yang, the light, the formless)—we have another way of understanding it.

It is interesting to note that, usually, when reference is made to these polarity forces, they are voiced or written in just that order: yin and yang, the dark and the light. In the Judeo-Christian scriptures Genesis follows the same prescription in phrasing its account of the creation. The same principle of evolution which was expressed by the men who gave us *I Ching* was also understood and recorded by the authors of the Bible. *"And the evening and the morning were the first day."* [32]

Could it be that the practice of expressing significant events in terms which follow the order of yin and yang, dark and light, is something that is rooted as an archetypal image in the 'ever-conscious' of man? After all, a twentieth-century popular song speaks of a significant love under the title "Night and Day." Also there is the colloquial expression: "Don't make a commitment unless you have it down in black and white." It is not irrational to suspect that there is a profound realization behind the order of this traditional expression.

Let us make a summary review of what we have covered so far. Out of the potential in 'non-beingness' that precedes existence and consciousness, there issued forth the condition making form possible. We call it yin. What inner-contained potential in 'non-being' that did not become (that which was not *manifested* as yin) remained as a residue of complementary balance, called yang. This yang has a vitality, but it is different in degree and in its equativeness to the vitality of Wu Ch'i. However, it follows the pattern of expressing itself in polarity. The new polarity it enlarges into is pictured in the diagram as D and C. If we measure the combined areas of yang 1 and subdivisions C and D, we find that it is a compound of three-quarters yang and one-quarter yin. The identical process of development which we have just described as happening with yang 1 is also true and followed by yin 0. And when we measure the combined areas of yin 0 and subdivisions A and B, we find that it is a composite of three-quarters yin and one-quarter yang. Thus from the arithmetic of the proportions alone, it is obvious why A is called great yin, B lesser yang, C lesser yin and D great yang.

We can now turn our attention to the makeup of the fourth stratum. It is certainly one of the most important bands in the "Diagram of Cosmic Evolution." It is sectioned into eight subdivisions, each of which receives one of the constructs and names of the pa kua. These three-line constructs are basic configurations which are indispensable for expressing the wisdom of *I Ching*. It is this fourth band that symbolizes man's activity and involvement with life. Let us study it carefully.

Receptive	Keeping Still	Abysmal	Gentle	Arousing	Clinging	Joyous	Originating
K'UN	KÊN	K'AN	SUN	CHÊN	LI	TUI	CH'IEN
k 8	k 7	k 6	k 5	k 4	k 3	k 2	k 1

| A | | B | | C | | D | |
| 0 | | | | 1 | | | |

The insights of *I Ching* are expressed in terms of yin and yang. As we study the eight subdivisions in this diagram, let us keep that fact in mind. Section D, the great yang, divides into K1 and K2. The odd number is the yang aspect; the even number is the yin aspect. As we study the combined areas of D, K1 and K2, and associate it with the linear images ≡≡≡ and ≣≡≣ above, we see a graphic expression of the intellectual motivation that determines the order of placement of the yin and yang lines of each structured kua. The bottom line expresses the yang of 1. The middle line expresses the yang of D. The top line expresses the yang of K1. The kua is called Ch'ien, "The Originating." The kua K2, is composed likewise, the bottom line expressing the yang of 1, the middle line expressing the yang of D, and the top line expressing the yin of K2. The kua is called Tui, "The Joyous."

The areas C, K3 and K4 derive their linear structures ≡≡≡ and ≡ ≡ in the same way. The bottom line of Li expresses the yang of 1, the middle line expresses the yin of C and the top line expresses the yang of K3. It is called "The Clinging." The K4 kua's bottom line expresses the yang of 1, the middle line expresses the yin of C, and the top line expresses the yin of K4. It is called Chên, "The Arousing."

We have just completed a very primitive survey of the yang half of the "Diagram of Cosmic Evolution." How can the information furnished by these graphically illustrated insights be meaningfully applied to everyday life? What kind of self-understanding can we develop by studying these four yang symbols?

To begin, Ch'ien, ≡≡≡ , "The Originating," symbolizes the unknown and unknowable origin of 'beingness'. This applies to individual persons and to all other kinds of 'being' which can be classified as organic and inorganic. Ch'ien is that dynamic projection of energy-intelligence, the divine principle Tao, that culminates in the manifestation of things. Ch'ien is that part of us and everything that is mystery. Ch'ien is the impenetrable "Before-the-beginning," the anteriority that was before the anteriority that was 'before-the-beginning'. [33]

Next we progress from beginning to being. 'Beingingness' (form), is symbolized by K'un, ☷ ☷, "The Receptive," located at the extreme opposite end of the fourth stratum of the "Diagram of Cosmic Evolution." It is the yin factor. While it is the secondary stage of phenomenation, it must be regarded as the first stage for every instance that deals with human comprehension. It is an existentialist practicality to begin all speculations with existent things. When one has explored all the areas of what-is and what-is-not, then one may be considered equipped to seek after sources.

Until then we would be wise to recognize that all that is issues from a mystery. In a sense, all things are products of 'change' and 'chance'. Chance never happens by accident; but accidents may happen by chance!

The "Diagram of Cosmic Evolution" is a statement, an archetypal statement that can lead to the comprehension of the human situation via revelation. Revelation, or the intuitive consciousness, is a direct path to understanding. It seems, often, to be closed to many; perhaps because of its independence from rational thought. Archetypal statements express, define and/or describe a principle that can be observed to be operating in a great multiplicity of phenomena. Among these we will mention celestial, animal and plant life, man, societal systems, national cultures, world civilization and the newly evolving planetization.

In a recent article titled "Planetary Vistas," Dr. William Irwin Thompson wrote:

An epoch begins with a divine consciousness
of cosmic myth in the age of the gods.   Wu Ch'i

By the time of the following age of heroes,
half the cosmic myth is gone, and with it
half the divine consciousness.   Age of gods

By the time of the age of men, the myth and
the consciousness halve again, leaving only a
quarter of the original.   Age of heroes

Finally in the ultimate age of barbarism and
chaos, little of the original myth or divine
consciousness remains at all.   Age of men

Lecomte du Noüy, explaining his system of reference and
scale of observation, is quite adequately defining what is meant
by "a special kind of consciousness" when he writes:

Let us suppose that we have at our disposal two powders.
One white (flour) and the other black (finely crushed
charcoal or soot). If we mix them we will obtain a gray
powder which will be lighter in color if it contains more
flour and darker if it contains more soot. If the mixture is
perfect, on our scale of observation (that is, without the
help of a microscope), the phenomenon studied will
always be a gray powder. But let us suppose that an insect
of the size of the grains of flour or soot moves around in
this powder. For him there will be no gray powder, but
only black and white boulders. On his scale of observation
the phenomenon, "gray powder," does not exist. [34]

In a like manner, archetypal images and words will communicate to us in accordance with the kind of consciousness we
use in experiencing them. This is an epoch for the development of
new consciousness, a heightened and expanded consciousness.

But as entropy reaches its limit in chaos
there is a reversal in the cycle,   kua 63
an inverse entropy, in which the chaos   kua 64
creates the fertile decay for a new cosmic
myth and a new age of gods. We spiral back
to the past in a future on a higher level of
order. [35]

To illustrate the archetypal nature of this "Diagram of
Cosmic Evolution," let us apply it to another area of
phenomena—the psychological. The realization of this correspondence exploded upon my consciousness, once again, while
reading Dr. Thompson's intriguing article.

. . . we can also spiral back psychologically
to realize that the mind of mankind is a
collective and interpenetrating field.

Wu Ch'i
(ever-
conscious)

The unconscious is not personal, but in
order not to be swamped by infinite information, the brain functions as what Aldous
Huxley called "a reducing valve." It shuts
out the universe (Wu Ch'i) so that the individual can do what is in front of him. The
million signals a second must be reduced to a
few. But the intuition and imagination maintain an opening to the unconscious which
contains all the information which could not
register in "immediate consciousness." Since
the immediate consciousness must work in a
step-by-step incremental sequence of events,
its perception of time is linear. [36]

yang-yin
(ever
conscious)
Wu Ch'i

pa kua

As a third exhibit, let us read the diagram as a statement on
man. Let us remember that each line of a pa kua has a correspondence: the bottom line with earth, the middle line with
man, and the top line with heaven. It has also been expressed as
object, subject and content. When man came upon the scene of
the infinite, heaven and earth were preexistent to his arrival.
The third stratum of the diagram (A, B, C, D) constitutes the
five elements, in that it symbolizes the earth containing the four
agents of water, wood, metal and fire. This was the provision
for man's arrival on the scene of the infinite. All of the forces
involved with the creative process are here existent. However,
man cannot embrace or handle the totality of infinity. He
cannot create a universe within this infinity. So he fragments,
he shatters the universe in which he finds himself (in the
diagram this phase is represented by the continuing ongoing
process of the amoebic-like division of yin and yang), and from
these manageable chunks he carves a small Buddha, a little
Jesus, a graceful Qwan Yin, an intense Shiva, to symbolize his
consciousness of the infinite. This is our heritage. Out of
Wu Ch'i (Beinglessness, the Before-the-beginning), came heaven

and earth. From the first moment of consciousness man finds himself enveloped by a totality he cannot embrace. So he splinters heaven and earth and manipulates the slivers, attempting to become himself in chips or sawdust.

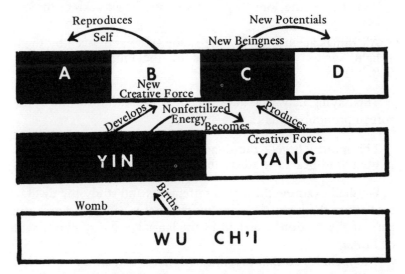

As you study the processes depicted by this diagram of cosmic phenomena, you will notice that it indicates a pendulum-like movement (a forward and a backward energy direction) graphically replicating the evolutionary sense of life. It pictures a lumbering giant who sways from right to left and left to right as life trods on, being the great implacable thing that it is!

The directional flow of the cosmic forces pictured by the arrows in this fragment of the "Diagram of Cosmic Evolution" emphasizes the dialectics of negation as a principle underlying everything in our universe. At the same time it is a graphic declaration of an existentialist conviction. 'Being' comes out of 'non-being'. 'Non-being' is not the same as nothing or nothingness. 'Non-being' identifies the unknowable state of all things before they have 'beingness'. That means not only their state before they have form; but also the state that they are in before they can even possibly be mentally visualized, or thought of, or capable of being conceptualized as an idea. It is the hidden Tao!

The forty-second chapter of *Tao Te Ching* reads:

Tao begets one; one begets two; two beget three; three beget all things.

All things are backed by the shade (yin) and faced by the light (yang), and harmonized by the immaterial breath (Ch'i). [37]

This saying may well have been the inspiration for the Pythagorean pronouncement:

The monad begets the duad; the duad begets the tetrad; the tetrad begets number, and number begets all things.

We shall examine these two statements and study the diagram to disclose the kind of cosmic insight that is a vital and enduring part of the wisdom couched in the language and symbolic signs of *I Ching*.

Tao includes all that ever was, all that is and all that ever shall be. Wu Ch'i, "Before-the-beginning," "The Ultimate Form Because It Has No Form," "The Supreme Ultimate," "The Ultimateless," etc., etc.—these all are names for the nameless and ever-hidden Tao. "Tao does nothing, yet through it all things are done." [38] Ch'u Ta-Kao interprets chapter four to read:

Tao, when put in use for its hollowness, is not likely to be filled.
In its profundity it seems to be the origin of all things.
In its depth it seems ever to remain.
I do not know whose offspring it is;
But it looks like the predecessor of nature. [39]

This Tao that "looks like the predecessor of nature," is graphically symbolized by the large, undivided rectangular form that is the foundation for the "Diagram of Cosmic Evolution."

There it *is!* It does nothing, yet in some mysterious way movement commences within it and direction is determined. Direction not so much in the sense of compass movement, nor of from-here-to-there, but direction in a phenomenal sense of from-this-to-that! This movement goes from right to left. (Of course, it must be understood that these expressions that graphically fix the route of movement are only symbolic, a necessary means of enabling us to glimpse a thin suggestion of what the cosmic process is. In a final analysis, where will you find up and down, or in and out, or left and right in infinity?) So we observe that there is a "phenomenation" (do forgive me for coining this term), that directs its movement from right to left. It is a process that establishes the requisite conditions for the distinction and the recognition of things. From out of the light (Wu Ch'i), the blinding light, there comes the difference of darkness that gives relief to our seeing. The seeing is not only optical, but includes auditory, sensory, olfactory, palatal, emotional, intellectual or psychical recognition. It is recognition made possible by the establishment of the requisite conditions for distinguishing things from each other.

An objection may be voiced that defining the initial movement in nature as being one to the left is wholly arbitrary and designed to accommodate the conclusion. After all, when drawing the arrow-line one need but slant the rule in the opposite direction to have it indicate the initial movement as being to the right. However, there is something deeply basic, a kind of cosmic heredity, contained within the *I*. The ancient sages declared that it was a key to understanding the totality of all that is. Many of the diagrams used to express its content are circles and/or the interrelationship of circles with circles. In the circle you have both movements, irrespective of what direction you may go in. So, with thoughtful perception, we will find other persuasive and supportive evidence to suggest that our description of what is being symbolized is a valid description, founded upon the truths contained in the archetypes of ideas and cultural habits.

The Chinese written language at the time in history when this diagram came into being, was customarily stroked from the upper right corner of the sheet downward, and in columns which ran from right to left. It would seem that there may have been something in the psyche that gave the initial movement in this diagram to the left. There may even be some significance to the practice of several great cultures, both in antiquity and presently surviving, which designed their literary matter so that it is read from right to left. Again, what explanation can one give for the tradition that marching begins with the left-foot-forward step? This suggests the idea that stability is founded upon the right foot, and movement into a change of position is made to the left. Consider that while most Americans eat holding the fork in the right hand, it is traditionally placed to the *left* of the plate. This necessitates an initial movement to the left in order to grasp the fork for supplying nourishment to the mouth. In plumbing, American houses are customarily (there are exceptions) fitted with the hot water faucet to the left. Heat and moisture are conducive to the production of living things. Cold and moisture are associated with barrenness and fruitless nonproductivity. One may continue to accumulate a great many references of movement and placement to the left, and may rationally infer the possibility that there is some deep meaningful arcanum in this fact.

I mention this miscellany not to state a principle, but to suggest that there is an intelligent and serviceable significance to these facts, which is demonstrable through the insights of *I Ching* as expressed in the "Diagram of Cosmic Evolution." The suggestion is not as fanciful as it may have been thought to have been some fifteen to fifty years ago. Today's fact, by scientific definition and declaration, is that we are individually and collectively composites of intelligence and energy' of varying intensities and compactness, existing in a universe of multiple force fields. The direction of flow of specific energy-bands in many instances is now known to determine what will be manifested. It is recognized that there is a correspondence between macrocosmic and microcosmic phenomena. This new scientific knowledge of our twentieth century was part of the inherent 'knowingness' of the ancient wise men in both highly evolved civilizations and simpler, so-called more natural cultures of tribal and clan traditions.

I have just touched upon the growth of our new scientific knowledge in that it now entertains concepts which were a part of early man's inherent 'knowing'. There is something to be gained when we recognize a distinction between knowledge and 'knowing'. I see knowledge as a halfway house between ignorance and 'knowing'. We are born in a state of 'knowing'. All creatures are born in a state of 'knowing'. One does not have to send an infant to nipple-sucking school to train it to feed from the mother's breast. The 'knowing' is inherent to the organism. It is during the process of individuation that the infant is separated from the whole. There are two ways in which this individuation occurs. First, by a gradual focus of the consciousness upon selected avenues of awareness, such as body comfort, nourishment satisfaction, physical associative experience—such as being reared in an environment of music or business or sports or religion or antireligion or politics or academia or illiteracy, etc. The other is through the beginning of indoctrination and training, so that the infant is slowly brought to focus upon what is expected of him; not in terms of the thing crying inside for expression and manifestation that is uniquely him, but rather in terms of what will be pleasing to those upon whom the child is, for the present, greatly dependent. In this way we are trained away from the harmonious path of natural 'knowingness' into the turbulent way of arbitrarily determined knowledge.

The diagram expresses the dynamic ambivalence that is exercised by nature in the process of its ever-evolvingness. Out of Wu Ch'i comes yin, the manifestation, the 'beingness'. That part of Wu Ch'i that did not become yin stands as a force field of tremendous potential, called yang. It alone maintains the only direct communication with Wu Ch'i.

Paul Carus's rendering of chapter 42 of *Tao Te Ching* gives another fascinating insight into the content of *I Ching* as imaged in the "Diagram of Cosmic Evolution." The first part reads:

Reason begets unity; unity begets duality; duality begets trinity; and trinity begets the ten thousand things. [40]

As Carus defines it, Wu Ch'i is commensurate with *"Reason so long as it remains latent is unnamable. Yet Reason alone is good for imparting and completing."* [41] "Imparting" is instigating and "completing" is fulfilling. Reason is thence the cause which accounts for something. Therein is the unity. Next Carus says "unity begets duality." That which is dual is that which has two forms: yin and yang. The phrase next following, "duality begets trinity," expresses several phenomenal developments.

We know that the A, B, C, D strata symbolize, among other things, the four seasons of the year: winter, spring, fall and summer. Winter is the severely cold season. Summer is the season of extreme heat. Between these two seasons is the interlude of temperateness. That is the trinity: cold, moderate and hot. The spring season is winter modifying itself, enticing, as it were, the passions of summer. The autumn, likewise, is summer putting a rein upon its zeal for activity and consenting to enter into quiet repose and the recreating dream tide of winter. Spring and autumn are, then, the seasons of transition. They are the dawn and dusk that separate day from night and night from day. In this way we see how "duality begets trinity."

Ch'u Ta-Kao quotes Yen Fu on this same chapter (chapter 42 of *Tao Te Ching*):

Tao is the primordial; it is absolute. In its descent it begets one. When one is begotten, Tao becomes relative, and two comes into existence. When two things are compared, there is their opposite, and three is begotten. [42]

At this point let us look at the diagram depicting the directional flow of cosmic forces on page 63, and study the schemata of phenomenal force fields as they have been observed by the ancient sages and *I Ching*. As we study the diagram we will discover that it significantly mirrors the nature of every human being. To make this discovery we must consider most thoughtfully the variety of phenomenal aspects of *I Ching*, as expounded by a long line of masterful commentators, and seek to understand what is hidden in them. When we begin to develop an understanding of the forces of energy and intelligence at play—which in some instances touch us, in others penetrate us, and in still others which emanate from us—we will then be merely on the threshhold of enlighenment. *I Ching* is a map of wisdom which, if properly comprehended, will direct us to this same threshhold.

As to what lies beyond that threshhold, I will not hazard to suggest either the beauties or the terrors. Each person, as he approaches the experiences that come with the expanding of one's consciousness, becomes aware of his singularly unique infinity. It is at this point of comprehension that one may awaken to the realization that, not only is there unity in diversity, but, also, that by experiencing multiplicity one discovers the secret key that reverts it into the indissoluble unity. Indeed, it is my hope to define and explain many principles of *I Ching* which deal directly and immediately with each of us. When we come to understand that *I Ching*'s linear images and words represent the very forces of energy, intelligence and intuition which are both for our use and for our being used by, we will become the *I*. When we become the *I*, we will have no anxieties about tomorrow, no need for divination, for we will be one with the 'changes' and living in the consciousness of 'now', experiencing pleasure and pain, knowing joy and sorrow, yet remaining detached from all.

Look again at the "Diagram of Cosmic Evolution." From out of the mysterious and indistinguishable realm of chaos and cosmos (Wu Ch'i), there emerges the material, yin (that which is manifested, the principle of beingness). This yin is counter-balanced by the immaterial, yang (that which is nonmanifested, the principle of potential, the faculty of becoming). Yin and yang constitute the nature of the finite universe. Yin is the manifested material universe of matter, the consequent of energy and intelligence having been projected out of the non-manifested immateriality of Tao. Hence, all matter is both that material thing which it has become, and the immaterial thing from where it originated. This demonstrates a principle of bifurcation. A part of matter's energy flow is directed toward sustaining, enlarging and preserving its material condition and character. The immaterial part of matter inherits the need to express itself in new avenues of manifestation, even though that must entail the disintegration of its present recognized character as it evolves into a wholly different condition of new 'beingness'. "When two things are compared, there is their opposite, and three is begotten." [43] This comparing results in the establishing of the great yang and lesser yin. These are represented by the linear structures of ⚌, great yang, and ⚍, lesser yin. These stem from the bifurcation of the primordial yang. The same process of bifurcation of the primordial yin principle yields us the great yin and the lesser yang. These are represented by the linear structures of ⚏, great yin, and ⚎, lesser yang.

This bifurcation continues until the great yang expresses itself as Ch'ien, ☰, "the Originating or Projective," and as Tui, ☱, "the Joyous." The lesser yin bifurcates into Li, ☲, "the Clinging," and Chen, ☳, "the Arousing." The lesser yang evolves into Sun, ☴, "the Gentle," and K'an, ☵, "the Abysmal." Great yin realizes itself as Ken, ☶, "Keeping Still," and as K'un, ☷, "the Receptive." It is these three strata of the diagram which images the terrestrial and celestial aspects which are inherent in and indispensable to man.

Strata 0 and 1 indicate the conditions of mysterization prevailing in each instance that involves man's conscious awareness, namely his activity-of-response to the phenomenon of manifestation (yin), and his eternal ensconcement within the machinations of what is not yet manifested (yang).

That there is an aura of profound mystery that envelops the entire process of life is immediately obvious whenever we try to give a logical and satisfying answer to the question: "What is the purpose of materially manifested, experiencing, living consciousness?" There is no way yet known to man (other than the esoteric attainment of a state of *samadhi*, or enlightenment), which satisfies rationally, emotionally and spiritually the wonderment of the becoming, being and 'begoning' of consciousness.

What is life but a puzzling process that expresses itself in patterns of energy and intelligence (thoughts)? Thought, by its nature, contains both the formlessness and the form of itself. Another of life's puzzling processes is what we, as humans, call the materialization of energy and intelligence (form). Form is a definement of life limited to the compactness of energy. This limitation (yin form) tends to conceal the intelligent (yang nature) aspect inherent in all life.

Intelligence is manifested as behavioral patterns, emotion and spirituality. The behavioral pattern is expressed by a mechanical utilization of the manifested form. Emotion is expressed within the form. Spirituality is experienced by transcending the form.

This, then, is a brief explanation of what is meant by the above paragraph. As we become aware of a mystique that envelops life, we will more easily avoid taking as absolutes those errors of illusion which come with pursuing the leads of logical reasoning. On the surface, it would appear that a logical approach to understanding the laws governing the group behavior of human beings would be to study the circumstances, qualities and characteristics of the individuals who make up the group. However, the truth is as Lecomte du Nouy observed. Turning the attention from the group to the individuals composing the group leads one into an entirely different field of information. It will not take long to discover that the psychology of a group cannot be determined by the deductions drawn from the psychological studies of the individuals composing it. [44]

The concept that admits there is an 'unknowable'—preexisting the "Before-the-beginning" (Wu Ch'i) and the yin-yang principle of polarity—is truly a premise that, with skillful use, enables one to embrace all things with understanding. When one arrives at the realization that things are simultaneously what they seem and not what they seem, then one is at the threshold of cosmic insight.

Charles-Eugene Guyes is reported to have declared: "The scale of observation is what creates it. In nature, different scales of observation do not exist. There is only one immense, harmonious phenomenon on a scale which in general escapes man because of the structure of his brain, a structure which necessitates dividing into arbitrary compartments, and cutting up into isolated pieces."[45] Perhaps *I Ching* is that single man-made scale of observation that most closely approximates that "one immense harmonious scale" that nature uses in expressing itself. Thus oriented, let us return to the diagram.

Strata A, B, C and D are graphic illustrations of what may be called container and content. In this philosophy, the earth (itself a symbol of 'located consciousness') is the container, while the other four elements (water, wood, metal and fire, the 'phenomenating' forces of life) make up the contents that fill the receptacle earth. In order to understand the very process of this experiencing, the sages imaged and defined the two natures of each of the elements in the pa kua (the eight trilinear constructs which are basic to the entire canon of 'changes'), four of which deal with natural phenomena and four with states and conditions of man.

A rather mystifying realization is that a great deal of information comes down to us through the commentaries concerning what, for convenience, are identified as strate 0, 1, 2, 3 and 6 of the "Diagram of Cosmic Evolution"; yet nothing is written about the significance or indications of strata 4 and 5. That there was no importance attached to these strata is exceedingly unlikely. One of the complaints of many Western scholars is the excessive attention and emphasis given to minutiae by the Chinese sages in their studies and treatments of these classical diagrams.

We sometimes hear of the oral tradition as synergic to the Oriental learning process. This tradition of orally passing insights on from master to merited disciple may have had its origin in necessity, due to the absence of the invention of writing. Whatever the case, it was, in time, hallowed as a means of protecting treasured information, and keeping it from falling into use by unqualified or undesirable persons. It will serve no useful purpose to argue the pros and cons of the oral tradition. We shall be content with the observation that there is a singu-

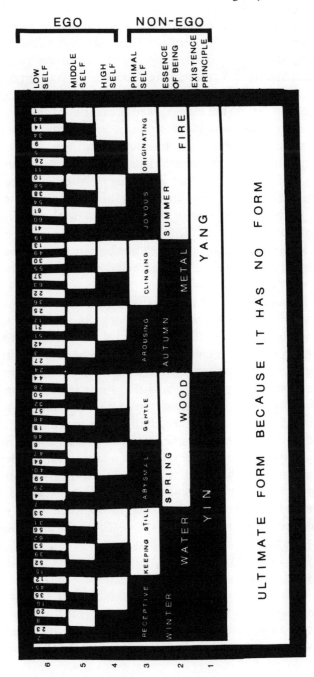

larly unique absence of explication concerning two strata in the "Diagram of Cosmic Evolution": one, stratum 4, immediately following stratum 3, which expresses the nature of the pa kua; the other, stratum 5, immediately preceding stratum 6, which particularizes the relationships of the kinds of forces of 'change' that are manifest as the experienced actualities of life.

Let us accept these silent strata as a challenge designed to encourage us to search them thoroughly for keys of new understanding and enlightenment. The benefits we derive from *I Ching* will be all the greater if, through a study of these strata, we can awaken to the untried potentials of dynamic being within ourselves. He who is concerned first with the discovery of insight and then with the using of insight becomes the "great man." With this as a goal, we need not be concerned about what an alleged oral tradition may have hidden regarding the silent strata.

When properly used, *I Ching* affords a means of going beyond patterned, traditional ways of thinking. It will not do your thinking for you; but it most certainly can incite you to new levels of consciousness which can be experienced as intriguing and creative. Here is a suggestion, using the *I Ching* "Diagram of Cosmic Evolution," for working out a method of comparative analysis that may open doors to self-understanding without which there can be only a very limited self-development. Think of 'self' as a yin-yang phenomenon consisting of a physical aspect which is complemented by a nonphysical faculty. The physical aspect is involved with all the problems which are a part of our mundane existence. We will call it the 'crude self' or 'low self'. It is expressed as contingent upon the sixth stratum of sixty-four identifiable processes of 'change' which constitute life in the sphere of causalistic phenomena.

As you look at the sixth, topmost stratum of the "Diagram of Cosmic Evolution," you find thirty-two dark areas alternating with thirty-two light areas, totalling sixty-four symbolic expressions of the forces of yin and yang. Each of these areas represents a kua. Each kua has a number and a name. Each name depicts a condition with which an individual may be involved in the process of living through their life. These sixty-four kua express aspects of 'change', and suggest that they succeed one another in various ways and, from time to time, serve as stimulating challenges that tax the ingenuity and imagination of one's will to survive and progress.

An entire book could be written on the sixty-four kua as symbolic expressions of forces (yin and yang) operative in the human experience. For the purpose of showing the vast indications discoverable in each kua that such a book would hold, I shall synoptically expound upon Chun, the third kua which is translated as: "Difficulty at the Beginning."

"Difficulty at the Beginning" is a statement that gives one a useful perspective when approaching any new concept, be it a thought, situation, relationship, thing, undertaking, etc., etc. The Judgment for this kua reads:

> Difficulty at the beginning works supreme success.
> Furthering through perseverance.
> Nothing should be undertaken.
> It furthers one to appoint helpers.

The initial phrase, "Difficulty at the beginning works supreme success," is something more than the mere recognition that the starting of things is begotten with difficulties. It clues one as to the kind of attitude one should adopt when inaugurating anything. The psychology of this is good. When a new undertaking is thought to be difficult, we immediately fortify ourselves to make a greater effort (in whatever way and at whichever level required) in order to progress. Because of this, each forward move is made with greater ease. In *Tao Te Ching* it reads:

> He who regards many things easy will find many difficulties. Therefore the sage regards things difficult, and consequently never has difficulties. [46]

It is said in *I Ching*, that to be mindful of difficulty at the beginning is to arm oneself with most of what can possibly be needed (routinely and emergency-wise). Thus one's preparation and initiative are structured to "work supreme success." The rationale that encourages such a great and meticulously instrumented anticipation is that anything which has the characteristics of a 'first birth' (new thing, beginning, radical departure from what is established, etc.) contains within itself a great profusion of potentials all "struggling to attain form." [47]

"Furthering through perseverance" is the next phrase. 'First birth' phenomena usually present odd and unfamiliar situations which, because of their unexpected strangeness, stimulate within one a sense of danger. These dangers are not necessarily threats from without; they may be dangers that are formed because of uncertainty within as to the way to handle the external situation. The situation itself often registers zero on a safety-danger scale, its only truly important attribute of distinction being that it is unique. But once the 'first birth' thing has begun, development comes only by contributing energy to the on-flowingness of the creative process "in spite of the existing danger." [48]

The third phrase advises that "nothing should be undertaken." Here we are confronted with what seems to be a contradiction. The law of 'change' has just finished telling us that "everything is in motion: therefore, if one perseveres there is a prospect of great success, in spite of the existing danger." [49] In the very next clause it says: "Nothing should be undertaken." A paradox?

From one point of view all truth or actuality is contained in and defined by the paradox. This is the meaning of yin and yang, each containing the seed of the other within itself, in the T'ai Chi Tu. To fulfill its role as a source of wise counsel the *I*, like a good attorney, examines both the pro and the con of each case. The sages were probably very aware of a tendency, common to most people, of generalizing indiscriminately. For this reason a careful distinction is made between the man who voluntarily begins something new and "when it is a man's fate to undertake such new beginnings. . . ." [50]

Let us take a play and two actors to illustrate the point. Actor A has a strong desire to play a particular role in this new play. He studies his lines, the situation, the period, and he familiarizes himself with the set and the costumes, etc. On opening night he stands in the wings awaiting his entrance cue. It comes—and he stands paralyzed. The danger from within. Someone pushes him on-stage. It is then that he realizes that he must now act and so, through perseverance, great success is surely furthered. Actor B has been engaged as the understudy. He has had the script for only a day or two. He has watched each of the three or four performances so far played. Actor A is taken ill. It is now actor B's fate to perform the role according to his contract as understudy. Since he has not had time to learn his lines, nor had the benefit of rehearsing with the other actors in the cast, he will do best by not undertaking the performance at this time. Instead, he will request that the stage manager read the role from the script during the performance, until he had had adequate and proper rehearsal.

A fourth and final clause of this Judgment counsels: "It furthers one to appoint helpers." It is, of course, a basic commonsense procedure. Whatever one is doing, assistance is required. "Helpers" are not necessarily other people. They may also be other things, other conditions, other places, other attitudes, etc. All such things as these can constitute "helpers." As you relate things through interpretation, these passages of *I Ching* become revelatory with meaning to any specific situation. One must learn to use the wisdom of *I Ching* as a metaphoric indicator of action to be taken. *I Ching* is a literary device that can activate an intellectual process that becomes responsive to the direction of the intuitive sense. This is the beginning of processing the self to become conscious of Tao. Consciousness of Tao is being in harmony with the cosmos. Being in harmony with the cosmos is to be in a state of 'nature-ness'. 'Nature-ness' is living at a plane of consciousness that transcends the three-dimensionality of 'low-self ego-beingness' and awakening in the state of 'primal being' which is separate from, yet one with, Tao.

There is a component of self which is most expressive of ego. One cannot become centered and know an inner peace until it has been brought under control. When the ego is out of control, one moves through the experiences of life with erratic difficulties, very much like a spastic whose locomotion over an irregular and obstacle-strewn terrain is uncertain and dangerous. Perhaps what is meant will become clear if one adopts the Kahuna view of the ancient Hawaiian pre-Christian religious tradition. The nature psychology of the Kahunas held that the 'ego-being' was a trinity of 'low-self', 'middle-self', and 'high-self'. The 'low-self' is basically the physical body. It is that part of our beingness which is most deceptive. We feel and think of it as our ultimate self, rather than as a thing the self uses. The physical body acts like a lodestone that draws to itself our sensations and our psychic consciousness, so that we become experientially convinced that 'ego-being' is our true being. However, the "Diagram of Cosmic Evolution," as we are using it, shows that 'ego-being' is a by-product generated out of the 'primal self', as it moves farther and farther away from 'essence', 'principle' and Wu Ch'i (the Before-the-beginning).

There is hidden in the fourth and fifth strata of the "Diagram of Cosmic Evolution" an individual revelation of self-nature for each person who will painstakingly delve into it. The true or 'primal self' originates in 'non-ego'. It (non-ego) may be thought of as a composite of mystery (Wu Ch'i), 'principle' and 'essence' which manifests as the 'primal self'. The 'primal self' is pictured as contingent upon the third stratum of the diagram that expresses the two long-enduring forces of manifested things and the six short-enduring forces of manifested things. The two long-enduring forces of manifested things are heaven and earth, known as 'principle'. 'Principle' originates out of Wu Ch'i and is expressed as a polarity of omnivalence and quiescence. This polarity sustains its identity and simultaneously produces 'essence'. 'Essence' is expressed as a tetrad that constitutes the five elements: fire, water, wood, metal and earth (consciousness). In order for fire, water, wood, metal and consciousness to coexist, there must be an interaction between them. The envelopment of the five elements by interaction introduces the phenomenon of "The Arousing." Together, the five elements adhere through the phenomenon of "The Arousing," and so establish the six short-enduring things. These, with the two long-enduring things, are known as the symbolic pa kua, the eight emblems of all phenomena.

When these correspondences are attached to the "Diagram of Cosmic Evolution," we begin to see hints of a psychological character perceiving the nature of the self. Contrary to many popular Western attitudes, 'non-ego' is not a concept alien to human nature. Indeed, the ultimate 'primal self' of human consciousness is fundamentally rooted in 'non-ego'. 'Principle' is an impersonal and nonsubjective thing. 'Essence' is without conscience and so it too is nonsubjective. These faculties constitute the 'primal self' as a nonsubjective energy force operating with 'non-ego' consciousness.

When the consciousness of the 'primal self' metamorphoses into a psychic consciousness, the 'non-ego' (our infinite beingness), commences to devolve into an 'ego' (our finite beingness). At once, 'ego-consciousness' begins its work of restricting our potentialities within the confinement of forward-directed causalistic limitation. At the same time, however, in accord with the principle of yin and yang, the evolving psychic consciousness remains as a dormant force, always on call, that can help us escape the limitations of forward-directed causality and tune us to experience the infinite possibilities of simultaneously coexisting in the sphere of backward-directed causality.

With these suggestions, one may begin to work with the yin and yang forces as they symbolically indicate directions, degrees, qualities and intensities of 'change' (which is development) in the "Diagram of Cosmic Evolution." With diligence and tenacious application, one will come to experience the cosmic consciousness that accompanies every instance of meaningful self-confrontation. Many are the subtleties required to perfect this reawakening to our 'primal nature'. How will one accomplish it? It is accomplished in the doing. Just as no one can taste for you, so no one can awaken your 'primal nature' for you. To know the taste of a fruit you must bite into it. To know the 'primal self' you must discover your 'self'!

The Pa Kua

The preceding exploration has dealt with selected facets of the Image of Origins, and it has expressed some ideas important to understanding the dynamics of yin and yang. We shall next take up a study of the pa kua. These have come to be known, by unfortunate circumstance, as the eight trigrams. I shall not, except in quotations, ever refer to "trigrams" or "hexagrams" in the text of this study. A "gram" is a geometrical figure of lines which touch or cross. The linear images of *I Ching* never touch and never cross. They are symbols of parallel forces of energy and intelligence which go forth infinitely—never touching, never meeting. In the original Chinese the word for both three-line images and six-line images is *kua*. Richard Wilhelm, who contributed the most brilliant translation of *I Ching* to the Western world, held true to the Chinese practice of using a single term to denote both kinds of linear images. He used the German word *Zeichen,* meaning "sign." The terms "trigram" and "hexagram" were introduced by the scholar James Legge, in his translation of *I Ching* (Yi King), which became a part of *The Sacred Books of the East,* originally edited by Max Mueller, the distinguished scholar, commentator and interpreter of Oriental wisdom and scriptures. So much for "grams." As you read on, it may be helpful to remember that *pa* means eight, and *kua* means sign, to divine.

The pa kua is a graphic representation of the life experience. As archetypes they challenge the ingenuity of any single person to exhaust the range of interpretation, symbolization, indication, inspiration and visualization they can excite. It is certain that the effort about to be made here will not be an exhaustive one. The purpose of the variety of delineations which are to be made upon the pa kua is only that of serving as an example of the countless directions and limitless dimensions in which these linear constructs may excite one's mind to move. In the "Diagram of Cosmic Evolution" the pa kua assume the following order:

As noted elsewhere, four of these kua represent conditions in nature. The remaining four symbolize conditions experienced in man. This division expresses a deep significance when it is juxtaposed with Carl Jung's diagrammatics used in exploring the nature of 'synchronicity.'[51] This division should not be confused with that described in the Shuo Kua, section iv of chapter 2. We will not concern ourselves with the pros and cons of 'synchronicity'; however, Jung's diagrams are displayed to awaken the reader to an awareness of the inspired revelations that may come out of such a comparative study. For now, the correspondences will be merely touched upon in order to show a few important basic aspects which are inherent in these pa kua. The Chinese have a tradition of mapping things compass-wise with south at the top, east to the left, west to the right and north at the bottom. It is essential to adhere to this tradition in order correctly to understand much that is written and diagrammed in *I Ching*.

There are a number of explanations for the Chinese arrangement of the compass points. One account reminds us that the altar or shrine tablets in a Chinese temple face north. Therefore, when the emperor leaves the temple his back is to the north, and he faces the people and the conditions of the kingdom as he looks south. Another way of seeing it is that when one turns from the divine (the shrine tablets), one is confronted with the problems of life—people and the things involving them. Still another explanation is to visualize the T'ai Chi Tu as standing upright in such a way that the yang force images the maximum of its form at the top, and the yin force images the maximum of its form at the bottom.

One interpretation of this is to read the yang as the sun, rising to high noon, the yin to be read as the sun descending into midnight blackness. In Chinese thought there is an old expression that goes: "The sun at high noon is the sun setting."

In the "Primal" arrangement pictured below, the four kua which represent conditions in nature constitute the N-S and E-W axis of a compass pattern. By placing this diagram of the vertical and horizontal axis of the primal arrangement between

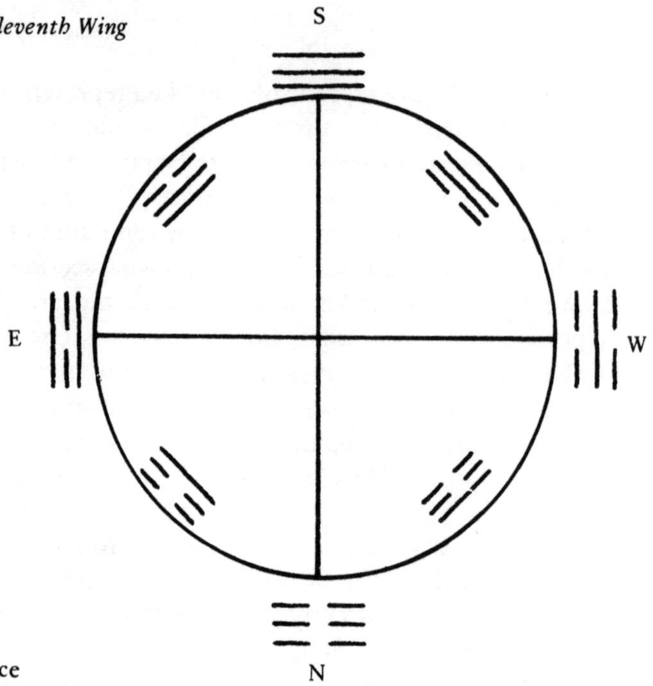
S
E
W
N

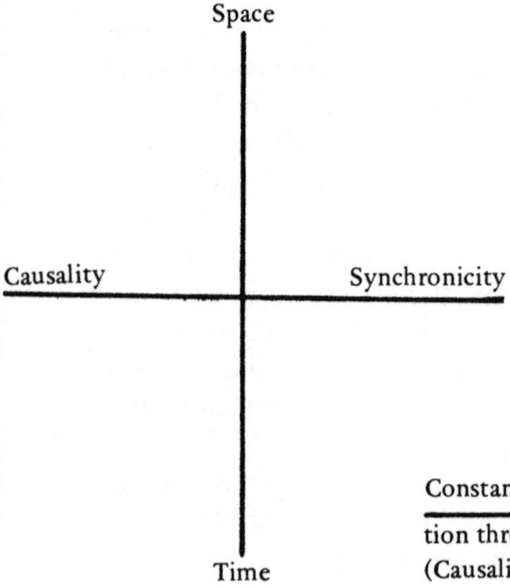
Space
Causality
Synchronicity
Time

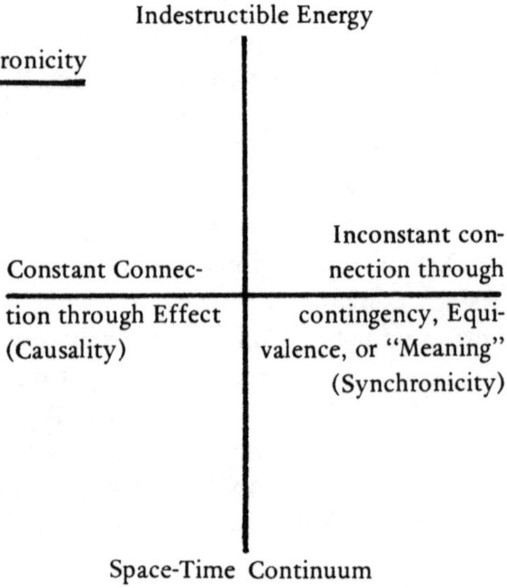
Indestructible Energy
Constant Connection through Effect (Causality)
Inconstant connection through contingency, Equivalence, or "Meaning" (Synchronicity)
Space-Time Continuum

Jung's two diagrams dealing with synchronicity, we provide a most interesting correspondence that lends itself to a wide range of speculative concepts and their multiple implications.

☰, Ch'ien (heaven) corresponds with 'space' and 'indestructible energy.' ☷, K'un (earth) corresponds with 'time' and 'space-time continuum'. Thus we can read in the "Primal" arrangement of the pa kua the statement that heaven, the realm from whence all things emerge, is above, is 'space', is 'indestructible energy'. Above, not in the sense of being up or over, but with the meaning of being a higher, a more refined and etheric element and/or force. Beneath is earth, the other factor of the polarity. Earth is a manifestation that had a beginning and that, it is foretold, will have an ending. Having a beginning and an ending, it is a product of time. Time may be defined as an awareness of the duration of experience upon

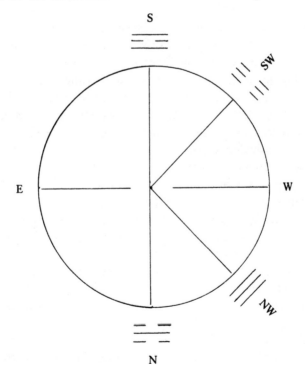

consciousness. This manifested earth floats or pursues a fixed movement in the 'space-time continuum'. 'Space-time', incidentally, is not a concept that only recently evolved with Einsteinian relativity. Indeed, the Chinese have a phrase which is used for "the universe": *Yu-chou.* It expresses the idea of space-time. It is a very ancient term and was written of as long ago as 120 B.C. in the eleventh chapter of *Huai Nan Tzu.*

> All of the time that has passed from antiquity until now is called Chou; all of the space in every direction, above and below is called Yu. Tao is within, yet no man can tell where it dwells. [52]

That is an initial and very minute projection of what is symbolized by the N-S axis of the "Primal" arrangement of the pa kua.

We will find a meaningful correspondence continuing between the east-west axis of the "Primal" arrangement and Jung's diagrams dealing with synchronicity. In the east, is ☰ , Li, (The Clinging, Fire); it corresponds with Jung's 'causality,' and 'constant connection through effect (causality).' In the west, there is ☵, K'an, (The Abysmal, Water), which corresponds with 'synchronicity' and 'inconstant connection through contingency, equivalence, or meaning–(synchronicity).' Causality contains all phenomena which may be defined as manifesting a relationship through cause and effect. Li (The Clinging, Fire), is a marvelous example of this condition. What an infinite variety of causes and effects there are imaginable which manifest a relationship that may be expressed as "clinging." It is no happenstance that the quality of "clinging" has for its element fire. Fire effects the transformation of a substance through a process of burning. The flame that is associated with fire 'clings' to the substance that is being transmuted. Because of this relationship there is that which we call an act of causality. The product of this kind of causality is ash, or cinder, or heat, or gaseousness. Yet there are other kinds of causality which have all of the characteristics of "clinging." Though it may be of a different kind, they too leave ash, or cinder, or heat, or gaseousness as a final product. For example: there is the clinging-vine relationship between a parent and child, doctor and patient, teacher and pupil, person and drug, religion and conscience, and so on, and so on. In every instance the requisite composites of cause and effect are easily discernible.

Lest we convey the idea that Li (The Clinging), is a negative kind of causality, let us demonstrate the yang aspects of fire: "Clinging," according to the principle of 'change', is a special kind of attachment that terminates in a constructive and on-going causality. When one learns to "cling" to the wisdom and not the teacher, one will come to experience freedom. When one "clings" to the target and not the weapon, one will master the art. When parent and child both "cling" to the principle of becoming, begetting and "begoning," they will experience maturity and happiness and a greater fulfillment of their potential. When one "clings" to the Tao and not the products of it, one will move and be moved harmoniously through life. These are some of the yang, the positive aspects of "clinging."

☰☵ ,K'an (The Abysmal, Water), corresponds with 'synchronicity' and 'inconstant connection through contingency, equivalence, or meaning (synchronicity).' The west is the direction of the setting sun. With the setting sun comes darkness. "The Abysmal" is surely the immeasurably deep, the unfathomable, the dark and mysterious sea. 'Synchronicity' may be defined as the connection of acausal events through meaningful coincidence. A series of distinctly different causal events, each comprised of a singularly unique cause and effect, may originate in the east and terminate in the west as components of 'synchronicity'. 'Synchronicity' is the domain of acausality.

There is another traditional circular arrangement of the pa kua. It is known as the "Sequence of Later Heaven," or the "Inner-World" arrangement. In the former "Primal" arrangement, the pa kua were positioned in pairs of linear opposites.

The "Inner-World" arrangement presents them in what is called a 'phenomenal sequence'; that is to say, the forces represented are arranged in an ordered sequence that depicts the order in which changes are experienced by man. The "Primal" arrangement is basically a symbolic statement of the eternal and balanced completeness within which the process of dynamic balance 'phenomenates'. Keeping our attention with the four kua that represent conditions in nature, let us see what their position in the "phenomenal" arrangement suggests.

Water and fire (The Abysmal and The Clinging) become the north-south axis of man's experiential beingness. What an interesting comment: life, emerging from a dark, immeasurably deep and unfathomable mystery to which it must return, is the phenomenon of "clinging" to the identity it discovers in the being as which it emerges. But life is a perplexity. As it tries to cling to its identity, it responds to an uncontrollable compulsion to evolve, to grow. This growth direction is imagined to be a straight-line direction, when in reality it is a cyclic curve. Thus life is always returning to its source—the Great Mystery, Tao! That is the first statement made by *I Ching* in the "Later Heaven" arrangement of the pa kua.

It was observed earlier that creative and evolutionary movement is from the right to the left. A kua, whether structured through the use of coins or stalks, is built from the bottom up. In the same way, the meaning of this arrangement may be discerned by moving clockwise, from the bottom up, in interpreting the signs. A concept of 'being' is projected from the abode of infinite potential, Ch'ien, into K'an (The Abysmal), the womb of mysterious darkness. There it germinates and receives the natural limitations of what it is to be. It is manifested, develops and then seeks to cling to its 'beingness'. It does this by being receptive to that which gives it sustenance, little realizing that the very acceptance of sustenance is the means by which all things evolve into their opposite. Development is the energy of negation.

I call attention to another interesting observation. In Chinese, the character 人 stands for man. However, when used in conjunction with another ideogram it is uprighted to appear as 弋 . Look at the diagram on page 86. You will see that the placement of the four kua which represent conditions in nature form the English letter K. In Chinese 兀 indicates a firm basis. If we follow the practice used in combining 弋 with another ideogram, and upright 兀 so that it resembles the form K drawn in our diagram, we could read the second statement made by the "Later Heaven" arrangement. It indicates that the individual internal experiences of man, such as his contemplativeness ("Keeping Still"), his happiness ("The Joyous"), his agitation ("The Arousing") and his docility ("The Gentle"), all take place against the background of heaven and earth through its powers of water and fire, interacting to 'phenomenate' becoming and 'begoning'. The four basic conditions in nature, fixed for the duration of the manifestation, become the background for the fluctuating conditions of temperament and behavior in man.

The kua symbolizing the conditions of temperament in man are Kên ("Keeping Still"), Tui ("The Joyous"), Sun ("The Gentle") and Chên ("The Arousing"). As we observe their placement among the other kua in the "Earlier Heaven" or "Primal" arrangement, any number of statements can be read. When we recall that the literal meaning of the "Primal" arrangements is "Before-the-World Sequence," [53] the interpretive readings promise to be even more fascinating. We have already noted that the "Primal" arrangement is a symbol of the eternally balanced and complete infinity within which the multiple finite processes of dynamic balance are acted out. This is why it is written: "To understand fully, one must always visualize the "Inner-World" arrangement as transparent, with the "Primal" arrangement shining through it." [54]

Perhaps by listing a few of the symbolic indications contained in the "Primal" arrangement, it will suggest and stimulate enlightening statements in each of us. Man's joyous temperament (Tui) is situated in the southeast octogant wedge between Li and Ch'ien. Li is the natural element of fire. It represents light, clarity, sun, eye, perception and understanding. It is set in the east, a symbol of rising, beginning, a starting point from where there is ascendance. Above, in the south, is

Ch'ien (The Originating). Ch'ien is the source of all phenomena, projective, the root of power. "It means that here the dark and the light arouse each other." [55] An inference: Man experiences the joyous state when he perceives without a doubt that he functions as a rising expression of heaven's power, and with this conviction he has merged into the will of heaven.

Man's gentle temperament (Sun), is located in the southwest octogant, midway between Ch'ien and K'an of the "Primal" arrangement. Ch'ien is the source of all phenomena, projective, the root of power. "It means that here the dark and the light arouse each other." K'an is the sign of "The Abysmal." It means water and signifies toil to which all creatures are subject. It indicates the time of gathering in the harvest, the period of concentration. [56] Inference: Man expresses his gentleness when he recognizes that while he is an expression of heaven's power, and will experience the pleasure of expansion and evolvement, he also is destined to succumb to contraction and devolvement. When this aspect of the universal phenomena is accepted, one comes to be at peace with oneself. A man at peace is without fear. Being without fear, his thoughts, words and deeds become projections of gentleness. "The Gentle" is penetrating. It is boundless like wind "to make things flow into their form," and like fine roots "to make them develop and grow into the shape prefigured in the seed." [57]

Man's meditative and reflective nature (Kên), rests in the northwest octogant between K'an and K'un of the "Primal" arrangement. (K'an is the sign of "The Abysmal." It means water and signifies toil to which all creatures are subject. It indicates the time of gathering in the harvest, the period of concentration.) K'un is the sign of "The Receptive." It is the earth and brings about shelter. After completing the cycle of life, everything returns to shelter. In the sign of "The Receptive," creatures serve one another and all things are nourished. Kên is "Keeping Still," the mountain. It begins the backward movement by stopping further expansion. It is the beginning and end of all creatures, therefore it is said, "under its sign all things are brought to perfection." [58] Inference: Man's meditative and reflective nature becomes the source of energy that motivates his thoughts, words and deeds, once he recognizes that he lives in the sphere where all creatures are subject to toil and he accepts the conditions of being sheltered in the earth. To volunteer to serve one another while sharing a common shelter brings happiness and bliss. This is the outgrowth of meditative reflection; all effort is made without effort, all labor is performed without pain.

Man's innate vehemence (Chên) in the northeast octogant is aroused between K'un and Li of the "Primal" arrangement. (K'un is the sign of "The Receptive." It is the earth and brings about shelter. In the sign of "The Receptive," creatures serve one another and all things are nourished.) Li is the natural element of fire. It represents light, clarity, sun, eye, perception and understanding. It is set in the east, a symbol of rising, beginning, a starting point, from where there is ascendance. Chên is "The Arousing," thunder. It brings about movement. Chên is "the electrically charged force," [59] awakening the seeds of what flowered earlier. Tao manifests itself through the sign of "The Arousing." Chên is to be decisive and vehement. It is young, green bamboo. Inference: The on-going genetic intelligence and energy that are expressed through man as temperament and behavior are basically attitudes acted out in degrees by his innate vehemence. Innate vehemence is impetuosity of action and feeling. Thus, when one has served others and been served by others while sharing the common shelter, he experiences the interdependence of things and creatures. Meditating upon the experience he is drawn into a clearer vision that awakens within the self new dimensions of understanding. New understanding calls for new expressions, new actions, new words. Hence, one is moved by intense feeling to impetuous action. Through man's innate vehemence, he evolves with the forces he sets evolving.

So far we have interpreted, step by step, the "Diagram of Cosmic Evolution" up to where it composes the basic pa kua.

We have explored the implications of an original grouping of the pa.kua as they stand in the "Primal" arrangement, thereby gaining the benefit of some important insights. These insights suggested certain innovations of study which further clarify the significant indications of the *I* as an explanation of man's role in Tao. The Chinese have used various subtle methods to extract many elixirs of knowledge from *I Ching*. This is exampled in part four of chapter two of the Shuo Kua (Eighth Wing):

> Thunder brings about movement, Wind brings about dispersion, Rain brings about moisture, the Sun brings about warmth, Keeping Still brings about standstill, the Joyous brings about pleasure, the Creative brings about rulership, the Receptive brings about shelter. [60]

In quoting the above I have capitalized the word used to signify each particular kua. To the quotation from the Shuo Kua, Richard Wilhelm added his personal comment:

> Here again the forces for which the eight primary trigrams stand are presented in terms of their effects in nature. The first four are referred to by their images, the last four by their names, because only the first four indicate in their images natural forces at work throughout time, while the last four point to conditions that come about in the course of the year. [61]

After studying this portion of the Shuo Kua and Wilhelm's comment, my thoughts turned to exploring other techniques of extracting meaning from *I Ching*. While engaged in this adventure, I struck upon the idea of analyzing the relationship between the kua of the two major axes (N-S intersecting E-W), being symbolic of the universe which harnesses within itself the kua of the two minor axes (SW-NE intersecting NW-SE), symbolizing the range of action and reaction of man.

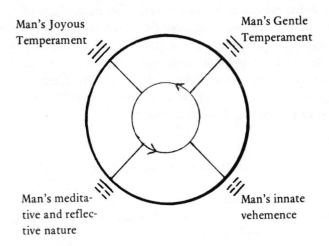

Man's Joyous Temperament

Man's Gentle Temperament

Man's meditative and reflective nature

Man's innate vehemence

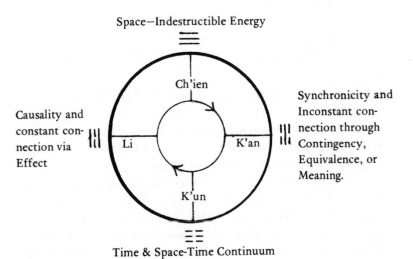

Space—Indestructible Energy

Ch'ien

Causality and constant connection via Effect

Li

K'an

Synchronicity and Inconstant connection through Contingency, Equivalence, or Meaning.

K'un

Time & Space-Time Continuum

The product of this study can serve as a Geiger counter to guide us through the minefields of a universe that creates by the forces of fire and water and the endless sequence of phenomena, which it locks between the polar caps of heaven (ideas) and earth (ideas manifested). Those who seek to discover the meanings indicated by this graphic representation of man-universe relationships will come upon their own revelations and awaken to what is uniquely important to their individual 'beingness.' This is the marvel of *I Ching* study. It is a source of endless inspiration and enlightenment.

Attributes of the Pa Kua

There are appended to each of the pa kua a variety of different attributes. Some of the important ones I have catalogues under seven headings.

1. Nomenclative
2. Adjectival
3. Anatomical
4. Familial
5. Chromatic
6. Animal
7. Elemental

But before becoming involved with any specific attribute of the pa kua, it will be well for us to define what an attribute is. Next we will observe how it functions. Then, through examples we will be ready to demonstrate how the attributes may be used to heighten our interpretations of *I Ching*.

The importance of the attributes has been left unstressed in all translations of *I Ching* save that of Richard Wilhelm. Yet even in this work the attributes, while very carefully listed and catagorized, are not given a necessary and merited commentary. This is not the place to expound exhaustively upon the attributes of the pa kua as given in *I Ching*. However, it will be purposeful and rewarding to touch energetically upon the nature, role and function of the attributes.

Each attribute is an archetype. An archetype is not only "an original model from which copies are made"; [62] it is also, according to Webster, "one of the ideas of which existent things are imitations." In Jungian psychology, archetype is defined as "an inherited idea or mode of thought derived from the experiences of the race and present in the unconscious of the individual." The attributes of the pa kua fulfill all of these definitions and may be taken as legitimate archetypes. We must always bear in mind that the attributes are never substances or things. They are ideas symbolizing conditions, forces, nature, tendencies, etc. They are like the pointing finger of Zen, which must never be mistaken for the moon. These are gentle works to caution us not to mistake the teacher for the wisdom.

Since Chinese mythology and legends abound with many wonderfully bizarre creatures, let me add one of my own making. I shall call it a "kua-de." Without describing the rest of its form, I will reveal that it has an appendage resembling a man's arm and hand. However, the hand has seven fingers instead of our usual five. To indicate something not immediately attached to itself, it will use one or more of these fingers in pointing to what it wishes to indicate. The finger or fingers pointing will not be that which is pointed at. Yet by the act of pointing, a meaningful relationship is made between the "kua-de," the pointing finger or fingers, and the thing or things pointed at. I've described this creation from the bestiary of my imagination in order to spell out a parallel which should make clear the meaning, function and use of the attributes traditionally assigned to the pa kua of *I Ching*.

A kua, like the hand, is an instrument or organ constructed with features of mobility that enable it to perform an endless variety of tasks, both luxurious and necessary. It is the flexibility of the fingers which greatly enables the hand to perform such a variety of functions. With *I Ching*, the attributes are the fingers of the pa kua. Each attribute awakens the intuition to an all-encompassing dimension of psychological meaning and significance. It is the attributes that empower the kua to be fountain-heads of revelation whereby *I Ching* has survived as man's oldest continually utilized cybernetic wisdom. We have said that an attribute is an archetype. Among the definitions made of an archetype is: "one of the ideas of which existent things are imitations." Let us examine this statement and see if it helps us to understand more about the function and use of the attributes in our various applications of *I Ching*.

We will select a kua at random by placing, in a covered bowl, folded bits of paper numbered from one to eight: Ch'ien = 1, Tui = 2, Li = 3, Chên = 4, Sun = 5, K'an = 6, Kên = 7 and K'un = 8. Now the bowl is shaken vigorously. Then, with eyes closed, I take off the lid, reach into the bowl, and remove one of the folded papers. Upon unfolding it, I read number five. Five is the kua Sun, "The Gentle." By exploring some of the ramifications indicated by its seven attributes, we will gain a better sense of the nature and use of archetypes.

Sun is imaged as two yang lines resting upon a yin line, ☴ . It pictures strength that modifies itself when it comes to basic confrontations. It can modify itself because it possesses authority and power that is reinforced with authority and power. A truly strong man can always be gentle, knowing that in a final challenge he has the authority, power and strength to become severe. When dealing with archetypal images, whether objects or words, it is important not to get hung up on the object or the word. Wang Pi, [63] who died at the early age of twenty-three, left a number of important works to posterity. One that we must regard to be of monumental importance is the *Chou Yi Lueh-li* ("Outline of the System Used in the Chou Changes"). In this work he delineates the theme that all ideas are expressed by symbols and they in turn are described by words.

Therefore the purpose of words is to explain the symbols, but once the symbols have been grasped, the words may be forgotten. The purpose of symbols is to preserve the ideas, but once the ideas have been grasped, the symbols may be forgotten. . . . [64]

Therefore he who clings to words does not get the symbols, and he who clings to symbols does not get the ideas. The symbols are intended for the ideas, but, if clung to, are no longer the symbols (of those ideas). The words are intended for the symbols, but if clung to, are no longer the words (of those symbols). . . . [65]

. . . the lines are multiplied in order completely to express the qualities, but the lines themselves may then be forgotten. Therefore in keeping with the category, the symbol thereof may be made; in agreement with the concept, the graph thereof may be made. If the concept consists of firmness, what need for a horse (to explain its meaning)? If the category is one of compliance, what need for a cow? If a line expresses compliance, what need for K'un to be made into a cow? If the concept corresponds to firmness, what need for Ch'ien to be made into a horse? [66]

With the above in mind, let us now approach the seven attributes assigned to Sun:

Nomenclative	The Gentle
Adjectival	penetrating
Anatomical	thighs
Familial	first daughter
Chromatic	white
Animal	cock
Elemental	wind/wood

First, regard each attribute as a finger of our seven-fingered hand. Now if we were to hold this hand with the fingers spread apart, each finger would point to something different in our immediate environment. So it is with each of the attributes attached to any particular kua.

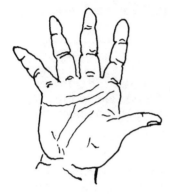

A Man's Hand

The Gentle
[Penetrating—Wind]
(with 7 attributes or fingers)

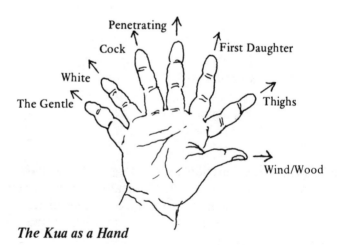

The Kua as a Hand

Just as the finger is not the thing it points to, so with an
I Ching kua; the attribute is not the reference it awakens in our
consciousness. That is simple enough to understand. The analogy is clear, as far as it concerns one finger and one attribute.
But what about using a different finger to point to the same
object? This tightens the metaphor between finger and
attribute. Obviously, using a different finger to point to an
object doesn't change the finger into the object. Not so obvious,
however, is a correct conclusion to the question: "Does using a
different finger to point with change the object?" The answer
must be yes and/or no. A further study of what is involved will
make the point clear.

Whether the answer to the above question is "yes," or "no,"
or "yes-no," or "no-yes," is strongly dependent upon the degree
of sensitivity that can be consciously experienced by the individual. The chance of understanding how these attributes
function will hinge partly on one's ability to become aware of
the subtle nuances of relationships in 'beingness'. As a test of
one's own chances to understand, try the experiment which I
will outline below. The pragmatic worth of this old, old wisdom
can only be proven to oneself by oneself. As Jung observed:
"The *I Ching* insists upon self-knowledge throughout." [67] It is
only by what one can prove to oneself that this ancient wisdom
can be understood to encompass the universe of man's experiences, be they occult, psychological, spiritual, intellectual. I
will introduce the personal experiment with this very relevant
quotation from Jung's foreword to the Wilhelm/Baynes translation of *I Ching.*

> . . . the *I Ching* does not offer itself with proofs and re-
> sults; it does not vaunt itself, nor is it easy to approach.
> Like a part of nature, it waits until it is discovered. It
> offers neither facts nor power, but for lovers of self-
> knowledge, of wisdom—if there be such—it seems to be the
> right book. To one person its spirit appears as clear as day;
> to another, shadowy as twilight; to a third, dark as night.
> He who is not pleased by it does not have to use it, and he
> who is against it is not obliged to find it true. Let it go
> forth into the world for the benefit of those who can
> discern its meaning. [68]

Experiment To Test Awareness Of Inner Nuances

Wherever you may be, with your eye select as a focus-target an object or person at a distance of fifteen or more feet away. Now point toward it with your index finger and adopt the thought: "I want to get closer to that (him or her), to see if I can find out what the attraction is between it (him or her) and myself." Review now the internal feeling—mental and sensory, etc.—that you can detect. Make some written notes about them. Now, using the same target, repeat the process, with one exception: point with the little finger of the same hand. While pointing, speak aloud the adopted thought: "I want to get closer to that (him or her), to see if I can find out what the attraction is between it (him or her) and myself." Once again review the internal feelings—mental and sensory, etc.—that you can detect. Write down your comments. Now compare the first with the second experience. Are there differences in the experience? What are the differences? How do you explain the differences to yourself? If there were no differences, how do you explain that?

All meaning of this exercise must be discovered by the individual. There is nothing that can be appended here, by way of report or analysis, that can in any way awaken in you what has not already been discerned within yourself. If you experienced no differences on any level at all, it would indicate that your sensitivity-awareness is, in all probability, sluggish. If you experienced differences on physical, psychological, emotional or spiritual levels, then your sensitivity-awareness is active and influential. This would suggest that you will increase your effectiveness by applying *I Ching.*

If by the preceding exercise, you discover that you have an active sensitivity-awareness, there will be no difficulty in understanding the nuances of meaning indicated by the attributes of any kua in regard to a given situation. For example: we have likened a kua to the hand. Symbolically, this is a declaration that a kua is that part of *I Ching* which enables us to grasp, handle, and/or manipulate something. This ability is provided by the maneuverability of its seven fingers or attributes. When appealing to the wisdom of *I Ching* in connection with a given situation or thing, we are furnished with two hands and fourteen fingers, identified as the upper and lower kua, or the inner and outer kua.

Keep to the metaphor of a kua being a hand. Consider each attribute as a finger of that hand. In this way you will develop an adequate intellectual understanding of how the kua functions symbolically in *I Ching*. The deeper understanding that comes with 'knowing' develops more slowly and less spectacularly.

We speak of the index finger as the "pointing finger." Of course, as our experiment has shown, any finger may be used for pointing with some interesting internal results. [69] But now evaluate the obvious fact that the "pointing finger" may point at an unlimited number and range of things. In a word, the finger may be used to indicate many separate related and unrelated things. It is this way with the attributes of a kua. This is the intellectual understanding. The intuitive, or understanding of 'knowing', is developed as we master the art and science of interpreting the things indicated in a way that is meaningfully significant within the context of the given area.

This may be crudely illustrated by exampling some directions of interpretation that are possible using the attributes of our randomly selected kua, Sun, ☴. We will proceed to take up the attributes according to their order of listing, the first being the nomenclative: "The Gentle"—this name is associated with the idea of "winds following one upon the other." [70] The wind itself may symbolize many things: spiritual forces; intellectual influences; gentle physical persuasion or empathetic encouragement; subtle, light but steady pressure. It may recommend a passive acceptance of something or someone, or a passive rejection. It should always be remembered that each attribute has its yin as well as its yang quality.

To illustrate, take the familial attribute of Sun which is "First Daughter." One of the more obvious indications is that of second-in-command, at an administrative level rather than at

an executive one. That is, the first daughter is usually recognized as the one to assume maternal authority in the event of
the mother's absence. In the family context, the mother's
authority (yin) is administrative, which serves as a complement
to the father's authority (yang) that is of an executive tenor.
Another consideration to be recognized is that of determining if
the first daughter is also the first child or a subsequent child.
This positioning in family life is important to the Chinese.
Therefore, it is important to consider its placement symbolically in the situation in which *I Ching* is being involved. In
other words, this consideration helps to determine how much
yang movement must be made with a substitutive yin force in a
given situation.

Viewed as a part of the anatomy, Sun is said to be symbolized by the thigh. Many of us visualize the foot as a symbol
of movement and speed. We see examples of this kind of
association in our Western mythology: the winged heels of
Mercury, the fast-pacing messenger of the gods. Again, interest
is stirred when we note that the idea is suggested in our
language when we use phrases such as: "quick-footed," "light-
footed," "fleet of foot," "feet of lightning," and so on. However, the foot is not the anatomical part responsible for
movement. It can merely, for a period of time, anchor a
movement and thus enable a successive complementary or
equating movement to be made. The actual physical movement
of the body is generated by the angular articulation of the
thigh. While it is not unseen, it is the unrecognized fulfiller of
movement. This may be viewed as the hidden yang force in the
yin kua, Sun.

The color attributed to Sun is white. In Chinese culture,
white is the color of mourning, of death. However, there is no
sharp distinction made between birth and death. They are
phenomenologically accepted as different aspects of the common phenomenon of 'change'. This attitude is expressed as the
fourth thought in Hui Shih's ten paradoxes: "Besides, where
there is life, there is death; and where there is death, there is
life." The sage Chuang Tzu wrote:

How do I know that the love of life is not a delusion? And how do I know that the hate of death is not like a man who lost his home when young and does not know where his home is to return to? Li Chi was the daughter of the border warden of Ai. When the Duke of Chin first got her, she wept until the bosom of her dress was drenched with tears. But when she came to the royal residence, shared with the duke his luxurious couch and ate delicious food, she regretted that she had wept. How do I know that the dead will not repent having previously craved for life? [71]

In chromology, white is regarded as the reflection of all colors. Sun's white may be taken to symbolize a wide yin-yang view of the situation at hand. This may be taken as a recommendation to explore the positive and negative qualities, so as to be able to determine the time and place in which to activate the proper aspect of force as required by the situation. Whatever action is appropriate to the situation should be administered gently in order to have a deep and penetrating effect.

The rooster is the animal symbol of Sun. This again expresses a yang action of a yin force. The rooster announces the dawn. He brags about his domain. He is an image of pride and a strutter. These are qualities which a mother often exhibits when she has brought the seed of the womb to a safe delivery and reared the child in health and happiness. Obviously, one should not crow if there is nothing to display. But to crow, one must work industriously, produce grandly and care for the products of one's labor.

We have taken a series of attributes and spelled out their yin and yang intentions. But let us not forget that each of these is an expression of a qualitative aspect of the phenomenon of 'change'. The aspects we have touched upon are the nominative, familial, anatomical, chromatic and animal. These, in themselves, are keys to insight and metaphoric equatives which can help us to encompass a situation with understanding. The situation which is clearly understood is one that becomes an instrument by which we bring into manifestation the desires of conscious will. Situations which are not clearly understood often become instruments which force us to experience manifestations which are the potential products of our unconscious fears. Therefore it is important to adopt *I Ching,* or any other philosophical discipline that can, in conjunction with meditation, help us enlarge our understanding of every important situation that becomes a part of our life experience.

An error often indulged is that of reading the kua in terms of "good" or "bad." Many novices to the philosophical psychology of *I Ching* have mistakenly interpreted Wilhelm's paragraphs on "Correspondence" [72] to mean certain itemized kua were "good" ones and others itemized were "bad" ones. The occurrence of the terms "good fortune" and "misfortune" in the translated text have also helped popularize this misconception. One will escape this trap if it is constantly borne in mind that *I Ching* interprets *forces,* not moralities. Forces are neither "good" nor "bad." The end-product resulting from the use or application of a force is the thing that may arbitrarily be defined as "good" or "bad." The sense of this can be expressed in the nonsense phrase: "An *I Ching* kua is neither good nor bad, because it is both good and bad."

Three
Life: An Adventure in Changes

Becoming What You Are

'Change' is *becoming what you are! I Ching* is a philosophical psychology that elucidates the nature of 'change'. Through its archetypal symbols, *I Ching* becomes a valuable aid to those who are engaged in the "ardent striving for universal identification."[1] However, one should clearly understand that there is a difference between an aid and a miraculous panacea.

Often people planning to study *I Ching* approach me and ask: "What will *I Ching* do for me?" I look at them pointedly and reply, "Nothing." Too many of us seem to be going through a period of lazy initiative. There is less and less that we wish to do for ourselves. The highly evolved machines of our technology operate with such expert efficiency that they have sapped from us much of the natural desire to do things for ourselves. America, like every great society in history, was built by pioneers. Pioneers are men and women who look at a great expanse before them, not asking will these hills, rivers, mountains and valleys make us a kingdom, but declaring, instead, "We will make a kingdom out of these hills, rivers, mountains and valleys!" It is not within the province of this book to explore the psychological or sociological reasons for this metamorphosis of human initiative. However, I must mention its existence, because so many people approach *I Ching* with a lazy expectation. And, unfortunately, many writers evidence this attitude in their presentation of *I Ching*.

Though it may be done unconsciously, I feel that it is important to correct inaccurate descriptions of *I Ching*. For example, it has been described as "an instrument of transformation."[2] It would be constructively more accurate to define *I Ching* as an instrument *that both registers and indicates the nature or processes* of transformation. Also I must differ with the view that *I Ching*'s "... aim is to aid the individual ..."[3] etc. As I see it, *I Ching,* of itself, has no "aim." It is like the sight on a firearm which, having no aim, may be used to aim at any target. Again, we may liken it to a vehicle which, having no destination, may be used to reach a destination. On the other hand, Ponce, touching upon the potential that may come from using *I Ching,* is brilliantly perceptive when he writes: "... it quietly leads him (the user) toward the hidden unity within, managing to achieve this without demanding he adhere to any fixed societal formula. It leaves such matters to the conscience and creativity of the individual."[4]

It is this characteristic of *I Ching* that has made it so attractive to each person who seeks to discover and fulfill himself. Elsewhere Ponce writes: "Man's task is to find and let this spirit express itself naturally. Recognition of this principle is the first step; a dialogue with it is the second; a successful integration of it into our daily experiences is the third, and final step."[5] This present commentary will endeavor to deal meaningfully with these three steps—recognition, dialogue and integration.

The capsular sentence that opens this chapter is a key to understanding what 'change' is. When we come to know what 'change' is, we will have enlarged our understanding of *I Ching*. Let us then explore the meaning of this opening phrase.

'Change' is becoming what you are. Since we can only recognize 'change' by setting it against that which is recognized as 'non-change', actualities must be accepted as being unified states of a harmonious interplay of motion (change) and stasis (non-change). To refer it to the individual, this concept is powerfully expressed by Pierre Teilhard de Chardin, who wrote: *"I must continually change in order to remain myself."*

Through the ages there have been many continuing philosophical conflicts about the nature of life and the universe. One such antagonism has continued between the proponents of 'becoming' and 'change' and those of 'being' and 'permanence' Two classical names from the period between 600 B.C. to 400 B.C. are Heraclitus and Parmenides. The former is renowned as a spokesman for the 'all is in the motion of becoming' concept. The latter spoke eloquently for the view that held life to be static permanence. Modern Western science has, for a long time, been ensnared in this Parmenidian web. It holds as fact only what it can produce repetitively in the sterile and unnatural confines of the laboratory. In such an empirical climate the only things in man's experience deemed worthy of study and understanding are those events which subscribe to the laws of causality. Truth becomes the consensus of statistical facts, and thus restricted.

Scientific inquiry into the nature of man can go no deeper than the length of his fishing line of psychological bias. Jung is emphatic on this point when he writes:

> We have not sufficiently taken into account as yet that we need the laboratory with its incisive restrictions in order to demonstrate the invariable validity of natural law. If we leave things to nature, we see a very different picture: every process is partially or totally interfered with by chance, so much so that under natural circumstances a course of events absolutely conforming to specific laws is almost an exception.[6]

The prejudiced view that causal events are the only valid experiences of life has penetrated deeply into most areas of our culture. Because of this, excessive emphasis is put upon subscribing to the practice of competition to the point of annihilating one's competitor, which draws us into the brutal warfare of competing ideas. We state, with demanding persistence, that one must choose between this or that. All things come to be labeled as either good or bad. This is all a part of the ensnaring emotional morass that engulfs many of us today. No wonder it is difficult for some to grasp the concept propounded by *I Ching* that all things simultaneously manifest being and non-being. Hence, the things in our universe are all beyond the realm of restricting partialities.

I Ching has been the source for the view that holds that life is a unified phenomenon of 'being' and 'non-being', of change and permanence, of coexisting 'becomingness' and 'isness'. It symbolically replicates these processes of life and expresses them as forces of cyclical change, sequential change and non-change.

In the "Appended Remarks" of the commentaries on the *Book of Changes* it reads:

> Essence and material force (Ch'i) are combined to become things. The wandering away of spirit (force) becomes change. . . . Change has no physical form. [7]

And in another chapter it reads:

> . . . Change has neither thought nor action, because it is in the state of absolute quiet and inactivity, and when acted on, it immediately penetrates all things. If it were not the most spiritlike thing in the world, how can it take part in this universal transformation? . . . Only through spirit is there speed without hurry and the destination reached without travel. . . . [8]

These quotations reflect the concept that all phenomena are an interrelated unification of 'becomingness' and 'isness' (being). One way to understand this individually is to think of your own personal development. Say to yourself: "I was born, and one of the early changes was that of being given a name (say your given name) which is other than me. I developed, grew up and matured. I now realize that I have been changing for all these (say your age) years." Now think upon what you have just said and what you felt. It is something similar to realizing that there is a focal identity for each of us—this 'I' that we talk and think and feel about—which is essence. It is being. Our infancy, childhood, adolescence, adulthood, on through senior citizenship and old age are all states of 'change'. Everything that happens to us and through us are other conditions of change. All of the aforementioned—and others here left unmentioned—are changing aspects of the 'I'—the enduring essence of each individual being—and of each of these changes it may truly be said: "This is me!"

We must come to recognize that we have experienced these changes, that we *are* these changes, because for each of us there is this essence of being—this non-changing 'I'. In this way we can understand how the 'I' exists independently as the essence of our 'beingness'. However we endure through the changes of which we are both conscious and unconscious, is part of the actual process of becoming what we are.

A. Cornelius Benjamin argues with Aristotle's supposition that "an infinite regress necessarily arises if we admit that there can be a 'change of change'." [9] He refutes this idea, astutely observing:

Acceleration, for example, is a change of motion, which is itself a change. But motion is a change of position in space, and position is not itself a change. [10]

In the same way, aging and experiencing are kinds of changes, but the essence of being—the 'I'—is non-change. This is the yin and yang of all existence, the movement and the keeping still.

Chance, Causality, and Change

"No intelligent person would go for *I Ching*. It's an unpredictable gimmick, too chancy." This paraphrases a frequently heard rejection of the *Book of Changes*. The two rituals, one of manipulating yarrow stalks, the other of tossing coins, appear to be wholly unrelated to either the wisdom recorded on the printed page, or any situation experienced in the mind of the person consulting this ancient literature. The causally oriented mind finds that consulting *I Ching* for advice on matters of importance is ridiculous, as well as irrational. Armed with this negative prejudice against *I Ching,* they argue that the principles are as whimsical and baselessly optimistic as the hunch sense that motivates a gambler.

Yet these same persons will readily concede that there is a definable system of law at work throughout all nature. However, the word "law" fashions in their minds an idea that the predictable is a kind of positivity. All things being governed by law, it is assumed that there can be no happenstance. "Nothing that exists occurs by chance" is a conviction of many who hold a hard and inflexible empirical view. At the same time they will give you the statistical ratio of the chances of such-and-such a thing happening under specified circumstances, quoting all the while from tables listed under the laws of probability. Here on one hand we have the declaration, "nothing that exists occurs by chance," while on the other there is an active concern with making projections predicated upon the laws of probability.

Be that as it may, let us turn our attention now to analyzing this so-called gambling aspect, the "chanceness" of *I Ching.* Which laws, if any can be discovered, will explain the effective usefulness of *I Ching* to countless people throughout three to four thousand years?

We need first to arrive at a feasible definition of "law," "chance" and "causality" that will enable us to function perceptively on several levels of consciousness. Most instances of intellectual shortsightedness are traceable to an unwillingness to step up or down, or to the right or left of where we are. This does not mean that in doing so one is required to surrender one's convictions in order to accommodate another experience. To the contrary, it may happen that through accommodating another experience one strengthens and reinforces his original convictions. At the same time, by accommodating other experiences, one is allowing for the possibility of personal growth and the evolving into new and exciting dimensions of being. Growth is, among other things, a result of energetic thinking.

In order to excite students into thinking, as opposed to recalling, I sometimes assign them a flippant phrase to mull over in response to a question. One such phrase has proven to be stimulating and never fails to provoke an abundance of varied responses. It is put to students when we encounter the challenge of coming to understand what chance is. Because our dictionaries list among several synonyms for chance the word "accident," it is always offered as an explanation of what "chance" is. But at the next class session fresh things are said. It becomes obvious that many of the students have had new thinking experiences. In between the two meetings of the class, I've asked them to think out the implications of this declaration: "Accident may happen by chance, but chance never happens by accident!"

To report just a few of the results of this exercise would only thwart the reader and keep him from having an individually unique experience. The value of the exercise is realized after the labor of intellectual refinements (the making of distinctions between the definitions of "chance," "accident," "happening," etc.), when one has moved into the beingness of the concept itself. In brief, the accident of encountering the challenge of this phrase is a product of the chance factor that one is a student in one of the classes I conduct (or, now, a reader of this book). But the unique individual experience of moving into the phrase and, by chance, becoming the concept, will be no accident. What rests in the consciousness of each individual becomes the phenomenon of singular realization for each, as he develops the 'mirror-mind'.

In *Nan-hua Chen-ching* ("Pure Classic of Nan-hua," another appellation for the *Chuang Tzu*), it is written:

> The mind of the perfect man is like a mirror. It does not lean forward or backward in its response to things. It responds to things but conceals nothing of its own. Therefore it is able to deal with things without injury to (its reality).[11]

In both Zen Buddhism and neo-Confucianism, the mirror figures importantly as a symbol for the mind. The Buddhist concept is that external reality has to be transcended. The neo-Confucianists accept external reality as a challenge to be responded to naturally, as though one were a mirror objectively reflecting all that is before it.

Someone once defined chance as "an actuality for which the cause has not yet been discovered." This rather accurately describes the kind of "chance" that is involved with *I Ching*. Most everyone who has taken to *I Ching* on whatever level—be it philosophical, psychological or divinatory—has become aware of having had a deep and remarkably meaningful experience. The resulting counsel understood by, or provoked in, the individual embracing this ancient text defies all rationalization. One becomes conscious only of the actuality. That actuality is that there is some unknown and inexplicable relativeness effected between the intellectual and literary pronouncements of this old book and the situation that an individual brings to it, and the psycho-intellectual consciousness of that individual. Because it challenges our empirical intelligence and confounds our talents for explanation and reasoning, we call what happens with *I Ching*—'chance'!

Neither the most ancient nor the most avid adherent of *I Ching* would claim that it functions solely as an acausal force. Because it is partly founded upon the principle symbolized by the T'ai Chi Tu (yin and yang), it has, in addition to its acausal nature, a causal side. Most Westerners who have become acquainted with the Wilhelm/Baynes translation are familiar with Carl Jung's concept of 'synchronicity'. He expertly uses 'synchronicity' to explain and make understandable the acausal nature of *I Ching*. Later, we shall give some attention to synchronicity. For now, we turn out thought and study to seeking some clarification on *I Ching*'s causal nature. We will search for an answer to the question: "In what way is *I Ching* a force of cause and effect operating in the realm of man's environment, so that he is able better to understand and cope with himself?"

As the heart functions through a systolic and diastolic action, so *I Ching* is expressed through acausal and causal events. The noun 'causality' is defined as a "state of being a cause." The causality of *I Ching* is manifested when the words associated with a particular kua are interpreted by the individual into action. For it must be remembered that *I Ching* is at all times a prescription for *action*. This means that, contained in its words and in its linear symbols (the kua), is a prewritten wisdom revealing the most advantageous, nature-conforming action, behavior or attitude to be followed in any given situation.

Examples of the causal action of *I Ching* are found in the lore and history of this ancient tradition. Many inventions came about when the linear structures of a kua caused many of the ancient culture's heroes and inventors to reexpress what the kua had awakened in their intuitive consciousness in another physical form. Thus it is said:

> Nets, textile-weaving, boat-building, houses, the crafts of the archer, the miller and the accountant, all are derived ingeniously from Adherence, Dispersion, Massiveness, Cleavage, the "Lesser Topheaviness," the "Break-through," and the like.[12]

As one gains an understanding of *I Ching*, there develops an ability (perhaps it is more a heightened intuition) to recognize situations in terms of the linear images and quickly have one's own action harmonize with that action which is expressed by the words accompanying the kua. A case in point: At times during the writing of this book, I found that I could not correctly formulate the words to convey what I wished in a particular paragraph. On one such occasion I had been sitting at the desk for a long period of time, struggling inwardly and outwardly with dictionaries and thesaurus. Yet for some reason or other the needed words would not come. Suddenly I realized that to sit and press on exhaustedly was a futile commitment. At the same moment I recalled the thirty-third kua, "Retreat." I remembered the wise counsel for "nine in the fourth place":

Voluntary retreat brings good fortune to the superior man
And downfall to the inferior man. [13]

I got up from the desk, put on a jacket and went outside to busy myself with pulling down old dead vine growth from some of the trees on the grounds about the house. After a while, as I was absorbed in devining the trees, what I wanted to say shaped itself in my mind. Then I returned to the battlefield at my desk and won the encounter. This also is an instance that illustrates how *I Ching* functions as a causative factor in the affairs of men. The value of *I Ching* is not in being able to run to the book a dozen times a day for advice, but in studying its wisdom so that behavior patterns befitting specific situations become an active part of your involuntary motivation. In any final analysis of life, its problems are not resolved by suppressing changes, but in managing them masterfully. This is a proper use of *I Ching*.

We have now touched upon *I Ching* as an acausal and causal dynamic involved with the phenomena of 'change'. And what is 'change'? 'Change is the fulfillment of 'what is'. 'What is' is the manifestation of potential. All manifestation of potential is less than a limited focal microspeck of infinity. Potential is the unfulfilled "what-can-be', a vast and boundless-limitless infinity of possibility. Potential is either both good and bad, or it is neither good nor bad. But that is another argument.

In recognizing that 'change' itself is the only unchanging dynamic, we must awaken to the character of *I Ching*. It has been called an oracle. As an oracle it stands out uniquely, for it is not a cornucopia of certainties, an altar-fountain of infallible predictions, but rather a vane indicating direction, a profferer of clues. Submitting to the discipline of *I Ching* means heightening the awareness of one's intuitional sensitivities and allowing them to be the cause of action which effects the nature of the resulting change. This, briefly, is the principle of *I Ching* at work as a phenomenon of chance, causality and change interacting on innumerable levels of beingness.

Chance, Change, Cause: Interrelationship

We have given some small attention which hints at the ways and degrees that we live out our lives in an environment of chance. In seeing that a proper use of *I Ching* can make chance our ally, perhaps we may develop a new and less fearful attitude toward it. Next we must examine the nature of causality. We have been told, for as long as we can remember, that everything has a cause. This point has been emphasized over and over again, especially by those who deny that chance can and does play a significant role in our lives. Voltaire stated it emphatically: "Chance is a word void of sense; nothing can exist without a cause!"[14]

Since he was known as an atheist (or deist), it is difficult to estimate how much study he gave to Judeo-Christian scripture. But surely he marched in locked step, arm in arm with the old Bible chroniclers as regarding attitudes to 'change' and 'chance'.

The term for "chance" occurs only six times in the Bible, and once as "chanceth," making 7 mentions in all. Chance is a vital part of our daily experience. "Cause" appears in the Bible text 272 times, and 32 times as "causeth," 7 times in the plural form of "causes," 4 times as "causing," and twice as "causest." Just to complete the statistic, the negative "causeless," appears twice. This makes some 317 mentions in the Bible, in one form or another, of the term "cause," as against only 7 mentions of "chance." [15] Is it any wonder that our Western culture has been so predominantly preoccupied with the concept of causality while spending most of its time trying to avoid the consequences of chance?

Dr. Siu relates Marcus Long's story of a scientifically minded chicken, which I shall offer here as a guide for our evaluation of the authority of cause and effect. Now to quote his quote:

A little chicken sitting comfortably in the henhouse without a care in the world was startled by the appearance of a man and ran away. When it came back the man was gone but there was some corn lying on the ground. Having a degree of scientific curiosity the chicken began to watch and it soon noticed that when the man appeared the corn appeared. It did not want to commit itself to any theory in a hurry and watched the sequence 999 times. There were no exceptions to the rule that the appearance of the man meant food, so it swallowed its skepticism and decided there must be a necessary connection between the man and the corn. In the language of causality this meant that whenever the man appeared the corn *must* appear. On the basis of this conclusion it went out to meet the man on his thousandth appearance to thank him for his kindness and *had its neck wrung.* [16]

The fact seems to be that scientific data is, after all, a report on only the degree of recorded measurement that has been made to the time of the reporting. There are those who hold the view that the events of chance merely constitute a swamp mist of ignorance that will be dispelled with the noonday sun of reason. What is overlooked, as recorded in the wisdom of the *I*, is that the sun at its zenith is the sun declining. The darkness falls again and reason is once more enveloped in the haze and mist of a night of new questions, new unknowns and new inexplicables. The 'chance' principle that functions throughout life is a part of the nature of becoming, being and 'begoning', and has very little to do with man's ability to make precise measurements. When we begin to think about chance, cause and effect, we cannot avoid the help we get from reason—which, as Jung says, "in point of fact is nothing more than the sum total of all (our) prejudices and myopic views." Our little chicken might still be alive if only the yin and yang potentials of chance had been its guiding caution as it went forth to thank its benefactor on the one thousandth visit!

One of the uses of *I Ching*, as mentioned before, is that of making an ally of 'chance' in order to afford us a degree of direction and control over those things we insist upon interpreting as being the events of causality. Let us examine the process of this development. We might begin by testing the formula: 'chance' + 'change' = 'causality'.

The manipulation of fifty yarrow stalks in the manner prescribed by tradition, or the tossing of three like coins six times, is a ritual or act that externalizes the process of chance which is hidden in nature. This factor of chance is then used to construct a kua, which in effect changes the relationship that exists between the individual and the situation he is momentarily concerned with. This is decidedly an emotional and psychological process, and it is important to understand it. Understanding is not a thing that can be given by one person to another. Each individual must seek for and develop understanding within himself. It is here that each reader must conduct an individual experiment, making personal observations and drawing personal conclusions.

In order for this experiment to have the greatest meaning to you, and be most helpful to me, I shall ask you to patiently follow the instructions that are about to be given. If it is convenient, use a sheet of carbon paper so that you may send me a copy of the experiment with your findings, and also retain a copy for your record. We shall conduct two experiments which are really just parts of a single experiment.

Experiment A

NAME	AGE
ADDRESS	GENDER
CITY – ZIP	DATE
WEATHER	TIME

(At the top of a sheet of paper
furnish the above information.)

Below the personal and statistical information write, on a single line, the following words: "What is situation with me at this time?" About half an inch below, draw a straight line across the sheet of paper. Below this line write the sentence eight times again, each time printing the next succeeding word all in capital letters, i.e.:

WHAT is situation with me at this time?
What IS situation with me at this time?
What is SITUATION with me at this time?
What is situation WITH me at this time?
What is situation with ME at this time?
What is situation with me AT this time?
What is situation with me at THIS time?
What is situation with me at this TIME?

Keeping the thought of yin and yang in your mind, silently read each line twice. When you have read all eight lines, return to the very first sentence above the line, and read each line (nine in all) aloud three times. This should not be done hurriedly, nor with an impatience "to get on with it." Relax, breathe normally and hold a feeling of pleasant peacefulness within yourself. Now toss your three coins simultaneously six times. (Should you have yarrow stalks and wish to manipulate them, do so.) With each toss of the coins, starting from the bottom and working upward (heads = 2 and tails = 3), draw the appropriate line in constructing the 'synchronic' kua. (What we identify as the 'synchronic' kua, is the one that is the immediate result of the *initial* operation of chance. By the ritual of coin tossing or milfoil manipulation, the kua is made synchronous with the matter of concern.) By the way, do not become upset about the grammar of the written phrase. There are reasons to express it in this manner and I must ask you, for the time being, just to accept it.

Look at the linear image before you. Read the phrase as it was first written by you above the line. Carefully analyze the thoughts you experienced when first reading the written phrase, and the thoughts you are experiencing now. Write down some of the impressions you have and your observation of them. Now refer to your text of *I Ching* to identify which of the sixty-four kua you have chanced upon. (For this reference it is most preferable to use the Wilhelm/Baynes translation, the Raymond Van Over rendering, the Z. D. Sung edition, or the Rev. Canon McClatchie translation, as these are the only ones, other than the Chinese editions, which have the Chinese ideograms that go with each of the kua.) When you turn to the page on which it appears, you will first be conscious of the kua's title in English (or, if you should be reading this volume in one of the European translations, you will be conscious of its title in your language). As this word or group of words which make up the name of the kua merges into your consciousness, new things begin to happen with how you see and feel about the interrogatory phrase we have related to *I Ching*.

Only a few will be able to do the next part of the experiment, unless you already read Chinese. If you know a Chinese scholar, go to him and ask him to explain the makeup of the ideogram to you. This will give you another dimension of understanding. This is to say, the chance factor has effected a change in what is now recognized as the significance of the phrase "What is situation with me at this time?"

For this experiment forget about any moving lines which you may have. Read the Judgment and the Image verses, and relate them to yourself in terms of the information that is responding to the question posed. Write down what you have experienced. Tell what seemed most important to you. Try to describe the feeling of change that you experienced during the various steps of the exercise. Finally, state your conclusions.

Experiment B

Use another sheet of paper and furnish the same information at the top. This time construct a phrase about a matter with which you are personally concerned. Now rework and rephrase it so that it is expressed in no more than eight words. Write it once above the line, and then eight times below the line, each time capitalizing all of the letters in the next succeeding word. When this is done, keep the thought of yin and yang in mind and silently read each line twice. When you have read all eight lines twice, return to the first writing above the line and read all nine lines aloud, three times each, unhurriedly. Breathe normally and imagine a great peacefulness taking over inside you. Next toss the coins, and from the bottom up construct the appropriate kua that is indicated by the throw of the coins.

Look at the linear image before you. Read the phrase as it was initially written. Analyze the thoughts you experienced when first reading the phrase and the thoughts you are experiencing now. Note some of the impressions you have and any remarks about them you may choose to make. Refer to one of the *I Ching* texts noted previously to identify the kua you have thrown, or as I prefer to emphasize, the kua you have chanced upon. As the word or group of words which make up the name of the kua registers with you, try to sense, feel and accept the new things which begin to happen. And even if you do not read Chinese, look at the ideogram that goes with the kua and somehow interpret it in terms that relate to the situation you have phrased and addressed to *I Ching*. Now write down your reactions, insights, feelings, and analysis.

When you have completed Experiment B, mail your papers to

International *I Ching* Studies Institute
P.O. Box 5018, Beverly Hills, Ca. 90210

They may be used in a forthcoming *I Ching* research and analysis report, planned for publication in the Institute Newsletter.

It is hoped that you will not read the following pages until you have completed both parts of the experiment above. What follows is a report on one student's compliance with Experiment A. It will be left to the reader to discover his own results for Experiment B.

Student: Lori Chin 5:25 P.M. January 25, 1972
Curious when I started, still am, not as much now. I started thinking about my present situation—besides what I am doing now. Problems and positive attributes that I am faced with presently. *Never knew a sentence could have so many meanings.*

At this point Lori removed the three ancient coins from a small red pouch in which they were kept along with a tortoise shell. She deposited the coins into the shell and commenced tossing them out to form the first line of a kua. There were thought processes of significance which passed through her mind with the marking of each line. To enable the reader to gain a hint of an idea of the internal thought and feeling state, I shall structure the kua line by line, commencing at the left of the page and moving to the right. Pause with each linear structure and become aware of your own inner reactions to the statement: "What is situation with me at this time?"

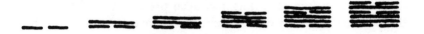

Here you should pause and consider the relationship that Sun (The Gentle—wind and wood, eldest daughter, southeast, penetrating, rooster, the thighs, white, 5 [it is the fifth of the pa kua], timely standard, and pleasure) has with the question, "What is situation with me at this time?" Apply these things to what you may regard as being "the inner" aspects of yourself.

You are now beginning to construct the kua that influences the outer aspects of your "situation—at this time." When the sixth and top line is drawn, consider it as K'an (The Abysmal—water, middle son, north, dangerous, pig, the ear, 6 [it is the sixth of the pa kua], timely development, liking, wisdom), and sense the significance these things bring to you in understanding the external aspects of yourself at this time.

Now look at the two kua as a total structure of K'an over Sun (The Abysmal over The Gentle). We pick up again with Lori's report, as she identifies the kua.

> When I first opened the book and found 48, Ching, "The Well," I first reflected upon the well as meaning health. I was very happy with this, until I started reading, then I had to focus upon a new dimension of content in the kua.

I placed myself in the image of the well and the town as people who will come to me for nourishment; and I seek them for survival also. If I or the town is not sincere with our feelings or honesty with ourselves, then we cannot exist.

I was no longer aware of myself as being a human being. A human being is the name of an animal with two hands, eyes, ears, a nose, mouth, etc. This is all physical. I was a human being without a form—I was I! Not a physical structure.

To quickly summarize what has happened: Tossing the coins was a systematized technique of utilizing the factor of chance to structure a kua. The kua has been pre-committed by us to the phrased situation with which we are involving *I Ching*. The phrased situation represents a concern with some condition that is important to us. As the kua begins to be structured, we are able to recognize that there is a change in the significance of both the phrased situation and the situation as we experience it internally. An analysis of this change can be explained as having been initiated by the introduction of the kua and its multiple symbolizations. This rationalization we accept as 'cause'. And so we have used 'chance' as an ally to enable us to give a direction to 'change'. Knowing that we are directing the change we have a comfortable feeling of living in an environment of causality. *I Ching* is 'chance'. *I Ching* is 'cause'.

Four
Chance Plays with Your Life

Your Experiences of Chance

Carl Jung saw "the chance aspect of events"[1] as a primary preoccupation of the Chinese mind. It is obviously a concern that stands in sharp contrast to the Western view which is committed to a world of causally sequenced events. However, more and more doubt is being thrown today upon the validity of the notion of causality as being the only and total explanation of experience. In our everyday life, as Jung observed, "an incalculable amount of human effort is directed to combating and restricting the nuisance or danger represented by chance."[2]

This question of chance, and the role it plays in our lives is important for understanding how *I Ching* can function as an extension of man's intuitive projections of psyche to further a harmonious directing of and caring for 'soma'. In any meaningful study of *I Ching*, it must be accepted and remembered that the underlying principle of *I Ching* is one that is blatantly inconsonant with our rigidly constructed causalistic concepts of reality. As an aid to easing into the sling of acausality, from where we can zoom out and explore the fascinating spaces of 'chance,' 'synchronicity' and cosmic happenings, let us reflect for a moment upon some of the many instances we experience daily in which we are exercising an effort to combat what Jung has described as, "the nuisance or danger represented by chance."

The examples to be given here are not profound, but are of a most simple, elementary nature. The intent is not to convince anyone that we live in chaos, nor by contrary deduction that all is an immense cosmos of clean and precisely cut order.

Think of the cost (we open with price, for it is an unfortunate reality of our culture that most of us have been raised to evaluate everything in terms of money—how much it costs—but that, as the saying goes, is another kettle of fish); think of the cost of purchasing, installing, operating and maintaining the thousands upon thousands of traffic-signal devices in our urban societies. The cost runs into millions of dollars a year. This gargantuan investment of public finances is made primarily, perhaps solely, to combat the chance of accident and injury; to force upon nature, which is acausalistic, a pattern of predictability for the sake of human convenience and easy comprehension. Yet it never wholly succeeds. For with all the red, green and flashing yellow lights, the death and injury toll at authorized crossings and intersections, to say nothing of the other areas of streets and highways, is painfully high.

In the area of economics our societies are in the process of evolving into giant "computerocracies." Part of the reason that motivates this change is the questionable concept that electronic machines will eventually be perfected to an extent that they will be error-proof and fail-safe. An explanation to rationalize this program of dehumanizing interpersonal relationships is that it will protect humans from the chance mistakes of judgment, coordination and simple, manually produced records made by other fallible humans. Is it so bizarre to ask: "If part of this premise recognizes the fallibility of human nature, can we expect this same fallible creature to produce a machine that will be the diadem of infallibility?"

To stave off the chance of disease, milk and other foods have, for many years now, been pasteurized. The ironic fact about this precaution against the spreading or contracting of disease is that the natural nutritional values which build the body's resistance to disease are destroyed. Thus, while warding off the chance of one kind of illness through the banquet of nutritionally deprived foods, we come to experience all manner of psychological, physiological and emotional ailments which may be traced to malnutrition.

This is not a popular view, because it rejects the concept that every single human life has a premium value of infinite importance. When we look to nature, we should suspect that there is a much grander plan in operation than that of sanctifying the human species as the epitome of divine invention. Indeed, if man is to be regarded as the noblest attainment of God's creative potential, it is time to look for a more divine god, who has a much higher aspiration. This is not to negate the natural urge of a species for self-survival. It is only to suggest that we, as men, recognize that we, too, are part of a grand scheme that totally eludes our ability and capacity to comprehend. As such, by turning to natural ways we may even speed up the forward-evolving process and get on with becoming whatever it is that Tao is forever becoming.

We each can find many instances to illustrate the point. So we will not belabor the issue, as it should be apparent that many of our solicitous programs to intervene between man's desires and their chanced negation are often self-defeating. It would seem that, try as we may, the great overpowering reality of life is that nature is primarily the phenomenon of acausal events. These examples are meant only to stimulate our thinking, to awaken our consciousness to a deeper awareness and recognition of the nature of the things we are regularly experiencing and doing. With this kind of awakening, we cannot help but realize how perceptively accurate Jung was when he wrote: "An incalculable amount of human effort is directed to combating and restricting the nuisance or danger represented by chance."

How all of this pertains to *I Ching* is, of course, our immediate concern. *I Ching* is the product of a civilization and culture that is fundamentally empirical. Thousands of years of experience, with the most astounding results, stand as a monument of verification attesting to the dependability of the wisdom and rituals of *I Ching*. Too often we are caught up in the need for a theoretical explanation of what we experience. For reasons I am unable to explain, it happens that a person cannot believe in his own experience unless it can be explained to him intellectually. Of course, this is a double-edged sword, for there are those who can explain in rational and intellectual language the most crass nonsense, which, unfortunately, may be accepted as fact. *I Ching* does not come laden with theories. It is a thing that one must use in coping with the 'chance' aspects of existence. Based upon one's own experience it will ring true or false to you, useful or useless.

I Ching speaks to us in a language of intensity and association. As a symbolic language, it catalyzes inner experiences, feelings and thoughts into an energy that can be expressed as sensory and tactile phenomena. The experiencing of *I Ching* is somewhat like a dream experience, in that it does not comply with the logical structures by which we guide ourselves in the waking state. When mind is in the dream state, it is in a condition of near maximum freedom. Restrictions of space, time and form are unknown. The dead can be alive. We can experience ourselves as being ourselves, animal and object all simultaneously. And, most significant, all of these experiences will have the total effect of what we call reality at the moment of their happening. At other times, the dream is experienced *as* a dream. We *know* that we are dreaming, and in a state of half-consciousness we may say to ourselves: "I must remember this dream when I awaken." But often upon waking, the most that we can recall is our wanting to remember. I have said that *I Ching* is somewhat like a dream experience—sometimes.

When one involves *I Ching* in a matter of concerned interest, the experience of relating what is imaged, symbolized and written is one of a sudden release from the confines of doubt, limitation and incapacitation. In a mysterious way the kua, resulting from whatever ritual act practiced, coincides symbolically and as an image with the matter you have at hand. What has happened in a given moment is experienced as containing, projecting or reflecting all of the qualities peculiar to that moment. The particular kua formed by chance events becomes a spying device that scans or penetrates, according to how it is used, the matter being observed at the time. The inexperienced may be puzzled, as they hold to the concept that words have a meaning within themselves, so how could the same words mean so many things to so many different people? Of course the meaning of words is in the consciousness of the person using them. Using words is a process of speaking, writing or hearing. It is possible that, in a conversation between two people, there may be at least three meanings to the words being used: the speaker's meaning, the listener's meaning and the language or dictionary meaning. Language is decidedly a phonetic of archetypes which is exercized on a yin/yang principle, enabling it to both reveal and conceal meanings.

Pierre Teilhard de Chardin, in one of the footnotes to his classic volume *The Phenomenon of Man*, writes:

It is only really through strokes of chance that life proceeds, but strokes of chance which are recognized and grasped—that is to say, psychically selected. [3]

One of the methods of psychically selecting a "stroke of chance" to help in our ongoingness through life is that of the ritual and wisdom of *I Ching*. Wish otherwise as we may, experience leads us to see the world through de Chardin's eyes as:

. . . the world proceeding by means of groping and chance. Under this heading alone—even up to the human level on which chance is most controlled—how many failures have there been for one success, how many days of misery for one hour's joy, how many sins for a solitary saint? [4]

With this recognition, we rock back and forth between the yin and the yang. And the Chinese Wu Ch'i (Before-the-beginning), becomes comprehendible because we can see a parallel between it and Jung's declaration that:

> . . . in all chaos there is a cosmos, in all disorder a secret order, in all caprice a fixed law, for everything that works is grounded on its opposite.

Slowly it may dawn upon us that our lives are lived for the greater part in the environment of chance. When it does, we will be appreciative of this remarkable wisdom that extends to us the possibility of making an ally of 'chance' so that we may befriend 'change'. After a deep study of this wisdom, one comes to realize that all the gods and powers are within us. We each have within us the godly in the form we deserve, and we nurture and preserve it by our daily expression.

It is the infinite consciousness, running through our finite beings, that utilizes the symbolic processes for communicating with ourselves. "The symbolic process is an experience in images and of images. Its development usually shows an enanti-odromian structure like the text of the *I Ching,* and so presents a rhythm of negative and positive, loss and gain, dark and light."[5] The way in which one becomes involved with *I Ching* is almost invariably characterized by one's getting stuck in a very difficult situation. One's strongest need and desire at the time is for the illumination or higher consciousness that will bring one through the situation successfully and with few bruises. The ancient *Book of Changes* answers to these requirements. Use it!

Before examining the foundations of causality, let us take a look at some selections from one of the poems of Saint John of the Cross. But in looking at it, let us read beyond the theological and religious meanings and consider the secular and totally human meanings communicated by the lines from "Por Toda la Hermosura" (Hunter's Quest).

The Hunter's Quest[6]

For all the beauty life has got
I'll never throw myself away
Safe for one thing I know not what
Which lucky chance may bring my way.

The savour of all finite joy
In the long run amounts to this—
To tire the appetite of bliss
And the fine palate to destroy.
So for life's sweetness, all the lot,
I'll never throw myself away
But for a thing, I know not what,
Which lucky chance may bring my way.

* * *

He that is growing to full growth
In the desire of God profound,
Will find his tastes so changed around
That of mere pleasures he is loth,
Like one who, with the fever hot,
At food will only look askance
But craves for that, he knows not what,
Which may be brought by lucky chance.

* * *

With love of One so high elated,
Tell me, if you would find great harm
If the servants He created
Did not rival Him in charm?
Alone, without face, form, or features,

Foothold, or prop, you would advance
To love that thing, beyond all creatures,
Which may be won by happy chance.

* * *

The man who strains for wealth and rank
Employs more care, and wastes more health
For riches that elude his stealth
Than those he's hoarded in the bank;
But I my fortune to advance
The lowlier stoop my lowly lot
Over some thing, I know not what,
Which may be found by lucky chance.

For that which by the sense down here
Is comprehended as our good,
And all that can be understood
Although it soars sublime and sheer;
For all that beauty can enhance—
I'll never lose my happy lot:
Only for that, I know not what,
Which can be won by lucky chance.

Three Kinds of Change

I Ching deals with three kinds of change, as most serious students know. They are identified as 'nonchange', 'cyclic change' and 'sequent change'. Each of these types of change has a significant relationship to every situation brought to *I Ching*. We shall try in this section to explore these things, and by discovering personal applications, we will be able to sketch out some universal guidelines, making this ancient wisdom better understood and felt. Finally, we will analyze how all three kinds of change are involved with nearly everything at all times.

What is 'nonchange'? Wilhelm describes it as "the background . . . against which change is made possible." It will be difficult for those who are used to thinking in terms of absolutes to accept the *I Ching* trinity of change. Yet it is important that it should be understood. Intellectually, it is indispensable to the understanding of traditional Chinese thought patterns which see the relationship between 'chance' and 'change' quite differently than many of us. Wilhelm's paragraph on this point is excellent in its expression and instructive in its content. I shall quote from it:

> For in regard to any change there must be some fixed point to which the change can be referred; otherwise there can be no definite order and everything is dissolved in chaotic movement. This point of reference must be established, and this always requires a choice and a decision. . . . At the beginning of the world, as at the beginning of thought, there is the decision, the fixing of the point of reference. . . . Experience teaches that at the dawn of consciousness one stands already inclosed within definite, prepotent systems of relationships. The problem then is to choose one's point of reference so that it coincides with the point of reference for cosmic events. . . . Obviously the premise for such a decision is the belief that in the last analysis the world is a system of homogeneous relationships— that it is a cosmos, not a chaos. . . . The ultimate frame of reference for all that changes is the nonchanging. [7]

This paragraph is crammed with many provocative thoughts. We shall try to deal with some of them, and in a somewhat orderly fashion. Think of what is being implied when Wilhelm writes that the act of establishing a point of reference "always requires a choice and a decision." This would indicate that the Chinese philosophy of 'change' *(I Ching),* is one that conceives of man as a free agent capable of exercising free will, as opposed to man as a pawn of fate. Choice is only possible in the context of freedom. For there to be choice, there must be alternatives. Decision is the act of cutting off one alternative from others. It is selection. This is interesting, because it distinguishes the

I Ching as an oracle from all other oracles we have known. It is not like fortune-telling that foretells what is predestined, but rather it is a prescription of action to be taken to deal with a given situation.

We know ourselves better than anything else. At least we like to think that we do. We are conscious of having undergone innumerable changes, from infancy to adulthood; we have changed in intelligence, in body proportions, in energy output, in our feelings about people and things, in our taste for foods, in our habits of dress and sleep, and in countless other ways. All of these changes we each have undergone. But how could we know this if it were not that there is something about us, in us, or of us that is fixed and *un*changing? This is what 'nonchange' is about.

'Cyclic change' is something we are all familiar with. The seasons of the year, night and day, the days of the week, the phases of the moon, the tides of the seas and oceans, our heartbeat, sleeping and waking, hunger and satiety, our respiration, all of these constitute instances of 'cyclic change'.

'Sequent change' is the ongoing, never-recurring kind of change, 'change' that is manifested as the aging process, the growing process, the acquiring of knowledge; all changes which happen *through* time rather than *in* time.

A very great many forms of life, like human beings, express both cyclic and sequent change processes. Trees, for example, age, grow old and become larger, while at the same time expressing seasonal changes. Certain kinds of fish mature, yet they regularly return to certain geographical areas to spawn. And perhaps on levels which escape man's awareness, even when abetted by his modern scientific instruments, such long-enduring things as rocks and mountains may manifest both kinds of change in addition to the fundamental of 'nonchange'.

Five
Two Languages of Knowing

Intuition—Its Nature, Its Use

Experimental research in biochemistry, physics and psychology is producing more and more evidence that there is a mysterious phenomenon, expressing information through the physiological being about directional and avoidable modes of conduct and feeling, which serves as guidance pressure helping to keep the individual in a state of harmonious participation in life. It is called intuition. When we are aware of it and respond to it, things go well. When we are aware of it and question it with our rationality, we more often become confused, and at best things go shakily. When we are aware of it and reject it outright as "a stupid idea," things go badly. When we are aware of it, almost without being aware of it, and we flow with that directional conduct and mode of feeling, things go quite well for us.

In any successful use of *I Ching*, intuition must perform importantly. How does it happen that a person reading one of the "oracle" phrases of *I Ching* understands it as an instruction for action or non-action that, upon later reflection, is found to be constructively consonant with the situation brought to the book? Is it because, as Dr. Karagulla wonders, there are things to be sensed which are not encompassed by our five senses? There is a universal acceptance of the concept that our five senses enable us to accumulate knowledge. Knowledge is that which is limited to the scope of rational and measurable definition. Our sixth, seventh and any other yet-undiscovered senses relate and connect us to primeval intelligence and elemental energy. When this relationship is established—or happens—there is projected to a conscious level the ability to intuit. Intuiting is to be aware of being in a state of 'knowing', almost involuntarily. Elsewhere I have elucidated upon the distinction between knowledge and 'knowing'.

Understanding this distinction is important in developing the artful talent of broadening one's useful application of the wisdom of *I Ching* so that it moves beyond the confines of anxiety about the future into the infinite vistas of 'Now'! Charles Hartshorne contributes a paper of exciting and revelatory insight to an anthology of *Theories of the Mind,* [1] which can serve as a supportive explanation of certain phenomena that take place within ourselves and *I Ching*.

I Ching is a method of experiencing the world. It is a system for determining our perception. In a section of his essay dealing with perception, Hartshorne writes:

> In looking at a photograph of a beloved person we may experience the shape of the light and dark masses on the paper almost as the very shape of the person, though what we literally see is the paper, not the person. And similarly in actual "seeing" itself, what we literally experience, I believe, is our own bodily state; but we evaluate what we experience as equivalent to an external state of affairs. And this for practical purposes it usually is, somewhat as when we see words of a book, and seem almost to experience the described happenings. [2]

Let us draw a parallel of looking at the picture of a beloved one with looking at the kua for a situation or problem that concerns one in using *I Ching*. Perhaps it should be noted here that not many Westerners approach the *I* at a level of image representation and archetypal significance. By this I mean that most Westerners, after constructing the kua, do not think first of the total image, but rather refer directly to the key (usually found in the back of the book) to locate an identifying number for the kua. (Incidentally, the key device does not appear in any of the traditional Chinese text of *I Ching.*) He then looks up that numbered kua and reads its name, as translated into English (or any other Western language). This registers at an intellectual level, and the reaction is usually either of pleasure, because it is a "good" kua, or unhappiness because it is a "bad" kua, or a rather fearful perplexity, because he cannot determine if it is "good" or "bad."

This kind of intellectual approach to *I Ching* is necessarily restrictive. It does not stimulate the development of one's intuition. It demonstrates how very much we are creatures of conditioning. We have been conditioned to experience a photograph almost as though it were the person or thing pictured. We seldom, if ever, think that a newspaper photograph is merely an arrangement of dots in varying densities on a white sheet of paper. On the other hand, we have not been conditioned to think of a dark unbroken line as being a yang force, strength, light principle, hard, assertive, projective; nor of a dark broken line as being a yin force, weak, dark principle, soft, receptive, yielding. The true miracle is that in spite of these differences of approach, the *I* still activates an intuitive something within, and so becomes very meaningful to us. For this reason, the kua is experienced as being equivalent with the external condition into which we have projected it. Of course, we may be inclined to believe with Hartshorne that what is actually experienced is one's own bodily state. However it may be rationalized, it remains, in fact, a way of knowing!

Knowing requires a quality of "simpatico," an aspect or tone of sympatheticness, that arises from a relationship wherein conditions conducive to some kind of productivity are inherent in the person(s), time(s), place(s) and thing(s), then in a proximate state. This challenges Hartshorne's assertion that: "A stone cannot be sympathized with because it is but a dense

swarm of molecules or atoms. . . ."³ Can anyone doubt that to
a sculptor, an architect or a gardener, a stone is something more
than "a dense swarm of molecules or atoms? . . ."⁴ It is part of
a potential that is composed of the dream, the vision, and the
promise and means of fulfilling it. In a very real sense, some
stones can be sympathized with by some people. The "sym-
patico" arises because there exists some wonderful state
wherein the person is able to perceive a relationship with the
stone that will culminate in a productive and creative expression, that instances change. This kind of sensitivity is a projection of the intuitive. The intuitive is the knowing.

The more we match Hartshorne's assertion to actual human
behavior, feelings and attitudes, the more pronounced its error
becomes. Earlier in the same essay he presents a quite different
view. He speaks of mind "on the higher or vertebrate level" and
the "further confirmation of our psychicalistic view."

> If "matter" is a form of mind, then the constituents of our
> bodies, such as cells and molecules, must consist of pro-
> cesses of remembering and of sympathetic valuation. What
> then can be our relation to these processes? It must be that
> of participation. Hurt my cells and almost immediately
> you hurt me, because intimate and continuous sympathy
> with my body is precisely what distinguishes my sequence
> of selves from all others. It is part of what makes my body
> mine and no one else's. That I depend upon the states of
> my body obviously follows; for the more intimate our
> sympathies with something, the more it can influence us.⁵

The important thought for an understanding of how *I Ching*
"works," is in the words: ". . . the more intimate our sympathies with something, the more it can influence us." So the
sculptor, having intimate sympathies with the stone, will be
influenced by it, and it, in turn, will ultimately be influenced by
him. When one experiences intimate sympathies with *I Ching*,
one becomes influenced by it, and in turn one will exert an
influence upon it. This is what has happened all through the
ages. This is the reason for all the different commentaries of the
past. It is the explanation for the burgeoning commentaries

appearing in cultures and languages other than Chinese today. People everywhere are experiencing a feeling of "simpatico" for *I Ching,* hence they are being influenced by it, and in turn are influencing it. There is a significant similarity to this phenomenon on all planes of human endeavor. An herbalist seeing a garden of growing herbs experiences "simpatico," and is influenced by the herbs he sees; in turn he will exert an influence upon them. An engineer seeing a river has "simpatico" and is influenced by the river into visualizing bridges or tunnels, shapes and forms, so that eventually he influences the river. And so it is throughout life.

Knowing is intuition. Knowing is also memory. Hartshorne says, ". . . memory is the way in which the past is possessed by present experience and thereby colors and influences that experience."[6] Those who embrace the philosophy of *I Ching* and its long extension back into the past enjoy an identity of comfortable continuity with a great antiquity. Because it is continuous to the present day, Chinese antiquity perhaps gives one a stronger sense of being in a closer proximity to infinity than any of the other cultural traditions. Through the archetypes, which the ancient sages used to express a wisdom of long enduring value, twentieth- and twenty-first-century man is able to use the past as a constructive influence upon the present. For the sticks, the coins, the book and the words are all essentially forms of matter. Matter is intelligence and energy manifested as form. Matter devoid of mind or intelligence is unthinkable. Every observed property entails the presence of intelligence and energy. The concept of a "phenomenal consciousness" that allows for the interflow of information between matter and organisms of different characteristics is no longer startling. Our present age has introduced us to new dimensions of cognition. Once again I shall draw from Hartshorne, who has expressed it so very well.

Physicists today generally concede that the notion of matter is not an ultimate explanatory conception. The notion amounts to this, that something or other is extended in space-time (or better, something or other is going on in space-time) of which we know through science certain geometrical patterns, certain forms of relationship. But what it is that is patterned or related, physicists do not pretend to know, though many physicists, biologists, and philosophers suspect that it is mind in various forms, mostly non-human.[7]

I believe that each individual has two reservoirs of past experience from which to recollect. There are the physical, intellectual and emotional experiences that immediately precede the present moment of consciousness. These perhaps can go back even to the fetal period. The other experiences predate the fetal stage. These are racial, genetic, and cellular intelligence experiences that influence the specific organism from before, through vast brackets of time and space. These also are drawn upon consciously and unconsciously.

The *Classic of Permutations* is a compilation of wisdom that is itself eternally evolving; thus, its endurance is indeed great. There are people of a dogmatic bend who will try to set up an *I Ching* orthodoxy, and there are those who are motivated by a passion for revolution against the shackles of tradition. Both camps only serve to vitiate the power that is in the *I*. Both camps should be resisted resolutely as we seek to find the unity between their difference.

The Use of What Is and of What Is Not

A great many of us, reared in the cultural pattern of the West, are unaccustomed to think in terms of unified opposites, such as symbolized by the *T'ai Chi Tu*. Most persons and things are regarded as being good or bad, hard or soft, short or tall, rigid or pliant, wet or dry, etc. This dualistic thinking is also to be found in some of the religious pronouncements recorded in Christian scripture: "He who is not with me is against me."[8] The custom of thinking in terms of isolated totality—as though people, things or qualities existed independently and unrelatedly—is alien to Taoism. Since Taoist thought was strongly influenced by the wisdom inherent in the *I*, there is justification to suspect that this thinking is also foreign to *I Ching*. In *Tao Te Ching* it is written:

> We put thirty spokes together, and call it a wheel; but it is upon the space where there is nothing that the utility of the wheel depends.
> We turn clay with a potter's skill, and shape it into a vase; but it is upon the space where there is nothing that the utility of the vase depends.
> We cut windows and doors into walls, and call it a house; but it is upon the space where there is nothing that the utility of the house depends.
> So as we recognize the utility of what is, we must learn to master the utility of what is not. [9]

There are many translations of *Tao Te Ching*, and each one affords another insight, another dimension to our understanding. Some of the footnotes, just by rephrasing as an explanation of the translated text, also add new values to our understanding. As an example, take this note from a translation by Ch'u Tu-Kao:

> Without space we cannot have the benefit of a carriage wheel, a vessel or a house. Without wooden spokes, clay moulds and walls, we cannot make use of the space in them. Existence and non-existence, after all are co-existent and interdependent. [10]

To this add the further paraphrase of R. B. Blakney:

> Is the Way real? Does it exist? Can one isolate it and say, "This is it?" It is as real as the hole in the hub of a wheel where the axle rests. The hole is a void in the hub. It exists as a window exists when part of the wall of a house is cut away. Similarly, the Way is like the empty place in a bowl. The advantage of a bowl lies in its walls, but its use depends on its emptiness. So with the Way. It is functional. It cannot be isolated, but you cannot be without it. [11]

Frank J. MacHovec translates the same chapter and here I quote from his last paragraph:

> So there is advantage in using what can be seen, what exists. And there is also advantage in using what cannot be seen, what is non-existent. [12]

And another shading of significance is to be found in Archie J. Bohm's interpretation:

> Every positive factor involves its negative or opposing factor; for example:
>
> In order to turn a wheel, although thirty spokes must revolve, the axle must remain motionless; so both the moving and the non-moving are needed to produce revolution.
>
> In order to mold a vase, although one must use clay, he must also provide a hollow space empty of clay; so both clay and the absence of clay are required to produce a vessel.
>
> In order to build a house, although we must establish solid walls, we must also provide doors and windows; so both the impenetrable and penetrable are essential to a useful building.
>
> Therefore, we profit equally by the positive and the negative ingredients in each situation. [13]

In rounding off this important point, I quote the final paragraph from John C. H. Wu's excellent translation:

> Thus, while the tangible has advantages,
> It is the intangible that makes it useful. [14]

My reason for such a lengthy variety of quotes of a single chapter in a single work is to set a reference inside each of us that will help awaken us to a necessary and proper use of the philosophical dicta of *I Ching*. One should always keep in mind that the verbal philosophy of *I Ching* is at the same instant a precise schematic of phenomenal process. We have quoted six different translators or interpreters on the eleventh chapter of *Tao Te Ching.* Spin it to the right or the left, there is an interesting correspondence to be found between this eleventh chapter of *Tao Te Ching* and the eleventh kua of *I Ching:* T'ai—"Peace."

Keep in mind what the message of the eleventh chapter of *Tao Te Ching* is; namely, that which is tangible has advantages to offer; however, it is the intangible that enables us to make use of the tangible. All experience on this plane of manifestation is a result of the proper or improper involvement with or use of the penetrable and the impenetrable. The eleventh kua is structured out of ☷, K'un, above and ☰, Ch'ien, below. The earth (the tangible) meets with heaven (the intangible). Peace is a condition in which one force has the compliance of a weaker force. One must always remember that peace treaties are always dictated by the victor, never by the vanquished. Thus it happens that imaged in the condition of "peace" is the basic fundamental principle of existence— negation of the negation. It is pictured in the T'ai Chi Tu as a dot of yin in the large body of the yang element, and a dot of yang in the large body of the yin element. This is the graphic representation of the fact that all things have seeded within them their opposite. In the condition of "peace," it exists only so long as the formerly vanquished cannot throw off the yoke of compliance. But there brews a new energy within, a new plan, a new dream that sooner or later will either overthrow the peace by vanquishing the former victor, or both, together, become a new matter and a whole new evolvement will begin to process itself. The text of the Judgment of the eleventh kua reads: "Peace. The small departs; the great approaches. Good fortune. Success." The negation of the situation imaged in "Peace" as expressed above is realized in the succeeding kua, "P'i," number 12—"Standstill (Stagnation)." The corresponding text reads, in part: "The great departs; the small approaches." "The small" that is departing in 11 now has gone full circle and becomes "The small" approaching.

Does this imply an inevitability? Not at all. *I Ching* stipulates that there is a pattern conceived within the tapestry of life. It does not say that one cannot work on different parts of the pattern at different times. Eventually each tapestry is completed. Each tapestry is a single, completed swatch in the patch-quilt of infinity. In a very real way the eleventh chapter of *Tao Te Ching* and the eleventh kua of *I Ching* prescribe the developing of the talent and know-how of utilizing the non-being element of every situation where its elemental composition is obvious and clearly sensed. This leads us to becoming masters of our fate.

As a completing touch to this study of the eleventh chapter of *Tao Te Ching* and the eleventh kua of *I Ching,* let us look into the numerological implications of the number eleven. The symbolic significance of numbers recedes far into the past of man. Preoccupation with number symbolism was considered an important scientific study to such ancient greats as Pythagoras, Plato, gnostic thinkers, cabalists and alchemists. Even before Pythagoras there was Lao Tzu, who stroked into the *Tao Te Ching:* "One becomes two; two becomes three; and from the ternary comes all the myriad things." Many numbers not only represent quantities, but they also serve as cogent symbols of ideas and forces. J. E. Cirlot in his book, *A Dictionary of Symbols,* writes:

> Apart from the basic symbols of unity and multiplicity, there is another general symbolism attached to the even numbers (expressing the negative and passive principle) and the uneven numbers (the positive and active). Furthermore, the numerical series possesses a symbolic dynamism which it is essential not to overlook. The idea that one engenders two and two creates three is founded upon the premise that every entity tends to surpass its limits, or to confront itself with its opposite. . . . [15]

We have mentioned the seed of strife hidden in the concept of Peace. Is it not interesting that the number 11 is held to be indicative of transition? Cirlot lists it as symbolic of "excess and

peril and of conflict and martyrdom." And if we take the 11 as
1 + 1 = 2, the 2 may be regarded as standing for echo, reflection, conflict and counterpoise or contraposition; all of which
are elementary qualities embodied in the condition of 'peace'.
The use of what is and of what is not is the lesson being
taught. How does one apply this Taoist principle to exercises
with *I Ching?* When one has completed the manipulation of the
yarrow stalks, or tossed the coins, the indicated kua is taken as
representing the situation as it is. The opposite of the kua gives
an insight on the situation's non-beingness. With some kua this
can be gotten by inverting it (like No. 11—T'ai, "Peace," K'un
over Ch'ien—its opposite, No. 12, is Ch'ien over K'un). With
others the opposite is attained by changing the lines. One then
makes use of the wisdom of "what-is" by influencing it with the
wisdom of "what-is-not." Which means that ideas are put into
action that effect the substances one must deal with. This is the
use of "what-is" and "what-is-not." The uses are complementary and thus productive.

What is meant by: "The opposite kua gives an insight on the
situation's non-beingness?" We and everything we can see,
touch, smell, taste and hear, are composed of 'being' and
'non-being'. A thing's 'non-being' is the limitation of manifestation that gives a thing its definition. In other words this dot
(·), A, can be distinguished from this dot (•), B, because the
former's beingness ceased to be manifested and became restricted by what we can call 'non-being'. The space about 'being'
(called 'non-being') is that part of a person and thing that is the
great unifier. Is is the 'oneness'. Another way of understanding
this is to picture 'being' as the individualization or manifested
identity of all that is. 'Non-being' is the unified totality of all
potential both in and about everything. The individual molecules which make up everything that exists float in a space
many times greater than the body of themselves. This is imaged
in *I Ching* by the yin and yang from which issue the broken and
unbroken lines. The linear images are structured by the lines
being in spaces (places), rather than flush one upon the other.

Without the spaces, which is the 'non-beingness' of the lines, an entirely different feeling and image is created. Experience it for yourself. Compare the feeling you have as you study the form of the lines composed one upon the other, and the lines spaced apart from each other in the illustration below.

Grace   Inner truth   Difficulty
at the Beginning

Three kua, each paired with its compressed form eliminating the intervening spaces, and demonstrating the different feeling conveyed by graphic forms.

Bio-Energy and Telecommunication (BET)

Bio-energy and telecommunication? How does this fit into a study of *I Ching?* BET sounds so technical and "computerish." Isn't *I Ching* a sacred book of oracles? Perhaps it is. The fact is, enough has been written about the supernatural powers of *I Ching,* leaving the reader more mystified than clarified. Excessive emphasis has been given to the idea that the book is difficult to understand and every contemporary commentator has dwelt upon its bewildering cryptic sayings. Its divinatory aspects have been so eulogized as to reduce *I Ching* to a charade of fortune-telling. If *I Ching,* man's longest lived philosophy, is to have a potency of meaning for today, we must escape from the limitations of yesterday's explanations. We need to seek an understanding of this vital wisdom by enlisting modern metaphors skilfully drawn with new words of tomorrow's vocabulary. While it is certainly true that we cannot yet use the full vocabulary of tomorrow's language because, as McLuhan put it:

Nobody yet knows the languages inherent in the new technological culture; we are all technological idiots in terms of the new situations. Our most impressive words and thoughts betray us by referring to the previously existent, not to the present. [16]

Nevertheless, we must try.

Today a great many persons throughout the world are developing an interest in *I Ching*. How does it happen that an ancient Chinese book should, so suddenly, be capturing the attention of so many Westerners? I believe their curiosity and interest are motivated by a reason issuing from a source within humanity that is itself beyond reason.

The belief that identifying signals are emitted by everything that exists—be it person, object, plant or other living organism— is no longer restricted to "kooks," occultists, metaphysicians and children. Indeed, no! More and more of the best productive minds in science are turning to explore our universe in new dimensions, a universe that is now believed to resound with an infinite number of message vibrations. A generalized way of describing this phenomenon is to say that everything that is and everything that happens projects the noise of its individual identifying energy transformations into the cosmic babble. And each separate thing and event functions as a uniquely refined selective receptor for only those messages which communicate meaning to it, while it either rejects or remains non-responsive to all other messages and stimuli.

However true this may be, it should not mistakenly be construed to imply that "scientists" are less prone to ridiculousness and error than "kooks." We need only to survey the state of pollution that infests our planet's natural resources to see how dangerously wrong science can be when its motivation is to conquer nature, rather than befriend it! Surely more is to be gained through befriending than through conquering. *I Ching* teaches that all things are interdependent or interrelated, and that opposites have seeded in each the nature of the other. It must follow, then, that we cannot destroy an enemy without destroying something of ourselves. But if we struggle to *be-*

friend an enemy, then we liberate a new dimension of potential within ourselves. All this is mere prologue to the purpose I hope to achieve here. My aim is to demonstrate to believer and skeptic some acceptable explanations of how "*I Ching* works." Yet I caution you to keep in mind that one must not mistake an explanation for the actuality.

Now I shall try to show what bio-energy and telecommunication have to do with *I Ching*. Bio-energy has to do with the energy forces of life. Energy is not isolated from intelligence. "Tele," derived from the Greek *tēlē,* means "far, far away; distant." "Communication" has its root in the Latin *communicatus,* past participle of *communicare,* meaning "to share, impart, partake." Hence "telecommunication" implies the phenomenon of sharing, imparting and partaking from far, far away. This introduces the idea of "distance." And what is distance? It is not only the measure of space between, but also the degree of incomprehensibility between organism and organism, object and object, or organism and object. *I Ching* may be viewed as a philosophical technique of utilizing life-forces in a process of sharing, imparting and partaking that transforms the incomprehensible into the comprehensible. I must reiterate, time and time again, that *I Ching* acts primarily as a catalyst, awakening the conscious mind to the content of the infinite 'ever-conscious'. With this image, it is perhaps easier to see what *I Ching* has to do with "distance communication" by using certain selected vibrations of life-forces to effect an evolution of our puzzlement into the understandable; our problems into solutions.

Lawrence K. Frank, in his volume *The World as a Communications Network,* writes:

> Through evolution, each organism has developed concern for those messages which are essential to its living functions and survival as a species, while ignoring what is not biologically relevant nor useful. Accordingly, in any geographical area, different species: bacteria in the soil, worms, insects, fish, reptiles, birds, amphibians, and the array of mammals, carry on their life careers, selectively

receiving and responding to the signals that are of concern to each species, while unaware of the many other messages that are being concurrently transmitted. [17]

In this passage Frank has described an infinite process with remarkable terseness. He has pictured a universe abounding in messages that are being concurrently transmitted to an astronomical variety of species. Yet each species selects only those signals which are concerned with its survival. But more than that, each individual identity of each species selects only those messages which are essential for *its* immediate individual survival. What a miracle! We will understand more about the nature of *I Ching* when we recognize that the ancient sages constructed this wisdom as a prototype of the universe described by Frank, the universe in which we live and enjoy our being. In the Shuo Kua it reads:

They put themselves in accord with tao and its power, and in conformity with this laid down the order of what is right. By thinking through the order of the outer world to the end, and by exploring the law of their nature to the deepest core, they arrived at an understanding of fate. [18]

And in chapter four of Ta Chuan it reads:

1. The *Book of Changes* contains the measure of heaven and earth; therefore it enables us to comprehend the tao of heaven and earth and its order. [19]

2. Looking upward, we contemplate with its help the signs in the heavens; looking down, we examine the lines of the earth. Thus we come to know the circumstances of the dark and the light. Going back to the beginnings of things and pursuing them to the end, we come to know the lessons of birth and of death. The union of seed and power produces all things; the escape of the soul brings about change. Through this we come to know the conditions of outgoing and returning spirits. [20]

3. Since in this way man comes to resemble heaven and earth, he is not in conflict with them. His wisdom embraces all things, and his tao brings order into the

whole world; therefore he does not let himself be carried away. He rejoices in heaven and has knowledge of fate, therefore he is free of care. He is content with his circumstances and genuine in his kindness, therefore he can practice love. [21]

Wilhelm here inserts a significant comment:

Here we are shown how with the help of the fundamental principles of the *Book of Changes* it is possible to arrive at a complete realization of man's innate capacities. This unfolding rests on the fact that man has innate capacities that resemble heaven and earth, that he is a microcosm. Now, since the laws of heaven and earth are reproduced in the *Book of Changes,* man is provided with the means of shaping his own nature, so that his inborn potentialities for good can be completely realized. In this process two factors are to be taken into account: wisdom and action, or intellect and will. If intellect and will are correctly centered, the emotional life takes on harmony. [22]

And most important is the fourth verse of chapter four of Ta Chuan:

In it are included the forms and the scope of everything in the heavens and on earth so that nothing escapes it. In it all things everywhere are completed, so that none is missing. Therefore by means of it we can penetrate the tao of day and night, and so understand it. Therefore the spirit is bound to no one place, nor the *Book of Changes* to any one form. [23]

John-Paul Sartre held that "The image envisions the object most of the time in its entirety all at once. . . . What is successive in perception is simultaneous in the image. . . ."[24] This may be taken as being descriptive of *I Ching* and its composition of sixty-four kua. It images this cosmic background 'noise', wherein the world in which we live resounds with countless diverse messages. Most men are primarily concerned with what is transmitted. Few, indeed, are those who focus upon the mechanism of selection that can pick out the messages essential for survival. As one develops a deeper understanding of *I Ching,* he will discover in the yin and yang principles which permeate each line of each kua a key to enable us to use more and more of all our senses. For there is, in the cells of every man, a potential to be realized that can free him to experience that which lies beyond the world of stone-deaf and color-blind impressions of our five-senses universe. Science today is once again returning its attention to the consideration of man as an integral part in a total universe.

In the October 1970, issue of *Psychology Today,* there was a report on some research conducted by Albert Mehrabian with people conversing. It turned out that only about 7 percent of a message's content was communicated by the words spoken. The greater percentage of the total impact reached the listener via nonverbal means, such as facial expressions, tonal quality of the voice, and postural attitudes. It seemed that the experiment confirmed the theory that feelings are communicated primarily through a diversity of nonverbal behavior. When one gets a "feel" of the *I*, the linear structure of a kua can be more meaningful for interpretation than the words. Let us remember that there is an old commentary that warns those who consult *I Ching* not to get hung up on the words, or the images, or the symbols. Words are good for describing images. Images are good for representing symbols. Symbols are good to remind us of things. But when one is familiar with the image, of what use are the words? When one knows the symbol, what need of the image? When you become 'at one' with things, how could there be a symbol?

I Ching is a meditative mechanism that enables us to share consciousness with the totality of messages vibrating throughout our world. With the development of skill, we can selectively pick out those messages most important to our individual purposes and desires for survival. Perhaps one of the barriers to successful experience with *I Ching* can be defined as: being corralled in the literal meanings. Buckminster Fuller observed:

> Better than 99 percent of modern technology occurs in the realm of physical phenomena that are sub or ultra to the range of human visibility. We can see the telephone wires

but not the conversations taking place. . . . Yet world society has throughout its millions of years on earth made its judgments on visible, tangible, sensorially demonstrable criteria. [25]

It is very much the same with *I Ching*. One sees the linear images and reads the printed words. What is missed are the phenomenal forces pulsating through the lines and through the words. It is important to be able to effect within oneself a condition of bio-energy telecommunication in order to experience the fuller meaningfulness of *I Ching*. We have to get in closer touch with ourselves. Remember, distance is not only the measure of space between, but also the degree of incomprehensibility between organism and organism, object and object, or organism and object. The *I* can be used to bridge this distance; it can be a key that opens us to a selective control of life-forces, so that we can accelerate the evolution of puzzlement into understanding, and problems into solutions.

Six
A Universal Prototype

A Psychological Catalyst

Any study of *I Ching* in the light of modern scientific research reveals that either the ancients had an amazing foreknowledge of where science would be in this age, or that we, in looking back, read much more into the knowledgeableness of the past than there was. Be this as it may, the actuality of the present is the same. It is very much like when it is said of a talented person that he has fulfilled the tendencies observed in him when he was an infant. Were these events in the early years of a person's life, now called observed tendencies, actually indications of one's future career, or have we forced into being a relationship between the behavior of one time and the behavior of a later time? In both cases the actuality is the same. It matters not whether the infant individually exhibited particular behavior patterns as an announcement of what it foresaw itself becoming or not. However, it does add to the romance that expresses the aesthetics of our understanding and chosen perspective of the fact.

All about us there is a variety of evidence, differing in quality, quantity and significance, which serves to demonstrate that a powerful potential for being a psychological catalyst has been built into *I Ching*. There are many deep and profound levels (as well as superficial ones) where we can recognize that the important principles being discovered by contemporary scientific research are indicated and defined in the intricate and encompassing system of *I Ching*. In modern parlance, this often is "a mind blower!" Let us look for correspondences between *I Ching* and the latest scientific research.

Gustaf Stromberg, the renowned astronomer of Mount Wilson, has authored many articles and books in which he has applied his knowledge of the physical universe as an explanation and insight into the nature of life and its essence. In one book he makes the observation that:

> ... with the introduction of an enlarged world frame, some scientists have begun to realize that there must exist a world beyond space and beyond time, and it is from this non-physical world that energy and matter have "emerged." It is not a world of matter, but of Spirit. [1]

The thirty-seventh chapter of *Tao Te Ching* opens with the lines: "Tao never makes any ado, and yet it does everything."[2] A few pages later in Stromberg's book it is written:

> There are reasons to believe that matter and energy suddenly came into existence at a moment in the history of the universe which has sometimes been called "the cosmic explosion," and which took place several billions of years ago. At that world-shaking moment in history, a definite amount of energy emerged from a nonphysical source beyond space and time, and the emergent elements were in the form of the uncharged elementary particles the physicists call neutrons. . . . During the following millenia, atomic nuclei of various types were formed, and they contribute the raw material out of which the matter in the earth, the sun, and the stars is built.[3]

Without a cyclotron, electroscope or laboratory the sage Lao Tzu is credited with writing down what has been variously translated into English as four terse lines:

> The movement of the Tao consists in Returning.
> The use of the Tao consists in softness.
>
> All things under heaven are born of the corporeal:
> The corporeal is born of the Incorporeal.[4]

Or, as another translator puts it:

> The movement of the Way is a return;
> In weakness lies its major usefulness.
> From What-is all the world of things was born
> But What-is sprang in turn from What-is-not.[5]

And still another:

> Returning is the motion of Tao,
> Weakness is the appliance of Tao.
> All things in the Universe come from existence,
> And existence from non-existence.[6]

"At that world-shaking moment in history, a definite amount of energy emerged from a nonphysical source beyond space and time. . . .[7] is the speculation of modern science, with its laboratories of highly sensitive instruments and its far-flung tentacles of rockets, moon modules, spaceships and instrument packets. One comes to feel that all this technology is not so much a willful invention of man, but rather a natural manifestation, involuntary in nature, of what is itself wrapped up in this small arrogantly strutting creature. It becomes a revelation of the things that are in us which we hide from ourselves. Take, for instance, the interest now growing in a concept of particles, tachyons, which travel at greater than the speed of light.

In a recent issue of *Science News* there appeared a further report on research into the possibilities that lie in a post-Einsteinian relativity. Back in 1969 a few theoreticians began to suspect that the relativity axiom that "nothing could go faster than light" was a false ceiling on the nature of the universe.

They argued that "Particles that are never at rest and always go faster than light seem to be possible."[8]

> If tachyons exist, they have a number of startling properties. One is negative energy. It is hard to imagine the meaning of a particle's having less than no energy, but that is what the mathematicians say, and it gave Jerome S. Danburg and George R. Kalbfleisch of Brookhaven National Laboratory an idea how to look for tachyons. If an ordinary particle, an electron or a proton, emitted a tachyon, the loss of the negative energy associated with the tachyon would result in a net increase in the positive energy of the emitting particle. That should cause a sudden change in the motion of the emitting particle, a sharp increase of velocity. They examined 5,000 bubble chamber pictures for such events but found none.[9]

Other speculations on the possible effect tachyons could have upon our life, once they have been identified, harnessed and directed, are most interesting as explanations of experiences many people now have within their own consciousnesses. They may also serve to explain the phenomenal dynamic of *I Ching*. Among these other speculations is one which envisions that once the tachyon particle has been harnessed, it will then become possible to devise a technique of sending information out to our astronauts in space, and have their response *before* the information has been sent. Surely this defies our understanding and seems to go in the face of all that we have ever experienced. But does it?

A few days prior to writing this, a young artist phoned and asked if I would look at some etchings he was making to illustrate the kua of *I Ching*. He told me that he had completed seventeen of the sixty-four to date. I agreed to see his etchings, and set a day and time for out meeting. He arrived about forty-five minutes early the day of our appointment. I was engaged with Irving Kramer, a Los Angeles attorney who has been legal counsel for our Taoist sanctuary since its inception. Realizing that I could not see him immediately, he asked if he might visit the sanctuary. I consented, excused myself for a moment from Mr. Kramer, and went to open the sanctuary for my visitor. I opened the doors for him, gestured for him to enter and immediately returned to my office. The attorney and I finished our conversation, and he left. I summoned the young man to my office. He entered rather wide-eyed, and shaking his head.

"Wow! That place blows my mind," he exclaimed.

"Oh? What happened to you?" I inquired, gesturing for him to be seated.

He sat down in front of my desk, placing a large folder of his etchings against the side of the desk. "Man, I dreamt about this place two nights ago. I had a dream in which I brought my drawings to be offered to some kind of shrine. When I went in, I saw an altar at the far end, and then I saw another altar to the side, but it wasn't an altar, it was a fireplace. And the place had some people in it. The sanctuary is exactly like what I dreamt, except there aren't any people in it. Wow!"

I told him about the theoretical concept of tachyons and the speed with which they are imagined to be able to travel. Then I asked him, "When was the first time that you saw the sanctuary?"

He said, "In my dream."

I wondered aloud, "Are you certain that your dream vision was the first time you saw the sanctuary; or was your dream vision a remembrance of seeing it now?"

From a scientific point of view, a tachyon is a mathematical, theoretical possibility. Is it not also possible, then, that the existence of such a particle is an amplification of a quality of intelligence-energy within ourselves to which we are only now beginning to reawaken? The phenomenon of déjà vu (dreams or visions of a place or event prior to being experienced in a conscious awakened state) is an example in the personal experience of many people of some kind of energy or intelligence that is actually a remembrance of the future. In Lewis Carroll's *Alice in Wonderland*, there was an exchange of dialogue between Alice and the White Queen, when the queen informs Alice that jam every other day means no jam *today,* because "it's jam every *other* day: today isn't any *other* day, you know."

". . . It's dreadfully confusing," says Alice.

"That's the effect of living backwards," the Queen said, kindly: ". . . but there's one great advantage in it, that one's memory works both ways."

"I'm sure *mine* only works one way," Alice remarked. "I can't remember things before they happen."

"It's a poor sort of memory that only works backwards," the Queen remarked.

"What sort of things do *you* remember best?" Alice ventured to ask.

"Oh, things that happened the week after next," the Queen replied in a careless tone. "For instance, now," she went on, sticking a large piece of plaster on her finger as she spoke, "there's the King's Messenger. He's in prison now, being punished: and the trial doesn't even begin till next Wednesday: and of course the crime comes last of all."[10]

The character was obviously aware of a kind of memory-energy that functioned with the speed of a tachyon. Lewis Carroll was a mathematician. Did he consciously or unconsciously suspect the existence of an energy particle like the tachyon? And is it possible that the ritual process of utilizing the wisdom of *I Ching* activates in the psyche of the individual an energy flow of intelligence that passes through consciousness before the event is experienced in wakefulness? Whatever the eventual answer to this question, the fact is that in the experience of countless thousands upon thousands of people, *I Ching* has been a source of wise counsel, helpful guidance and deep awakening

to a higher consciousness. It functions as a psychological catalyst; of this there should be no doubt.

A catalyst is an agent which helps to effect a reaction
without itself manifesting any change. As one utilizes the rituals
and wisdom of *I Ching*, one will experience a change of reaction
to whatever it is one has involved *I Ching* with. Yet *I Ching*
remains unchanged. In this way it is itself an exemplification of
the paradox "change is the only thing that doesn't change."

Lewis Carroll was not the only writer to exercise what I call
'predictable consciousness'. Louis T. Culling, in a succinct
manual concerning *I Ching*, recognized this tachyon-like quality
when he wrote:

> The concept and wisdom of the *I Ching* is milleniums of
> years old, but it is as modern as tomorrow. You have only
> to look over your shoulder to Walt Whitman's "Song of
> Myself" in which he states, "I am the acme of things
> accomplished, and I am the encloser of things to be."
> Whitman understood the interrelated change of *I Ching* as
> "Transcendentalism." He understood that he, in 19th-
> century microcosm, was part of the whole. Whereas
> Whitman and others of that school told us of flux, artists
> like 20th-century Picasso showed us flux, change from
> moment to moment. Listen to our avant-garde poets, com-
> posers, artists, writers, and actors in "happenings." [11]

It is very true that often the significant actualities of life are
revealed in an accident, in a moment of trivia, or in a comic
expression. We cannot always know when or how the 'beingness
of eternality' will express itself through and to us. A very
popular and most successful entertainer Victor Borge, has, on
occasion, referred to one of his fabulous relatives as being so
smart that he had many files filled with answers for which he
was seeking the questions. Yes, it is funny. But our scientists are
now speculating that there is a form of energy that would
enable us to receive answers from our astronauts in outer space
before we have sent the question. A psychological catalyst may,
in a final analysis, be a stimulus of physical energy-intelligence.

I Ching—Its Ideas, Symbols and Words

I Ching expresses a totality of ideas through its sixty-four symbolic images to which are appended a vocabulary of words serving as explanations. Surely it is important to know how to grasp the symbols and cling to the words. But it is more important to know how to release the symbols and forget the words. I am concerned with emphasizing this point because a great deal of sincere effort has gone into explaining the meaning of the words in the text accompanying the various kua. There is often, in the fellowship of Western adherents to *I Ching*, a tendency to intellectualize excessively. This compulsion for the cerebration of all conscious experience has the effect of depriving one of knowing the joy that comes with being 'at-one-ment' with experience. Chinese, as a written language, is one of symbols, and as a spoken language, it is one of words. For this reason, the writings of Wang Pi, who composed an outline of the system used in the 'changes' of the Chou era, are most important. In his *Chou Yi Lueh-li* he wrote:

> Symbols serve to express ideas. Words serve to explain symbols. For the complete expression of ideas there is nothing like symbols, and for the complete explanation of symbols there is nothing like words. . . . By examining the words one may perceive the symbols. . . . By examining the symbols one may perceive the ideas. The ideas are completely expressed by the symbols, and the symbols are explained by words . . . once the symbols have been grasped, the words may be forgotten . . . once the ideas have been grasped, the symbols may be forgotten. . . .

> Therefore he who clings to words does not get the symbols, and he who clings to symbols does not get the ideas. . . . Thus by forgetting the symbols one gets the ideas; by forgetting the words one gets the symbols. . . . The acquisition of the ideas depends upon forgetting the symbols, and the acquisition of the symbols depends upon forgetting the words. . . . The lines (of the kua) are (initially) multiplied in order completely to express the qualities (of things), but the lines themselves may then be

forgotten. . . . If the concept consists of firmness, what need for a horse (to explain its meaning)? If the category is one of compliance, what need for a cow (to explain it)? If a line expresses compliance, what need for K'un to be made into a cow? If the concept corresponds to firmness, what need for Ch'ien to be made into a horse? [12]

Perhaps a fuller significance of Wang's counseling may be understood if it is translated into situations of phenomena with which most of us are familiar. There can be no doubt that what he has written is a phenomenal thing of universal occurrence. We all know or have heard of instances succinctly described as "beginner's luck." It is an experience so common to men that it is puzzling that no thoughtful study has been given to it since the time of Wang Pi, who died ca. 844. However, with the advent of interest, experimentation and research into the nature and effects of bio-feedback, there is the promise of reawakened attention to this important area of human experience.

"Beginner's luck" is instanced, for example, when a person who has never been to a racetrack before is taken to the races and, with no knowledge of horses, jockies, past performances or track, picks a horse in several races and wins on all of them. This happens much to the consternation of his companions, who, as old enthusiasts, are experienced and knowledgeable in reading the charts on the horses' past performances, etc., from which they calculate how most wisely to bet—and lose. On the gloomy trip home they besiege the happy inexperienced winner with questions, wanting to know what made him pick those particular horses. Indeed, a great deal of scientific inquiry originating at the racetracks and gambling tables is never recorded and remains barren of conclusions. At this time the inexperienced winner is brought into a state of conscious awareness that he did something important, something sufficiently important that he might want to do it again. So he begins to analyze, through retrospection, his feelings, his motives, how he was standing, who was standing near him, who was in front of him in the line before the betting window, etc., etc. And when he has the situation pretty well reconstructed, he hopes that he can return and repeat his "past performance." But somehow it doesn't happen, and the whole first experience is chalked up to "beginner's luck!"

Those who have produced legitimate alpha brainwaves via bio-feedback instrumentation as used by doctors Joseph Kamiya, Elmer Green, and Bob Beck are acquainted with this phenomenon. On first being hooked up to an electronic device that is capable of amplifying the bio-energy output of an organism and instructed to "produce alpha," one almost immediately responds with an impressively healthy burst that is registered by the electronic meter. No one is more impressed than the first-time subject. He or she is then told to "produce more alpha." The conscious mind searches through its recent experience, seeking to find the condition, the thing, the key, the "what-ever-it-was" that enabled the production of that first burst of alpha. Alas, nothing happens. The alpha burst is "nowhere!" Another actuality is chalked up to "beginner's luck."

This time the winner, who quickly became loser, asks the presumedly knowledgeable experimenters: "How was it that I did produce alpha the first time, but couldn't repeat the performance when asked to do it again?" It is here that we will find a parallel between the explanation of the bio-energy experimenters and the counsel of Wang Pi.

Flora Davis reported in an article on "Brain Training":

When he had wired up his first subject to an EEG, Dr. Kamiya explained to him that he was to guess, whenever a bell rang, whether he was at that instant in state-of-mind A or in state-of-mind B. . . . The object of the experiment was simply to see if he could learn to tell the difference between A, alpha, and B, all the other brain states.

The first day he guessed right 50 percent of the time, which he could have done by pure chance. But the second day he was right 65 percent of the time; the third day, 85 percent, and the fourth, 100 percent. . . .

But the subject couldn't explain what the internal signals were that told him whether he was in A or B. "Sometimes

I just feel I should say A, sometimes B," he insisted. However, it was clear that he did know the difference, for he guessed right four hundred times running. [13]

This is a most interesting thing about the alpha state and the unconscious-consciousness of it. It is wholly a yin-yang phenomenon, for the results show conclusively that one knows when the alpha state is being experienced, yet mysteriously one does not know *how* it is that one knows. And the harder one tries to know how one knows that he knows, the more impossible it is to achieve the alpha state-of-mind experience. Miss Davis recounts a personal experience that illustrates this:

At Kamiya's suggestion I called Dr. Les Fehmi at the State University of New York in Stony Brook, Long Island, and asked if I could come to his lab to try out alpha. . . .

Having wired me up, Fehmi told me to close my eyes and listen for the tone. Whenever it sounded, he said, it meant that I had just produced alpha. Then he left me alone in the darkened room. In a minute the tone came on, a gentle uneven beeping sound.

But it turned out that my muscles were reluctant to let go and images kept creeping into my head. . . . I tried to get out of my head and concentrate on body sensations. I imagined that I felt heavy and warm. I thought loving thoughts; peaceful thoughts; tried vainly to think empty thoughts, but nothing seemed to work.

Dr. Fehmi showed me my record . . . an object lesson in how not to produce alpha. It seemed I had tried too hard.[14]

The point to be understood here is that it is necessary to be able to let go and to let happen. For, as was said elsewhere in this volume, there is a distinct difference between a state of knowing and a state of knowledge. One can 'know' without being able to know how one 'knows'. Knowledge is the halfway house between 'knowing' and ignorance.

The condition that happens with the gambling, the alpha state-of-mindness, and the symbols and words of *I Ching*, is the same phenomenon. Wang Pi's counsel is the key to a successful experience in all three areas. Get into that state of being "at-one-ment" with the thing—let go, let happen—and there is no longer a need for intellectualization with words, or for remembering the symbol which is merely the shadow of the actuality.

Seven
Everyman's Computor

How is it that *I Ching* has recently met such an enthusiastic welcome by so many in the Western world? It is a question asked repeatedly both by those who accept it and those who reject it. And it seems strange that acceptance of *I Ching* by Westerners comes at the very time when it appears that most Chinese are turning away from it. As one studies the situation, there develops a sense of some kind of worldwide cultural phenomenon taking place, a phenomenon that exemplifies the inter-transference function of yin and yang. The "mystical" East is divesting itself of saffron robes, gilded shrines and temples filled with choking incense. The "materialistic" West, stunned by the mutilation of its land and natural resources, the ethical decline of its society and the moral and psychological bankruptcy of individuals, all of which has been evolved in the name of progress by its pragmatic technocracy, now turns to experience the psychological warmth of a saffron robe, the aesthetic pleasures of a gilded shrine and the spiritual excitation of temples filled with choking incense.

I do not believe that there is, or can be, any simple and single answer to the question that opens the paragraph above. In consequence, the possibility about to be explored should not be read as *the* answer; but rather as one small, yet important, contributing explanation for the growing popularity of *I Ching* in the Western world.

Elsewhere I mentioned that Gottfried Wilhelm von Leibniz became deeply interested in *I Ching* after examining the diagram of Shao Yung's sequence of the evolution of the sixty-four linear images. Leibniz saw in this diagram an expression of his binary principle of mathematics. He was the more fascinated when he learned that it had been structured by the ancient Chinese sages as a pattern for man's thinking. In a word, *I Ching* was the world's first computer. A few thousand years later man invented a machine computer. It is an attractive speculation to wonder about the possibility that by studying the binary structured wisdom of the past, we may learn how better and more creatively to program the mechanical computers of today to abet the growth of the total man. And what can be gained by the converse? Will an understanding of how the modern computer works give us deeper and more useful insights into the philosophical and psychological dimensional functions of *I Ching?* Let us make a stab at it and see. From a biased point of view, it appears that the kua of *I Ching* set the stage for the computer, and the computer is, in a sense, a technological fulfillment of *I Ching*.

In a fascinating book dealing with computers, the authors John Caffrey and Charles J. Mosmann present "A Prose Glossary" of the technical vocabulary used in computer communication.[1] When I first read this glossary, I was struck by the correspondence between the functions of the electronic computer and the linear philosophy of *I Ching*. Perhaps by selecting certain of the terms and their attending definitions from the glossary and matching them with the described functions of *I Ching* which are to be found in the ancient commentaries, we may, even as laymen, develop a better understanding of what computers and *I Ching* are all about. *I Ching* suggests a method of "getting one's head" into the most efficient place in this age of computers.

On the left side of the page will be quotations from "A Prose Glossary" of computer jargon, with some occasional embellishments of my own. On the right side of the page will be quotations from the appendices of the *Book of Changes*, which appear to be, if not identical in function with, then surely parallel with, the computer, evidencing a significant correspondence between the modern electronic computer and the ancient lineargraphed wisdom of *I Ching*. And, once again, these quotations are presented with an occasional personal thought or observation added.

From *A Prose Glossary*

1. "*A computer* is a machine for performing complex processes on information without manual intervention."

From the appendices of *I Ching*

1. *I Ching* is a thinking system for handling the complex processes of life experiences, without the limitations of causality. The *I* utilizes the intelligence-energy of the individual free-will human organism, so that the individual can function effectively on both the causal and acausal level of being.

2. "*Analog computers* perform this function by directly measuring continuous physical quantities such as electrical voltages." An analog computer is a calculating device that uses numerical aggregates to represent directly measurable quantities (as resistances or rotations). "The best-known analog computer is a slide rule."

2. *I Ching pa kua*, (the basic eight trilinear images), were constructed by the ancient sages to represent graphically the "intermingling of the genial influences of heaven and earth, and the transformation of all things . . . ."[2] Fung Yu-Lan elucidates the appendix quoted by writing: "A human being is produced by the union of man and woman, and

so by extension, the universe is also considered to have two prime principles: the male or yang, . . . and the female or yin." He notes that heaven and earth are the physical representations of these principles. "From the union of Ch'ien and K'un comes Chên, . . . the physical representation of which is thunder . . . Sun . . . the physical representation of which is wind . . . Kan . . . represented by water . . . Li . . . represented by fire . . . Kên . . . represented by mountains . . . Tui . . . represented by low marshes.

"The greatest things in the universe, in short, are heaven and earth. In heaven, the objects most noteworthy to man are the sun (☰), moon (☷), wind (☴), and thunder (☳). On earth they are mountains (☶), and marshy low lands (☱); and the things most used by man are water (☵), and fire (☲). The ancient Chinese regarded these objects as forming the constituents of the universe. . . ."[3]

The *I* is an infinite archetype expressing the eternality of its function through the pa kua, as a scale of infinity upon which all things (weighted and weightless), can be weighed, and by which all things (of form and formless) can be shaped, and with which all things (of substance and without substance) can be measured.

4. *"Digital computers* represent numerical quantities by discrete electrical states which can be manipulated logically and hence arithmetically. Digital computers are sometimes referred to as *electronic data processing machines, EDP, or processors.* A digital computer operates with numbers expressed directly as digits in a decimal, binary or other system."

3. *The derived kua* have their origin in the original pa kua, by combining any two of these into structural images of six lines each, making a total of sixty-four expressions, or the square of the eight trilinear kua which are basic to *I Ching.*

The squaring of the pa kua depicts what is described in Appendix III. "The way of heaven and earth is constant and unceasing. 'Movement in any direction whatever will be advantageous.' When there is end, there is beginning again. . . . The four seasons, changing and transforming, can constantly give completion (to things). . . .

"All movements beneath the sky are constantly subject to one and the same rule."[4]

Dr. Fung comments: "The underlying idea in these quotations is that all things in the universe follow a definite order according to which they move everlastingly."[5] This does not mean that the order is a static and fixed duration, but rather it is fixed as an eternal metamorphosis of movement. Thus it is that the sixty-fourth kua reads: "Things cannot be exhausted and therefore it is with Wei Chi that the sages brought the system of *I Ching* to the point of its recommencement."

From a numerological view, the sixty-four kua exhibit an amazing faculty of operating meaningfully as digits in both the decimal and binary systems of mathematical thought and analogy. For example: "Movement in any direction whatever will be advantageous." This is a reading given to kua 32 in the third Appendix: $3 + 2 = 5$. Five in Chinese cosmology is the number of heaven. Heaven is yang, projective. All movement emanating from yang gives advantage to its potential. Again, when one studies the Sequences, twenty-two reads: "Things should not be united in a reckless or irregular way." Hence, there follows PEN (No. 22); which is

Pi (☲☶), "Grace," in Wilhelm's translation. 2 + 2 = 4. Four is the number of the square. To square things is to put them in a proper order of relationship to one another. Such a task cannot be done recklessly without plan and a sense of order. These two examples are only samples of how each of the kua can be extended. So it may be said that the sixty-four kua are analogous to the digital computer.

9. *Hardware.* In order to distinguish the actual physical equipment from the programs which extend its usefulness, the former is called "hardware."

The Changes or *I,* with its components of linear images and language packaged in "The Book," must always be distinguished from the situations programmed to it via any of a variety of ritual processes. It is the latter that extends the usefulness of the former, making any experience with the book meaningful.

It is possible to go item by item through this computer glossary and find parallels existing between certain aspects of *I Ching* and specific functions of a computer. For instance, of the computer it is said: "The *core memory* is the main memory of most modern machines; it is normally the only memory directly accessible to the CPU (central processing unit). Its name derives from its composition: small ferrite rings called 'cores.' An aspect of *I Ching* that can be chosen to match this is that of the "Inner

World" arrangement, or as it is also known, the "Sequence of Later Heaven." This circular arrangement of the pa kua is the main reference in most interpretive dealings with *I Ching*. Frequently this arrangement is the only one used by practitioners of the 'changes'. It was structured by King Wen, circa 1120 B.C., who concentrated on an arrangement of the pa kua which, in its circular sequence, would more accurately reflect, through symbol, the events in life as living men more often see and experience them. Each kua is composed of a set of attributes.

Lines 92 and 93 of the glossary read: "A set of instructions to perform a specified function or solve a complete problem is called a *program*." With *I Ching*, each situation that one brings to it establishes a set of instructions. Thus it is enabled to serve as a prescriber of the proper action to abet the creative development or resolution of the situation brought to it. The way in which the situation is phrased and understood by the consultee constitutes the equivalent of what the computer receives as a "program."

As a wrap-up, let us take lines 115 to 119 of the glossary. "A *programmer* is a person who converts a problem into a set of directions to a computer for the computer to solve. The function is sometimes broken down into several parts, particularly if the problem is very complex. The task of stating the problem in a clear and unambiguous form is performed by an *analyst* or *systems analyst*." With *I Ching*, whoever formulates a question or structures a situation to which it must react is a "programmer." Sometimes a problem or situation can be quite complex. One may not know how or be able to phrase the matter effectively and efficiently. At such times, one goes to a person who is learned in the psychological use of the philosophy of *I Ching*. We might call such a person a hierophant, or an interpreter of esoteric doctrine, or an "analyst," or "systems analyst."

This should adequately serve to demonstrate for anyone interested that it is possible to study the computer nature of *I Ching* and so bring oneself into a harmonious alignment with the processes of this evolving "computerological" era. The sort of enlightenment that could result from such a study may even lead to discovering a higher morality or hidden spiritual modality in the archetypal values that obviously persist to be expressed through the binary and digital systems of computers. This computer thing, this computer science, is as remote from emotional involvement with man as God, being no respecter of persons, is removed from good and evil. And perhaps tomorrow God may be known as, if not the twin, then, very likely, as the substanceless shadow of, the computer; or the computer may come to be accepted as the materialized expression of the divine.

Eight
I Ching
Helps You
Help Yourself

Symbols: How to Associate Them

Edward Maitland, the writer and biographer, experienced the phenomenon that when he reflected on an idea, related ideas became visible to him, and that when he stayed with an idea, it would seem to extend itself until it encompassed its origin. An experience of this kind results from attaining a symbolic attitude that carries one beyond the reach of emotional entanglements and traumatic shock. It is to arrive at a state of consciousness that is detached from the world, where a symbolic attitude consciously associates symbols with experience.

A similar thing happens with *I Ching.* The important difference is that one does not have to go into a sort of euphoric unconsciousness in order to experience the relatedness of ideas. With training and practice one can easily reawaken to the multiple linkages that connect one thought with so many, many others.

I Ching is filled with many "signifying" words and phrases. To develop an understanding of the connection between these obscurities and our present concerns, it is necessary to develop a symbolic attitude that effectively embraces this wisdom as a vital adjunct to our daily experience. There are, of course, many ways to accomplish this. In this chapter we shall offer some suggestions as to how to develop such an attitude, and also give some attention to those symbols which either have, or appear to have, contrary meanings in Western culture to those signified in Eastern culture, especially in the Chinese traditions. Take pigs and fishes, as used in the Judgment verse to kua 61:

> Inner Truth. Pigs and fishes.
> Good fortune.
> It furthers one to cross the great water.
> Perseverance furthers.

Eva C. Hangen gives a brief but extremely fascinating account of some of the symbolic meanings attached to the fish. Used as an offering to the dead in the cult of Adonis, it symbolized "love's grievous separations." "In Syria and Mesopotamia, luck and life . . . in early Greece, good fortune, and happiness . . . an attribute of Saint Peter . . . in Chinese art, a fish may signify virility, a fruitful marriage . . . a triangle of fishes represents the Holy Trinity. . . ." Pig, she notes in a short sentence, symbolizes "from natural habits of the animal, gluttony."[1] Compare these with a few other recorded associations made by others to the same creatures. In Jung's, *Man and His Symbols*,[2] "pig" is connected with ideas of bestiality, lustfulness (Circe turned all the men who desired her into swine); a pig-man appears on an ancient Greek vase, and is associated with "dirty sexuality," as used by the artist George Grosz in his satirical drawings. In Juan-Eduardo Cirlot's, *Dictionary of Symbols*,[3] the pig is associated with "impure desires," and indicates the transmutation of higher into lower. The boar is linked to "intrepidness" and an "irrational urge to suicide," along with licentiousness. In this same volume fish is associated with concepts of "penetrative motion, the mystic ship of life." Other symbolizations given include: phallic, purely spiritual, bird of the nether regions, symbol of sacrifice, fecundity. "A fish with the head of a swallow was a harbinger of cyclic regeneration." Now let's read Wilhelm's comment on the pigs and fishes, as used in the *I Ching* text:

> Pigs and fishes are the least intelligent of all animals and therefore the most difficult to influence. The force of inner truth must grow great indeed before its influence can extend to such creatures. In dealing with persons as intractable and as difficult to influence as a pig or a fish, the whole secret of success depends on finding the right way of approach.[4]

Pauwels and Bergier, in a paragraph concerning the author Arthur Machen's belief that " 'man is made of mystery and exists for mysteries and visions,' " add their own significant comment, which may indicate to us how to go about "finding the right way of approach":

> Reality is the supernatural. The external world can teach us little, unless we look upon it as a reservoir of symbols and hidden meanings. The only works which have some chance of being real and serving some useful purpose are works of imagination produced by a mind in search of eternal verities.[5]

The Chinese *Book of Changes,* is a magnificent verification of their conviction. The fact that it is being picked up by more and more people in the Western cultures is an indication that here is a tome of wisdom that unites ancient and traditional insights, through the principle of yin and yang and the five agents, with modern research and speculations of science. Therefore every effort to become enlightened through its symbols and images is an intelligent recognition of the fact that:

> Psychology in depth has shown that a man's apparently rational actions are in reality governed by forces of which he himself knows nothing, or which are closely linked with a symbolism having nothing in common with ordinary everyday logic.[6]

I Ching is one of man's many thesauri of the infinite's vocabulary. It deals with eternalities. As such, from time to time it falls under the heavy hand of dogmatists. "Luckily," as Jung says, "symbols mean very much more than can be known at first glance." So it has happened through the thousands of years of its existence, each time attempts have been made to stiffen and concretize the indications of its symbols, liberators have arisen from the ranks of the intelligentsia and prevented the foolish attempts to picture-frame infinity. *I Ching* is a symbolic representation of nature and the universe; through it man is able to recognize his relationships. As Arnold van Gennep recognized for all of us:

> ... man's life resembles nature, from which neither the individual nor the society stands independent. The universe itself is governed by a periodicity which has repercussions on human life, with stages and transitions, movements forward, and periods of relative inactivity.[7]

The operation of all of these principles is expressed as phenomena through the linear and verbal symbols which structure its wisdom.

Let us return to Maitland's experience that when he reflected on an idea, related ideas became visible to him. One has a situation in mind or in feeling, the *I* is consulted, and it responds with the kua and its appended verses. One holds the situation before the mirror of image and verse and examines the situation as the reflected, discovering in it new dimensions of relationship revealed by the ideas contained and expressed by the kua and its verses. Then if one will stay with the ideas being expressed, one comes to a point where it is possible totally to contain the situation, and in this condition of "befriendment," direction, control and accomplishment are made possible.

In dealing with symbols, whether they be *I Ching* symbols or those of other disciplines, it is helpful to understand the types and kinds of imagery the human mind deals with in corresponding with its 'ever-consciousness'. One phenomenon with which *I Ching* is very directly concerned is that of prevision. It is this aspect that has caused it to be confused with magical divination and fortune-telling. That this should occur is understandable. There are many people who will concede that we regularly observe events before they occur, yet suppose that the phenomenon of prevision is a most singular and unusual event. This can only be because in our concept of the universe in which we live, being primarily causalistic, we find difficulty in admitting the possibility that cause could follow the effect. The idea is not unknown in Chinese thought, as I shall illustrate. With this awakening we shall have to consider our universe anew. J. W. Dunne puts it very cleanly:

> If prevision be a fact, it is a fact which destroys absolutely the entire basis of all our past opinions of the universe. . . . If that be the case, the sooner we begin to recast physics and psychology on such lines, the sooner may we hope to reckon with our present discontinuities and set out upon a new and sounder pathway to knowledge.[8]

It has been hinted that in ancient Chinese thought the situation had been conceptualized in which cause could follow effect. Joseph Needham touches upon this by noting:

> . . . in ancient China we hear that such and such a lord, in his lifetime, was not able to obtain the hegemony of the feudal states because, after his death, human victims were sacrificed to him. Both facts were felt to be part of a single pattern, not exactly timeless, but with time as one of its dimensions, in which causation could operate backwards as well as forwards.[9]

I Ching deals with many kinds of time and many kinds of images. Two books, which I would recommend as helpful in orienting one to this concept are: *The Serial Universe* and *An Experiment With Time,* both by J. W. Dunne. It is from the latter that I wish to introduce some definitions of concepts to help both in the understanding and more effective use of *I Ching.* Needham introduces a dimension of time "in which causation could operate backwards as well as forwards." This obviously introduces the idea of "regress" with a new significance. Here the phenomenon is one in which consciousness projects back from that which is not yet experienced to that which is being experienced now. The relationship to *I Ching* can be seen in the fact that the counsel of the *I* is always one that is a prescription for action (or non-action as the action), that will grasp and shape the event we are observing before it occurs.

Any number of the images used in *I Ching* date from a great antiquity. "Ridgepole," "Dragon," "Ten pairs of tortoises," "Ting (Caldron)," "Treading upon the trail of a tiger," these are some of the images used in the text. When these, or any of the more commonplace images come to be associated with a situation brought to the *I*, they often become "retrospective images." A retrospective image may be defined as "a visual representation of a past presentation to the consciousness, motivated by external sensory organs"; however, in a period of recall it originates from the internal motivation of will or desire.

When one reads the text of the kua that has been the response of the *I* to the situation brought to it, it often happens that the words set off a train of ideas connected to the situation. These may be identified as "memory trains." They are a succession of ideas, a particular pathway through the associational network of experiences recently impressed upon the consciousness. They usually progress as a recalling in the order in which they were experienced. This tends to cause one to see the particular situation as it truly is.

On some occasions students have been confounded by the fact that they have consulted *I Ching* regarding one matter, and found "answers" which were extremely satisfactory for some *other* situation which was a part of their experience, but not of concern at the time of working with the *I*. They have asked how and why this happens. I have suggested that at some other level of consciousness there was a need for release of tension. Tension, in this particular instance, refers to a condition where attention or awareness is entrapped, and cannot move on. At such times, the reading of the text triggers what can be called a 'train of ideas'. Dunne gives an example of the 'train of ideas' phenomenon.

Almost everybody has, at one time or another, amused himself by retracing the train of ideas which has led him, without any conscious aim on his part, to think of, or remember, a certain thing. "I saw this," he will say, "and that made me remember so-and-so; and that made me thing of such-and-such." And so on. [10]

He gives a specific example, starting with a teacup with a checkered black and white border. This leads to a memory image of a checkered linoleum floor covering, which leads to a book, a reading glass, a store, fishing tackle and finally a two-and-a-half pound trout, which he had acquired from a friend's stream two days earlier.

Another experience people have with *I Ching* is that of seeing their situation in other forms. This effect is similar to what Dunne calls "retiary images." These radiate like tentacles or root fibers from generic images. (Generic images occur when a number of partly similar impressions have been attended to at different times; there is observable, in addition to the several memory images pertaining to those several impressions, a vague, general image comprising nothing beyond the key elements which are common to all those separate images.) Thus, a single "retiary image" may serve as a multiple generic reference, which can be defined as associational image-constructs. They tend to function in this way: pipe = wood = walnut = table.

Dream images are less commonly experienced, but are very dramatic. These are incidented when people consult the *I* and can make little or no connection between the text and the situation they have brought to it. They close the book, go about their business, and, finally, at night, retire. In their sleep they have a dream that relates to the text (either to its words, the events described therein, or the images it structured). Whatever the form, they may be regarded as dream images. They are constituted mainly of experienced impressions in the category of associational image-constructs. They are distinguished, however, from mind-wandering by noting that the activity of logic and reason is at minimal function, if at all. Dream images present themselves as real yet significantly nonmaterialized episodes in a personal adventure of an only partially reasonable character. It is then that the text makes sense.

I Ching is a process of involving the remembrance of conscious, unconscious and genetic experience in a way that enables one to identify the corresponding cosmic pattern which a particular situation resembles, and thereby to blueprint the kind of action necessary to complete it. This principle has already been outlined by Aristotle in his treatise on memory. In touching upon some facts of geometry, he observed that we do not, for the purpose of a proof, make any use of the fact that the quantity in the triangle is determinate; "nevertheless," he emphasizes, "we draw it [as though it were] determinate in quantity."

Perhaps the most challenging problem that confronts the Westerner who is anxious to use the wisdom of *I Ching* as a guide in his psychology of living is to be able to skip rope, as it were, in two circles simultaneously. In one of his books Cassirer quotes a view originally expressed by Humboldt, the idea that man spins language out of his own being; however, in the process of doing it, he is ensnared.

> Each language draws a magic circle round the people to which it belongs, a circle from which there is no escape save by stepping out of it into another. [11]

As our technological computerized civilization continues to expand, there seems to be a decline in many of the social ceremonies and religious rituals. There has been a traumatization of the human temperament as a consequent. For this reason many people today are turning to new and ancient traditions of ritual and belief. Unable to achieve transitions from perplexity to peace, from confoundment to discovery, alone, many now reach for collective symbols such as can be found in *I Ching*. Every sincere experience with *I Ching* will enlarge one's ability to structure personal symbols and individual metaphors that will lead to the discovery of one's own truth. When personal truth is realized (not recognized, for that is merely to see it; realization is seeing plus acceptance that is manifested in actualizing), one is so liberated as to dance in two circles simultaneously!

Using *I Ching* as Metaphor and Symbol

There has developed a public tendency to confuse the terms "metaphor" and "symbol." In some quarters they have come to be regarded as interchangeable. Since *I Ching* uses symbols and metaphors, we will need to study the distinction and see how it affects our use of *I Ching*. Also to be taken into consideration is the fact that words are used to express many of the symbols and delineate many of the metaphors used in *I Ching*. So a few sentences on the place and function of words will be in order. Let us open this section of our study with two definitions:

Metaphor is a figure of speech in which a word or phrase denoting one kind of object or action is used in place of another to suggest a likeness or analogy between them. (An implied comparison in contrast to an explicit comparison.)

Symbol is something that stands for or suggests something else by reason of relationship, association, convention, or accidental but not intentional resemblance. A visible sign of something that is invisible . . . an object or act that represents a repressed complex through unconscious association rather than through objective resemblance or conscious substitution.

Words serve many functions in the various cultures. Those who have given study to them have posed challenging questions with the intent of being able to open up some secret about the nature of words. Such questions as: "Can one think in words?" "Are words images in themselves?" "Are words indispensable to language?" And so the questions go, and the scholars reason and argue and sometimes pretend conclusions. Rudolf Arnheim gives a quote from Edward Sapir's book, *Language,* which may help us into our study:

> Thought may be a natural domain apart from the artificial one of speech, but speech would seem to be the only road we know of that leads to it. [12]

When one has gotten deeply into the being and meaning of *I Ching*, speech is hardly a necessity for experiencing thought processes. The linear configurations frequently set off a sequence of thought images which are themselves devoid of word representation, yet dynamic in the conveyance of meaning. If one has had this experience, then the comment that Arnheim writes immediately after quoting Sapir is one that deserves some follow-through:

> Nobody denies that language helps thinking. What needs to be questioned is whether it performs this service substantially by means of properties inherent in the verbal medium itself or whether it functions indirectly, namely, by pointing to the referents of words and propositions, that is, to facts given in an entirely different medium.[13]

Those who have made use of *I Ching* will, I believe, share with me the conviction that the words are merely indicators that point us toward discovery. In *I Ching* there are two groups of words: those which together serve as a metaphor, and those which singularly or in groups act as symbols. There is, at all times, a symbolic or metaphoric relationship between the language of *I Ching* and any and every situation it comes to be applied to. This is so because it cannot be otherwise, for as Arnheim put it:

> Presumably there are no two things in this world that have nothing in common, and most things have a great deal in common. . . . Each individual thing would be explicitly assigned to as many groups as there are possible combinations of its attributes. A cat would be made to hold membership in the associations of material things, organic things, animals, mammals, felines . . . black things, furry

things, the pets, the subjects of art and poetry, the
Egyptian divinities, the customers of the meat and canning
industries, the dream symbols, the consumers of oxygen,
and so on forever. In the universe of theoretical logic all
these memberships are in fact constantly present when the
concept 'cat' comes up. . . .[14]

The talent of using *I Ching* as a psychological stimulus is to be
able to hit upon that aspect of a kua which is tangential to the
matter at hand. It is to experience the world of the senses as
one that is continually responding to the interplay of cosmic
forces. These forces rule the heavens and all the planetary
bodies therein. They rule the seasons of our year, and every
large and small thing and every action on earth. It is these same
forces which are represented by the lines composing the kua of
I Ching.

E. R. Hughes, the author, editor and translator of numerous
works of Chinese thought, in his paper "Epistemological
Methods in Chinese Philosophy," observed that:

Confucianist thought took the diviners' cabalistic figures
of divided and undivided lines and linked them by a sort of
science of symbolism to the yin and the yang and the five
h'sing. For many minds this symbolism was the key to the
march of history. For others it was an epistemological
method, a sure guide to all possible forms of knowledge. . . . Today they are, rightly or wrongly, despised by
the intelligentsia as having had a crippling influence on
Chinese philosophy.
. . . I have still to be convinced that this line of abstraction
had only a crippling influence on Chinese powers of ratio-
cination. The significant thing is that these symbols, i.e.,
the lines in the hexagrams and the trigrams, were regarded
as centers of energy continually acting and reacting on
each other according to their relative positions. We find,
also, the correlative notions of t'i (substance) and yung
(function) used in connection with them; but the impression I get is that greater importance was attached to the
functional side. The center of interest lay there, so that the
logic at work in these thinkers' minds led them to concentrate more on categories of relationship than on
categories of substance. . . . So also . . . is the fact that the

idea of a macrocosm's being paralleled by a microcosm in the human body was worked out in a kind of precise scientific spirit. [15]

Our Western science today is being repeatedly surprised by the discoveries it is experiencing through its highly evolved and complicated instruments and devices. The surprise is that its research is often a newly phrased confirmation of the insights of our folklore and the things we used to call foolish and ignorant superstition. In a recent issue of *Scientific American,* there is a report that presents the findings of a study of volunteer subjects who practice meditation, the indications being that there is a distinct physiological change effected through meditation. [16]

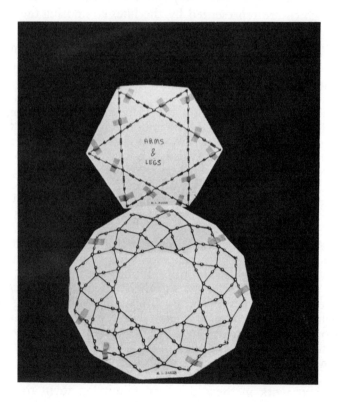

Picture of Elaine Jacobs' Diode Resinators Designed to Channel Yin Yang Forces.

Some time ago a manual was sent to me in which some experiments were listed dealing with iron bar resonators and *I Ching* patterns.[17] Later when we look at various study devices and diagrams as aids in the developing of our awareness and use of *I Ching*, Elaine Jacobs's system of using the iron bar resonators will be explained. I mentioned them here because they are an example of the use of symbols. Remember the dictionary definition of symbol: ". . . something that stands for or suggests something else by reason of relationship, association, convention, or accidental but not intentional resemblance; a visible sign of something that is invisible. . . ." In this way the various diagrams and study devices all serve as symbols which help us to integrate the philosophy and principles of *I Ching* into our daily living patterns. Might we not call a symbol, a "faithlet"? I mean in the Paulian sense: "Faith is the substance of things hoped for, the evidence of things unseen." [18]

An example of the metaphoric use of the text of *I Ching* can be seen in the Judgment verse of Hsiao Ch'u (The Taming Power of the Small). The last line of the Judgment reads: "Dense clouds, no rain from our western region." The explanation of the text tells of King Wen, who came from the west and was residing in the east at the court of the tyrant Chou Hsin. He had been plotting a revolt, but the time for action was not yet arrived. It was during this interim that King Wen endeavored to keep the tyrant in check by friendly persuasion. Hence the image of "many clouds, promising moisture and blessing to the land, although as yet no rain falls." A metaphor is "a figure of speech in which a word or phrase denoting one kind of object or action is used in place of another to suggest a likeness or analogy between them."

The kua for the same Hsiao Ch'u is a symbol of fundamental forces in a relationship that represents all instances and situations and feelings which may be observed or experienced as "The Taming Power of the Small." In another volume, Ch'ao-Li Chi and I shall deal with the significance of the ideographs as keys to the wisdom contained in *I Ching*. [19] To better understand the use of this metaphor, practice the same exercise that Arnheim illustrated with his cat. Take the idea of "The Taming

Power of the Small,'' and see how many things, situations and feelings you can associate it with. This is the function of metaphor. When you have made these associations you may be surprised at how much more penetrating your understanding of the subject probed by metaphor will be.

Nine

Putting
I Ching
to Work

Numbers in *I Ching*

The distinguished scholar E. R. Hughes felt that "the level of mathematical interest ... remained low" in China. We must agree that from a Western point of view this is especially so. But the significance of numbers was by no means a rarity in Chinese thought. "... in the Neo-Moist books (third century? B.C.) a number of geometrical definitions are given. A sort of Pythagorean playing with numbers is found in the Hsi Tz'u (sometime between the third century B.C. and the first century A.D.) and elsewhere, but it is not until early Sung times [A.D. 960-1279] that we can find such high-level calculations as produce an abstract theory of numbers." [1] It must be kept in mind that these evaluations are applicable only to the pre-Sun Yat Sen era. Today Chinese mathematicians rank equally with the mathematicians of the Western world. How else to account for their great technological advances? How else the development of nuclear power for energy, agricultural and other technological uses? It can no longer be said that China is scientifically backward. China may not yet have realized development equal with that of the West, but the ability and the potential for reaching it is there. It is at work right now! In the area of our interest, numbers have played an important role in the cosmological thought of Chinese tradition. It is our position that this facet of knowledge is still meaningful and productive in today's world.

We will consider the various ways in which numbers were used, and the indications which were attached to them. Since we are concerned with how these things fit into the system of thought encompassed by *I Ching*, we will commence by noting the most common ascription of numbers to the individual structures of the pa kua.

8	7	6	5	4	3	2	1
K'un	Kên	K'an	Sun	Chên	Li	Tui	Ch'ien

A fact that makes a striking impression upon anyone who is pursuing studies in *I Ching* is the remarkable correspondence between its wisdom and that of other ancient traditions and many of the principles established by modern science. We shall, in the course of the next few pages, attempt to present sufficient evidence to corroborate these claims. It must be left to the judgment of the individual if there are meaningful indications to the value and symbolism given to numbers. Now to get to numbers as used in *I Ching*.

Five is the most popular number in Chinese culture. Tea sets made in China and Japan, even now, feature service for five. Five is a pivotal number in both Taoist and Confucian thought: there are the five aspects of nature, the five Beginnings, the five canons, the five classics, the five colors, the five constant virtues, the five directions, the five elements, the tones, etc., etc. Surely it would be a mistake to write down as merely an "interesting coincidence" the fact that Chou En-lai outlined to President Nixon, on his recent visit to China, five uncompromisable points as being basic to any discussions which may hope to lead to an easing of tension between the United States of America and the People's Republic of China.

The "*I Ching* Monthly Commands," which date from about the third century B.C. and the *Huai Nan Tzu* both correlate the five elements with the five points of the compass, the five colors, the five notes of the scale, and the five phases of the planet's orbiting the sun, thusly:

Element	Compass	Color	Note	Phase
Wood	East	Grey	Chiao	Spring
Fire	South	Red	Chih	Summer
Metal	West	White	Shang	Autumn
Water	North	Black	Yu	Winter
Earth	Center	Yellow	Kung	Year

The five elements were also identified with the following numbers: Wood (8), Fire (7), Earth (5), Metal (9), Water (6). Another tradition assigns the numbers differently. For the time being, we will restrict ourselves to the system of the "Monthly Commands" and the *Huai Nan Tzu*.

The assignment of numbers to the principles of yin and yang is as follows: yin is given all the even numbers (2,4,6,8 and 10); yang is given all the odd numbers (1,3,5,7 and 9).

Ancient Chinese thought recognized a psychological and physiological importance in the relationship of the nature and feelings. The *Po Hu T'ung* (Comprehensive Discussion in the White Tiger Hall), ascribed to the historian Pa Ku (A.D. 79), poses the question as to what is meant by the nature and the feelings, and then answers it:

> The nature is a manifestation of the yang; the feelings are evolved out of the yin. Man is born endowed with the yin and yang ethers. Therefore he harbors within him five (aspects of the) nature and six (kinds of) feeling. The feelings mean passivity, while the nature means what is

obtained at birth. . . . What are the five (aspects of the) nature? They are love, righteousness, propriety, wisdom, and good faith. Love is the inability to bear (seeing the sufferings of others). It is manifested in affection for others. Righteousness is what is proper. It makes decisions in accordance with the mean. Propriety is to tread. This means to tread the moral path (Tao) and beautify it. Wisdom (chih) is to know. It is a special vision and fore-sight. This means not to be deluded by things, and to know, when one sees the abstruse, what it will bring forth. Good faith (hsin) is sincerity (ch'eng). It is unswerving singleness (of mind). Thus man, at birth, reacts to the forms of the eight (kua) (portrayed in the *Book of Changes*) and acquires the five forces as constant norms, these being love, righteousness, propriety, wisdom, and good faith.

What is meant by the six feelings? They are defined as joy, anger, grief, pleasure, love, and hate, and serve to com-plement the five (aspects of the) nature. Why is it that there are five (aspects of the) nature and six feelings? It is because man is born endowed with the forces of the six pitch pipes and those of the Five Elements.[2]

A study of this excerpt from the *Po Hu T'ung* shows how the ancient Chinese sages explained the processes that were mani-fested as the correspondences between the macrocosm and man as a microcosm. True this is a very evolved and complicated treatise, but when it has become a part of one's deeper con-sciousness, it serves as a stimulator to one's intuitive faculties. The study of texts such as the *Po Hu T'ung,* and *Tso Chuan,* etc., help to develop within the individual what I call a 'totality consciousness'. That is, one reaches a point where the "five notes," or the "five feelings" will bring into consciousness a whole panoramic image of all of the things indicated. This happens very much in the same manner that one learns speed reading, so that almost with just a glance at a page, one sees the content complete, rather than laboriously measuring each word separately. This is an important part of the practice that is necessary for developing an empathetic consciousness with *I Ching.*

The apocrypha which dealt with the study of emblems and numbers is, for the most part, lost today. In the *Tso Chuan* (an extended commentary covering the events and thinking in the State of Lu from about 722 to 481 B.C.), some attention is paid to the matter of emblems and numbers.

The tortoise shell has its emblems (hsing), the milfoil [yarrow stalk] its numbers (shu).

The two traditionally established methods of divination are here being referred to. The tortoise shell method was one of drilling a small hole in the back of a disembodied shell and then heating it over hot coals until cracks formed in it. These were then examined, read and interpreted by the individual who was divining. These lines or cracks, we are told, became the inspiration for the construction of the linear constructs of three lines each. Of these there were eight such constructs composed of broken and unbroken lines which were called the pa kua, or the basic eight emblems of *I Ching*. Those who have read extensively into the literature of *I Ching* may or may not have come across this origin of the eight emblems. There are several legends giving somewhat different accounts of how the eight linear constructs came to be. I would not claim that any one was more correct than the others. The authenticity of such matters rests more in the antiquity of the legend than in the verifiability of the facts.

The other method of divination was that which used the milfoil, or what is popularly known to us as the yarrow stalks. It was prescribed that the diviner use a total of fifty stalks. Through a process of ritualistic manipulation, one eventually ended with a collection of numbers which by instructed calculation would indicate the lines to be added one above the other in structuring a kua. Some recent writers on *I Ching* have scoffed at the "silliness" of the fifty-stalks prescription of tradition. They argue that one stalk is immediately discarded, so one works with only the remaining forty-nine stalks. Why not just say use forty-nine stalks? Such practical rationality only evidences that these critics are not familiar with the philosophic symbolism and principles attached to numbers in Chinese tradition. There is something to be learned and something to be experienced by becoming familiar with the ideas which underlie the whole complicated process of the milfoil method of relating to *I Ching.* If you are already familiar with Chinese cosmology and the *Yi-wei Ch'ien-tso-tu,* skip over the next lengthy paragraph. It will be a detailed explanation of the meaning of the moves that accompany the milfoil method of consultation.

In some of the ancient Chinese systems of thought there is a correlation between the numbers fifteen and fifty. Yin, the symbol for earth, carries the number ten. Yang, the symbol for heaven, carries the number five. The two add up to fifteen. In the *Ch'ien-tso-tu* it is stated right after the presentation of these facts: "therefore 'the number of the Great Expansion is 50.' " In Chinese the ideographs 5 and 10 are used to write the number 50 (五十, wu shih), and when they are reversed, they represent the number 15 (十五, shih wu). It is accepted that 5 represents the number of heaven, which is odd; 10 represents the number of earth, which is even. When the number of heaven is combined with the number of earth, it is called Tao, specifically, Tao of the universe. Thus, in the Chinese mind, 15 and 50 are both combinations of the numbers 5 and 10. The 50 yarrow stalks therefore symbolize the Tao of the universe, the great cosmos. In picking up the 50 stalks, a man simply signifies that he is approaching the cosmos, the all-knowing, the great totality, seeking aid. He sets one stalk aside to indicate that he does not expect the cosmos to become his servant exclusively. Symbolically this indicates that the cosmos, the all-knowing, is free to help others of his fellow beings. And from another view, it is a humble acknowledgment that the consultor is only one small fragment of the all, but he recognizes that the meaning of his individual being is contained in the grand macrocosm. One stalk set aside, the remaining 49 are now divided into two heaps. These 49 stalks, added numerologically are 13, which added equals 4. The 4 represents the four natures of yin-yang: great yin, lesser yin, greater yang, and lesser yang. Dividing them into two heaps, is to remind the individual that there are two forces eternally at play in the universe, yin and yang. The instructions tell us to select a stalk from the right-hand heap and to place it between the ring finger and the little finger of the left hand. Next, the left-hand heap is placed in the left hand, and with the right hand the stalks are removed from it in bundles of four, until there are four or fewer stalks remaining. This movement with the heaps of stalks and the hands manipulating them becomes a T'ai Chi Ch'uan-like movement. It symbolizes the placing of the dot of yin in yang, and of yang in yin, as it appears in the T'ai Chi Tu. It reminds one that each thing in the universe has seeded within itself its opposite, its own negation. The removing of the stalks in groups of four symbolizes the four seasons of the year. Man lives through, in and with the four seasons. It functions as an intercalary device in relation to the individual's matter of concern, their life and time. Each remainder of four or fewer stalks then following is placed first between the ring finger and the middle finger of the left hand, next between the middle finger and the forefinger of the left hand. The sum of the stalks now held between the fingers will add to either nine or five (in the textbook the range of numerical possibilities are given). Nine and five are both yang numbers, numbers of heaven. All things are conceived in heaven. How very appropriate that the first line forming a kua should have its origin in a number of heaven. The 9 is to be regarded as 8, and the 5 is to be regarded as 4. Each by reduction brings the number down to an even number. All even numbers are numbers of yin. Yin is earth. Again, how appropriate that the first line of the kua dealing with an individual's situation should originate in a number of heaven and be manifested in a number of earth. The particular stalks which have been counted out as either 9 or 5, are now set carefully aside. The remaining stalks are gathered together again and once more divided into two heaps at random. The same mechanical procedure is followed, only this time the total number of stalks remaining between the fingers will be either eight or four. How appropriate that once the kua has come to be manifested on earth, it then becomes an earthly problem in need of using all the forces of the universe in an earthly way. This basically, will give you an idea of the very beautiful symbology and feeling of highly refined sensitivity that is expressed in the tradition of the milfoil method of using *I Ching*.

We are told of the two movements symbolized in *I Ching*: the yang, forward movement, and the yin, backward movement. The significance of this representation can be grasped when we consider the number of things in the universe which utilize these two movements. There is the systolic and diastolic activity of the heart; the inhalation and exhalation of our respiratory systems; the opening and closing of the eyes, etc., etc. Some students have had difficulty understanding how the backward and forward movement was evident in the T'ai Chi Tu symbol. "No matter how one moves about the circle there is only one direction in which one goes," they pointed out. They didn't understand until it was explained that this was the illusion. Going in one direction is impossible if one is making a circle and completing it. One starting at the south (which is at the top in the manner of the Chinese) marks the outer perimeter of yin by moving either from left to right, or downward. When one reaches the north, at the bottom, to mark the outer perimeter of yang one is either moving from right to left, or upward. Thus it is clear that two opposite movements are required to complete the circle. This polarity of forces is essential to all living things. It is the same with electricity where we have the negative and positive aspects. In *I Ching*, this polarity is represented by the numbers assigned to the yin and yang. Yang is the forward moving force. It grows from 7 to 9, and there, having reached its maximum, it is ready to change into yin. Yin is 8 and shrinks to its maximum 6, when it is ready to change into yang 7.

In commenting on the fact that a kua has three and only three lines, the *Ch'ien-tso-tu* states that it symbolizes the principle that "things have their beginning, time of maturity, and end."

The Chinese have always been wise in the adoption of imported ideas or things. They have retained the valuable and indispensable essence, but have never refrained from making such refinements as would make it more consonant with the Chinese character, temperament, etc., as necessity seemed to indicate. I believe in this way one is able to preserve important and valuable things when they have been transported from one place to another. *I Ching* is a valuable wisdom, and it can serve Western man in the most rewarding ways. I think the gains to be gotten from *I Ching* will increase when we experiment and find ways of integrating some of the great principles of Western spirituality and metaphysics into the system of *I Ching*. Buddhism, which originated in India, has endured longer in China, while it is almost unheard of in India today. Even so, *I Ching* (which is fading in China today) may and can have an exciting new vitality and usefulness in the society of Western civilizations. It is for us to cut the garment to fit the man, not the man to fit the garment.

Charts to Aid Interpretation

The greatest collection of chart studies and *I Ching* diagrams is housed by the Ching Shih *I Ching* Institute Limited, where there is a treasure house of over three thousand pieces. These deal with the application of the philosophy and principles of *I Ching* to a vast range of subjects and disciplines. Arrangements are now in progress to secure copies of this library, so that we may afford an opportunity for interested Westerners to participate in these studies. I already have copies of a small number of the collection kept on file at the International *I Ching* Studies Institute, which is an adjunct activity of the Taoist Sanctuary, Inc. These can be examined by qualified persons at the offices of the sanctuary. At the present, all information about the diagrams is printed in Chinese. When acceptable translations have been completed they will be released periodically to the Western public, through the quarterly *Institute News Letter*.

The diagrams and charts which will be presented in this section of the book are selected from those used in the elementary *I Ching* study seminars conducted by the Institute. While there is neither space nor time to offer an exhaustive explanation of each of the charts, the information and descriptions which shall be furnished may prove to be of very good use. The serious student will be surprised to discover what a growth of insight comes just from studying these diagrams.

In Chapter Two, the "Diagram of Cosmic Evolution" in terms of the sixty-four kua is very thoroughly gone into. But even this treatment is not an exhaustive one. Diagrams, such as "The Sequence of Earlier Heaven," and "The Sequence of Later Heaven," are being omitted from this volume, as they appear in the Wilhelm/Baynes translation and nearly every other book dealing with *I Ching*. We shall follow the description given in the *Huai Nan Tzu,* and depict the "Annual Revolution of the Yin and Yang":[3]

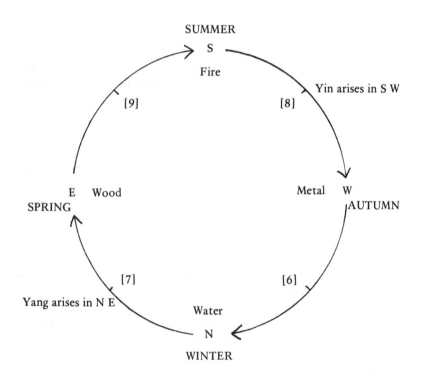

The *Huai Nan Tzu* describes the yang ether as arising in the northeast. It moves southward, upward, passing through the eastern quarter, where it encounters the presiding element of wood and helps it to flourish. In this way it produces spring. It progresses on to the south, where it encounters the presiding element of fire, which it also helps to flourish. In this way it produces summer. The yin ether moves in the same way. It arises in the southwest. It moves northward, downward, passing through the western quarter, where it encounters the presiding element of metal, which it helps to flourish. In this way it produces winter. The diagram contains the number [7], in brackets to picture the forward-upward movement to [9], where the yang force reaches its maximum. When it reaches its maximum, there is no alternative but that it must evolve into its opposite ether, yin. This yin is given the number [8], in brackets and is directed in a downward movement, backward, to become [6], where the yin ether reaches its maximum and must next evolve into yang [7].

If you can keep this simple diagram in mind, and the legend that goes with it, you will find that it pictures a great many things you experience every day. This is an initial step in learning to use *I Ching* as a key for understanding the situations and events that you experience in life from day to day.

This diagram that presents the cosmological theory of T'ung Chung-shu, regarding the annual movements of the yin and yang, will be found to disagree with the theory stated in the *Huai Nan Tzu*. It is included here to show that there are independent interpretations and theories expressed by the ancients on these cosmic matters. In a sense, this serves as a very modest confirmation of the correctness of each person trying to find his or her *I Ching*, which is really nothing more than finding one's own true nature.

The importance of timeliness in human affairs is a subject often treated in the Appendices to *I Ching*. The philosophy of the *I* holds that all things in the universe are eternally in a state

Yin and Yang in
summer meet in
the fore.

Yin goes toward the left; it returns to the N. and emerges at
Chen. Yin ether begins by
emerging in S.E. and moves N.
Yin daily increases and becomes
mighty.

Yang goes toward the right;
returns to the N. and retires a
Shen. Yang daily diminishes an
weakens.

S

Yin is precisely i
the W. in Spring

E

Yin in East
in Autumn.

Yang in
West in
Autumn.

W

Yang is precisely
in the E. in Spring.

Yin comes
W. from E.

Yang comes
E. from W.

N

Yang goes toward left; returns to
south, emerging at yin. Yang
ether begins emerging in N.E.,
moves south. Yang raises itself
and emerges in the East.

Yin goes toward the right; re
turns to the south and retires a
Hsu. Yin daily diminishes an
weakens. Yin holds itself lov
and retires in the West.

Yin and Yang in
winter meet in
the rear.

Tung Chung-shu's
"Theory of Annual Movements of the Yin and Yang." [4]

of flux and change. In the third Appendix there is a passage that reads:

> The *I* is a book which cannot be put far away. Its method (of teaching) is that of frequent changing (of its lines). They move and change without staying (in one place), flowing about into any one of the six places of the kua. They ascend and descend, ever inconstant. The strong and weak lines change places, so that an invariable and compendious rule cannot be derived from them. It must vary as their changes indicate (p. 399).[5]

It is apparent then that the accomplishment of anything, under such perpetually changing conditions, can only be realized if the necessary action takes place at the necessary time. Timeliness of action is important, and is treated in the timely mean.

The following diagram depicts a correspondence between the timely mean and the pa kua. By alternating between the yin and the yang, one reads the process of phenomena as starting with Ch'ien (The Originating) from where a thing is projected with the totality of its completeness in the very idea itself, a yang action. It is received by K'un, which now moves to fulfill and manifest what is projected from yang. This phase delivers a 'change' in the thing projected as the idea. It is now in the process of materializing. As it concretizes we are able to make more and more *use* of it. In using a thing we come to learn or discover its *meaning*. When we have recognized the meaning of a thing, we are then able to think in terms of its further *development*. After a thing is developed to its maximum, we should *release* ourselves from it. By releasing ourselves we establish the *standard* by which we and all things can harmoniously evolve with the cosmic order.

There are, of course, many ways in which one can use this diagram in bettering one's understanding of the principles of *I Ching* which govern the processes of change in our lives and in our universe.

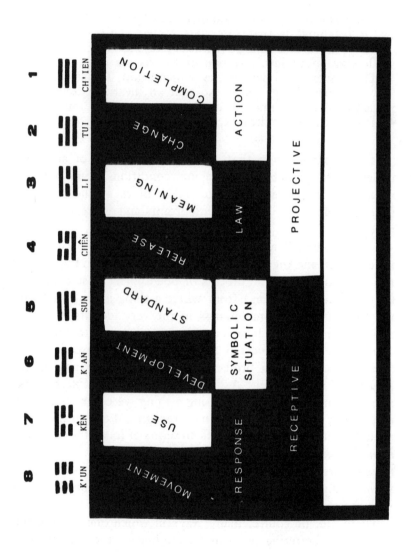

The next diagram is a black and white reduction of a large ten-color subject entitled "I Ching Meditation Mandala." This was structured a number of years ago in an attempt to synthesize graphically the primary principles and content of the *Book of Changes*.

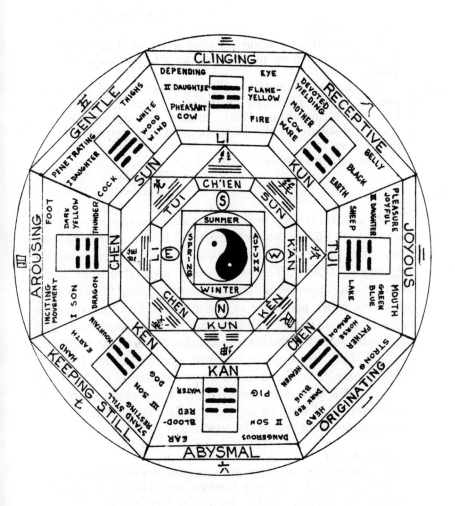

A copy of the large colored mandala was sent to Dr. R. G. H. Siu, the eminent biochemist and author of *The Tao of Science*, and *The Man of Many Qualities: A Legacy of the I Ching*, as a token of appreciation and admiration for his two remarkable volumes. I cannot express how overjoyed I was to receive the following letter from Dr. Siu.

November 16, 1968

Dear Dr. Dhiegh:

You were most gracious in your letter of October 17th as well as generous in sending the *I Ching* mandala of yours.

I studied the mandala again this morning and was impressed by the obviously deep thought that has been put into its formulation. Many thanks for this powerful graphic distillate of the plethora of words written about the *I Ching*.

With all good wishes,

Sincerely,
signed (R. G. H. Siu)

This mandala is used in the study seminars sponsored by the International *I Ching* Studies Institute. It is excellent to have beside one for ready reference when reading or studying the literature of *I Ching*. This is especially applicable when one is studying the appendices. There is another diagram which encircles the outer perimeter of the mandala with the sixty-four kua arranged in their monthly and seasonal sequences. This graphically amplifies the correspondence between the individual kua and daily, seasonal and annual cyclical events. It is not pictured here, but is used in the study seminars at the Institute. In closing this section of chapter nine, I will give a simple and brief example of how to use the mandala in conjunction with some passages from one of the appendices:

Appendix VI:
Between heaven and earth nothing goes away that does not return. When the sun has reached its meridian height, it begins to decline. When the moon has become full, it begins to wane. . . . When the sun goes, the moon comes.

When the moon goes, the sun comes. The sun and moon
thus take the place of one another in producing light. . . .
That which goes contracts, and that which comes expands.
It is by the influence, one upon the other, of this contraction and expansion that what is beneficial is
produced.[6]

If one looks at the T'ai-Chi Tu, in the center of the mandala,
you see yang (heaven) and yin (earth) interlocked. As you look
at the figure, you realize that it gives the picture of an endless
revolving, and because of the comma-like shape of each symbol
of yin and yang, an endless evolving of all that is. When you
study the expanding shape of the yang figure you see also that
when the yin begins, one has to become conscious of the yang
reducing as the yin expands. Yin is equated to the moon and
yang to the sun in the literature of *I Ching*. The phenomenon of
waxing and waning is forcefully depicted in the graphic structures of yin and yang. So by looking at this simple diagram, the
full content of the sixth appendix (the portions quoted for this
example) become evident. This single point could be elaborated
upon much further, but I would rather allow the reader to
enjoy the pleasures of further discoveries of correlations and
clarifications to be gained at his prerogative.

Developing Intuition and Interpretive Insights

A most difficult challenge to master is that of learning how
psychologically to use the philosophy and wisdom of *I Ching*. It
requires a heightening of our intuitive awareness and a bold,
daring expression of our interpretive insights. Among the reasons for these difficulties is that many of us tend to have an
excessive reliance upon words—the meanings of words. By
"meanings of words," of course, is meant the dictionary
meanings. In a word, too many of us are hung up on the
intellectualization of experience, rather than the sensing and
feeling of it. By not getting beyond the words we develop a
tendency to classify the kua into "good kua," and "bad" kua,
just as though the kua could or would make a moral judgment.

As long as we remain imprisoned in the dictionary definition of words, it will be difficult to put across the idea that there are no "good" or "bad" kua. The kua, like God, is no respector of persons. One must learn to look and listen to the *I* with new eyes, new ears and new sensitivities, for it is a vocabulary of archetypes—fingers which are pointing, but which are not themselves the thing at which they point!

In the elementary *I Ching* study seminars given by the Institute, students sometimes report: "I threw the coins and luckily I got a very good kua." As a rule I will ask what they got. A sample reply would be: "I got 'Abundance,' isn't that good?" It is then that one should be guided to recognize that the *I* is of an archetypal nature, that the ramifications of its symbols (whether they be in words or images), stretch from yang to yin, and from yin to yang! The *I*, in the person's opinion, has functioned as a soothsayer. They have accepted it as a thing wholly outside and removed from themselves, yet having some uncanny talent for knowing what is going to happen to them. Even though one feels they have been "lucky" and that the *I* has said they are to have an "Abundance," does it mean an "Abundance of luck?" And if so, what kind of luck— good luck or bad? The efficient use of *I Ching* is experienced after one is able to see, feel and experience *I Ching* as a component of his individual being and psyche; a component that in a very real way links one to the total happenings of the cosmos. One then relates to the wisdom of *I Ching*, not as prediction, but prescription. To develop this relationship, we have a practice in the seminar sessions called "experiential exercises." These are designed to heighten our awareness and help us to respond to more and more of the things which we are continuously experiencing mentally.

To those who have read more extensively than some into the literature of *I Ching*, and who are chained to the authority of the written word—who therefore will want to know the source-document and paragraph reference for what follows—there can only be this reply: "In the tradition of these teachings, the written word is but the skin covering the being, the heart is deep inside and must be listened to with the ear." These exercises are part of an oral tradition and even these are not fully explicated here. But what is here will be useful.

Experiential Exercise 1.

We begin with the assignment to experience a painting. Take a painting (preferably a classical Chinese painting of a nature scene, or a fan painting), set it before you and compose yourself. (For purposes of this training it doesn't matter if the painting be in color or in black and white.) Look at the painting for a full two minutes, then turn away from it, or place it face down before you, and write down what you have just *experienced*.

To illustrate how this exercise can be evaluated, we use the black and white reproduction of a work of the classical period which is shown on the next page (*Landscape* by Fu Pao-shih). The artist is a contemporary painter, who draws on traditional sources for his subject matter. He is especially attracted to the painters of the Sung Dynasty, yet his individual style is modern. Nevertheless there is a tremendous psychic force in his painting which can arouse an intuitive visionary response in the viewer. This is what constitutes *"experiencing the painting."* Study the painting for as long as you care to. Then write down what you experienced. The key to sharpening one's intuitive awareness of what is happening in oneself is to make a "description with" not a "description of."

Viewer 1. The painting showed a forest at the base of very high mountains. The trees became thinner as the mountains rose and became more barren. It seemed to contrast the feeling of yin and yang. It was lonely but peaceful.

Viewer 2. The scene is rich and elevating. There is an abundance of natural life (trees, bushes, rocks and water), and while I don't see any people, I suspect they are about somewhere, perhaps hidden in houses concealed by the trees—for there is a

Landscape by Fu Pao-shih

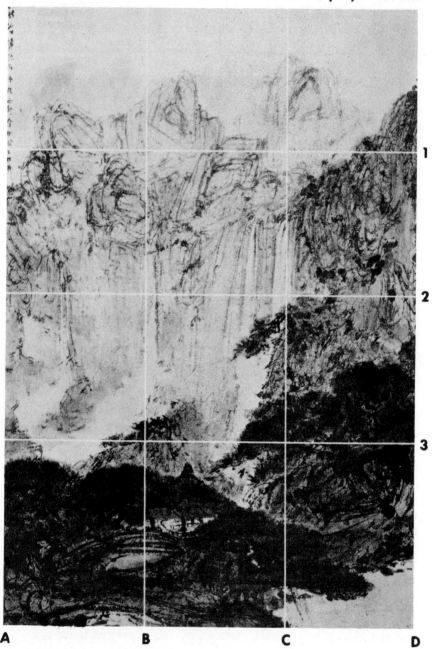

fence and what might be some animals grazing nearby. I get a feeling of spirits all about—or perhaps dragons—not the scarey kind, but friendly and protective.

Viewer 3. Objectively I would say this is a painting of forest, farmland and mountains; but that is more a "description of." When I merge into the painting I sense and see many things that are within myself. In the area between lines 2 and 3 bounded by C and D I see a demon head (such as are seen in Chinese paintings and used by actors in Chinese opera); it is friendly. Within the demon head itself, I see a dancing figure; I think it is a woman. The movements are graceful and pacifying. Also I notice that what I see as a dragon or demon head is part of a larger tree, except this tree has more the feeling of a whirling dervish dancer. In the area between 3 and 4 and lines B and C there is the profile of a pregnant woman, and behind her there seems to be a small baby dragon. In the upper center area of the same section I see a man riding a camel. The animal seems in the process of rising up. Line 3 runs right through a horse which is just left of where line B intersects line 3. There are many interesting faces, too many to describe them all. There is a strong figure of a man carrying a pack upon his back marching to the right. In fact one or two more steps and he'll be outside the frame of the picture. He is in the upper right hand corner of the bottom area of the picture between lines 3 and 4 close to line D, which is the right hand edge of the picture. The more I look at this painting the more things I see. I won't write down any more now. I want to list the things I've seen, and then see how they relate to my life and things that interest or concern me.

Viewers 1 and 2 are students which have just begun the elementary seminar. Viewer 3, is a student that took the seminar last year and has been attending some of the workshops in *I Ching*. This student, on the first introduction to this exercise with a different picture as the subject-stimulus, reacted very much the same as Viewer 1 did with this exercise.

At first glance you may not even see how the last viewer could possibly imagine such images as have been described. You may even decide that these are all pure hallucinations. It does not matter what evaluation you may give to the exercise, so long as you are able to remain receptive to the possibility that if it has been the real experience of the individual it has meaning and use to them. Another possible development is that you may return to study the picture and awaken to some of the images seen by Viewer 3, in addition to seeing some that are your own. The experience is something akin to a Rorschach, and on several levels contains the same kind of significance. This exercise is one for developing the sensitivity of the eye so that while it looks outward, it focuses inward. What we see outside is what is projected from inside. Thus it happens when we can see the formless in the form and a form in the formless, we are approaching self-knowledge.

Experiential Exercise 2.

The next target for awakening the intuitive is taste. You will have to secure the help and cooperation of another person to carry out this exercise in experiencing taste. Also, it is important that you keep yourself in a state of blissful ignorance about what the other person is going to get or do. Now request that they prepare an assortment of freshly ground spices (preferably some that you are not familiar with), and place a small pinch of each in a circle on a plate. The spices should be freshly ground with a pestle in a mortar. Each spice should be ground individually, and the mortar and pestle washed and dried each time before grinding the next spice. A selection of five to eight will be sufficient for a solo experiment. Have your helper place the plate with the small piles of spices in a box, so that you cannot see their color or texture. Now moisten the tip of one of your fingers and place your hand close to the plate and have your helper gently touch your moistened fingertip to one of the spices. Put the finger to your tongue and then salivate and spread the taste around in your mouth. Now write down what you have just experienced. Please do not read ahead until you have completed following the last instruction. Now that everything you wish to note has been written down, read on.

What often happens with this exercise is that the person tries to identify what they have been tasting. "It was salt," or "It was nutmeg," or "It was cardoman seed," etc., etc. This is not what the exercise required. No request was made asking that you identify what the substance was. The instruction is to *experience taste;* in other words, what happens to you and within you—physically, mentally and emotionally. Taste sparks off sensations of recall or of a newness that challenges one to make a decision. It is becoming aware of these things within one that is the intent of experiencing taste, the thoughts which pass through one's mind as one deeply and consciously tastes. How often we eat a meal and never taste it? Oh, we know the flavor, but we haven't bothered to taste with the consciousness of our whole being. And that is quite a different thing. Full tasting is another way of looking inside.

There are additional experiential exercises dealing with the faculty of smell, touch and hearing. I will not touch further upon them here. The pattern outlined in the two exercises which have been illustrated will be more or less basic to those in smell, touch and hearing. The important thing to keep in mind during these exercises is that one is not to identify something, but identify *with* something and *through* something. Practice will result in a great heightening of one's awareness to the intuitive guidance that is always at one's ready disposal, if only one will awaken to it, turn to it, and use it!

Ten
The Symbols and the Text

Meanings and Interpretations

I Ching is! All else is mere commentary. There can be no ultimate agreement on the meaning of any of the symbols or the texts which make up and express its wisdom. Whatever is said or written, by whomsoever it may be, is specifically a revelation of their individual enlightenment from the vantage point of their momentary perspective.

I open this chapter with the above statement to emphasize what is importantly in need of clarification and definition. The *I* is. It is all things to all people. The cynical find it illogical and ridiculous. To the hard-minded practicalist it is mystifying and perhaps of some quaint and charming literary interest. To some few it is truly a wellspring of stimulation and enlightenment. It is a wisdom that, I often feel, must be considered as being the shadowed side of Tao. Hence what is said of Tao is being said of

I Ching. The forty-first chapter of *Tao Te Ching* (41 = 4 + 1 = 5, the number of heaven, which may be a clue that this chapter is one of several having a universal significance) reads:

> When a wise scholar hears the Tao,
> He practices it diligently.
> When a mediocre scholar hears the Tao,
> He wavers between belief and unbelief.
> When a worthless scholar hears the Tao,
> He laughs boisterously at it.
> But if such a one does not laugh at it,
> The Tao would not be the Tao![1]

Were we to substitute *I* for Tao, we would have a rather accurate picture of its relationship to the people in our society of today. This verse of *Tao Te Ching* is a clue to how it should be used (including the use of *I Ching*). The complete instruction is contained in the first sentence: "When a wise scholar hears the Tao, he practices it diligently." A "wise scholar" is one who is capable of experiencing a state of 'knowing'. By a state of 'knowing' is meant a unification with something, be it an object, an idea or an experience. "He practices it diligently," suggests that when one realizes this "state of 'knowing'," he or she then flows with it. One should remember that one of the definitions of "diligence" is given by Webster III as being "a large, covered horse-drawn carriage used for long journeys."[2] This suggests that when one is in the "state of 'knowing'," he is wrapped or enclosed within the thing itself, and so is prepared to move with it until it reaches its destination. This flowing with the thing, the situation, comes after one "hears the Tao." Hearing the Tao is not merely a matter of auditory perception. It implies a total response of the organism, the intellect and the psyche to that something which touches or reaches the consciousness of the "wise scholar." Total response, in this instance, may be likened to the scent of a flower. Somewhere I read a lovely anecdote, which you will forgive me for crudely paraphrasing. It went something like this: "May I smell your flower?" "Why of course, for no one can smell all of a flower." The kind of total response mentioned here is that which is simultaneously total and in part. We say to a dear one, "You have all my love." Then we turn to another and say, "I love you very much." Yet there is no contradiction. The eternal things of life are those which we can give to any single receptor totally, yet it remains to be given to another, and another, and another, eternally as a total, yet always in part.

One should avoid putting forth ultimatums which deal with the words, images and symbols of *I Ching* and defining "how they should be interpreted." This is a difficult temptation from which to refrain. We have been so very well trained to seek after and accept only the rational, intellectual explanation of things as true, even when they seem to go against a secret inner feeling. And a great store is placed in the old canard "The truth shall set you free!" The wisdom of *I Ching* can enable us to envelop that canard and more. All ultimatums eventually come under the advice of Chieh, the sixtieth kua of *I Ching.* Ultimatums are limitations, and in the judgment of Chieh it is written: "Galling limitation must not be persevered in."[3] The last sentence in the Wilhelm comment reads: "Therefore it is necessary to set limits even upon limitation."[4] This is the principle of the Einsteinian universe that expands and then turns in upon itself. This is the nature of Tao.

In much of the recent literature (translations, interpretations, commentaries and explanations) involving *I Ching,* a great deal of attention has been given, with the very best intent, to putting down meanings for words, phrases, images and symbols used in *I Ching.* The aim has been so that the Western reader shall better understand the *I.* But that very noble aim is to miss the point of *I Ching.* Its aim is to enable one to understand oneself in the universe of consciousness where one is self-found. It is hoped that this will be more clearly indicated by taking some of these glossaries and putting them beneath the microscope of 'change'. Perhaps by so magnifying the view we may enlarge our understanding. Also I would like to state that I am not arguing against the interpretations and views given by various authors to selected words and phrases of *I Ching,* but rather expanding upon them in a way that, I hope, will leave them open for further extension by each involved individual. The validity of this position is confirmed by the fact that each of the sixty-four kua has a number of explanatory texts attached to it. Each text amends the meaning or indication of the kua, and the tradition of commentaries being appended to the *I* is a continuing one. Therefore there can be no fixed "how" that a kua should be interpreted. So let us explore the dangers of literal and fixed definitions.

In one volume the author has selected fifteen recurring passages which are "generally of great importance, and contain the essence of the oracle's message."[5]

> Supreme Success: The complete fulfillment of your hopes. This phrase implies that your actions are fully in harmony with the prevailing cycles of Tao.[6]

The word "success," appears thirty-eight times in the Judgment texts of *I Ching,* and once as the verb "succeed." Twice it appears preceded by the qualifying adjective "Sublime"; both are found in the Judgment for kua one and two. Eight times it follows the adjective "Supreme," in kua 3, 14, 17, 18, 19, 25, 46 and 49. Twenty-eight times it appears as a single noun in kua 4, 5, 9, 10, 11, 13, 15, 20, 22, 24, 28, 30, 31, 32, 33, 45, 47, 50, 51, 55, 56, 57, 58, 59, 60, 62, 63 and 64. In kua 29 it has a singular expression: "If you are sincere, you have success in your heart, and whatever you do succeeds." These are the statistics concerning the occurrence of the word in the texts. How does one give meaning to it blanketly?

We will commence by examining each use of the phrase "supreme success," as it is used in each of the eight texts.

Kua 3: Difficulty at the beginning works supreme success.
Kua 14: Possession in great measure. Supreme success.
Kua 17: Following has supreme success.
Kua 18: Work on what has been spoiled has supreme success.
Kua 19: Approach has supreme success.
Kua 25: Innocence. Supreme success.
Kua 46: Pushing upward has supreme success.
Kua 49: Supreme success, furthering through perseverance.

With the possible exception of kua 14, there is no use of the phrase "supreme success" that, even in a literal sense, can be taken to mean: "The complete fulfillment of your hopes." As for the phrase implying that "your actions are fully in harmony with the prevailing cycles of Tao," one is hard put to see how, when viewed in context, such a bold conclusion could be drawn. Perhaps the thing most conspicuous and most important is that the "supreme success" appears always to be dependent upon prescribed action or condition. In **49**, the *I* says that "supreme success," is furthered by the continuation of effort and analysis. Kua 25 announces that a condition of innocence is prerequisite to "supreme success." Kua 18 and 19 indicate that "supreme success," comes if one approaches a task, or if one reviews, and discovers his errors and then works to correct them, or to avoid repeating them. There is no promise by the *I* that announces "the complete fulfillment of your hopes." Always there must be action, change, a plan that must be carried out.

A random selection of five other of the fifteen "key phrases," listed by the same author as "passages [which] occur again and again" tally as below listed: "Crossing the Great Water" is mentioned in the Judgments seven times, not mentioned at all in the Images, and occurs three times in the Lines—a total of ten mentions throughout the text. "The Superior man" is mentioned four times in the Judgments; fifty-two times in the Images, and eleven times in the Lines. "The great man" has six mentions in the Judgments, a single mention in the Images, and five mentions in the Lines—twelve mentions in all. "No blame" is mentioned five times in the Judgments, never in the Images, and sixty-eight times in the Lines. The inclusion of "Blame" as one of the recurring "Key phrases," is the most baffling in this listing, as it never appears as a single word phrase in the text of *I Ching*. "Crossing the Great Water," as previously noted, appears three times in the text of the Lines: the 15th kua in the text for the bottom line, the 27th kua in the text for the top, or 6th line, which is also a ruling line, and in the text for the third place in the 64th kua. The criticism of the "indications of how (these important key phrases), should be interpreted" is that they are crudely elementary and are wanting in psychological and philosophic perception that would elevate them above a kind of soothsaying infantilism. That this particular list is thoughtlessly compiled is evidenced by the following fact: the eleventh of the fifteen repetitive "key phrases"—"Occasion to repent," which may be equated with "Cause to repent"—appears only once in the text for the 6th, or top line to kua 1, Ch'ien. There is no other appearance of the phrase in the text, or for that matter, of the word "repent."[7]

In conclusion, on this point, let us recognize that there can be no fixed interpretation to any of the words, phrases or symbols of *I Ching*. The words serve only as disinterested pointers in indicating an infinity of possibilities, discoverable in its archetypes yet knowable only to the individual. Dr. Argüelles hits the mark squarely in writing:

> It is this quality of impersonality, or anonymity, that makes it possible for each person who consults the *I Ching* to participate in the unfolding of his own consciousness: Reading and interpreting the (Kua) in a particular life-situation and carrying out the instructions revealed therein, are solely a matter of the individual psyche which addresses itself to the *I Ching*. It is this kind of dialogue which has given the *I Ching* such long life and vigor; by contributing to the evolution of him who consults the oracle, the *I Ching* perpetuates itself and achieves its own evolution.[8]

Resurrected Scholars

There are twenty different volumes of *I Ching* in English on the shelf above my desk. Of these, only one volume, *The Oracle of Change* by Alfred Douglas, lists a bibliography of some of the European and American translations of *I Ching*. It is unfortunate that so many have hastened to write about *I Ching* without giving some time to research the earlier attempts of a number of distinguished scholars to bring this wisdom of China to serve Western growth. The writings of these pioneers are vibrant with needful insights for our *I Ching* studies now. A few, whose writings have appeared in English, I will refer to in this portion of our closing chapters. By name they are: Joseph Edkins, F. Huberty James, James Legge, De Groot, Thomas McClatchie and A. Terrien De Lacouperie.

Joseph Edkins was a frequent contributor to the *China Review,* especially between the years of 1884 and 1889. He authored a number of articles on "The Yi King," some of which are scheduled to be published in the *News Letter of the International* I Ching *Studies Institute.* Of particular interest to serious students will be his paper on "The Yi King and Its Appendices," and especially the diagram depicting "The Position of the 64 Kwa on the Horizon."9

F. Huberty James gives an interesting history of *I Ching,* which appeared in the July 1898 issue of *The Chinese Recorder.*

Here is adumbrated the groundwork for the philosophy of divination and geomancy, the germs of all science, the laws of all being, visible and invisible. All inventions and knowledge are hidden within the mysterious symbols invented by Fuh Hsi and expounded by the "Literary King" Wen Wang, the Duke of Chow, Confucius and other illustrious scholars. . . .

I think this is a fair and correct summary of the views held by the majority of Chinese literary men concerning the *Book of Changes.* Job ought to have been the patron saint of students who have been blessed with the opportunity to devote happy days of toil to the above mass of occultism with its 2200 expositions. It certainly requires either immense imaginative power, or a boundless credulity to see in these eight trigrams and their variations, pictures of the mutations of nature or illustrations of the development of all things from the original elements. Yet the so-called unimaginative materialistic Chinese regard this book as a marvelous storehouse of sound and solid philosophy. 10 [A professional cynicism appropriate to the time.]

Of all the early English sinologists academically recognized, perhaps none was more bitterly argued with than the Reverend Canon Thomas McClatchie. His forays in the scholarly journals are every bit as exciting as the accounts of the fictional feuds between a stubborn, self-righteous Scotsman and his neighbor of the English gentry. Though he was officially dedicated to Christianity, the religion of love, he was quite adept at aggressively defending himself with a sharp vindictive phrase. In a response to one of his critics published in *The China Review* in 1875-1876, the editor found it necessary to preface the good Canon's reply with the following notation: [The following paper is inserted in accordance with the rule which enjoins giving a fair hearing to both sides of a question. We trust, however, that any future contributions on the same subject will be devoid of undue personal references. Ed. C. R.] .[11]

In the matter of *I Ching*, at the present time McClatchie does not enjoy the same degree of respectable prestige that Legge or Wilhelm do. However, it should be remembered that Rev. McClatchie was a Presbyterian and secretary of the Christian Missionary Society's Missions in China. It is possible there may have been some prejudice exercised against him. I'm hoping that sometime in the future I may be able to carefully study the Canon's translation and his commentary, to determine if there should be a reevaluation of his scholastic offerings.

A most fascinating, provocative and articulate of the earlier scholars is A. Terrien de Lacouperie. Doctor Lacouperie was Laureate of the Academy of Inscriptions and Biblical Literature; Professor of Indo-Chinese Philology at University College, London. In a three-volume work he treats with great thoroughness a careful and searching analysis of *The Oldest Book of the Chinese—The Yh-King and Its Authors*. No one who is seriously interested in *I Ching* can afford not to make the effort to locate copies of the work and study it. Next to the oral tradition, which communicates many things about *I Ching* never to be found written or printed, this is the most valuable reference for a Westerner.

In this work, the good doctor reveals that the basis of *I Ching* consisted primarily "of vocabulary lists or glossarial explanations of the ideograms forming the heading of every chapter, and that these lists had been framed by the early Chinese leaders for the benefit and teaching of their followers, in imitation of similar lists used in Anterior Asia, with which they were acquainted, explaining the various uses and meanings of the ideographical characters of the writing which had been taught them."[12] Lacouperie, in the introduction to his work *The Yh-King,* makes two very important points:

> A great danger in explaining the Yh-King is to take as bona-fide expressions and meanings in the language, such acceptations of words which have no earlier existence than this work itself, and no other meaning than that which have been attributed to them by the ancient commentaries whence they have taken an undue hold in the literature. Therefore little value can be attached to their case, and the instances are most numerous.

> A danger of another sort is to translate by their modern acceptations expressions which at the time when the work was composed had a different meaning.[13]

It is important to the work of developing *I Ching* into a philosophical instrument of practical usefulness to Westerners that the research and scholarly studies of the pioneers who brought *I Ching* into the world arena be reexamined, evaluated and harvested for whatever fruits they may have.

Appliers and Applications of *I Ching*

It is not possible to record all, or even most, of the prominent people who have made use, in one way or another, of *I Ching.* But it may serve a purpose to touch upon a few of them and some of the areas of human pursuit which have, in a greater or lesser degree, been influenced by *I Ching.* There are any number of ways in which this could be done. One way would be to present everything chronologically. Another more interesting way is to fashion a collage of persons, areas and events that have had a significant experience with *I Ching*.

I Ching is known to most Westerners as the *Book of Changes.* In China it is also known as the classic edited by the four sages: the Emperor Fu-hsi, circa 3000 B.C.; King Wen, founder of the Chou dynasty; the Duke of Chou, the youngest son of King Wen; and the world-famous Confucius, who was born in 551 B.C. *I Ching* is the world's oldest continually circulated literature. It is "a most mysterious work," wrote Kiang Kang-Hu, "and so allows of all kinds of interpretations." We shall shortly demonstrate how accurate this statement is by noting its applicability to medicine, astrology, cosmogony, geomancy, invention, architecture, agriculture, palmistry, physics, music, philosophy, divination and other areas.

Even from such a synoptic presentation as will be made here, it will become apparent how "each of the interpretations may express certain points of its truths to certain extents. . . ."[14] Kiang wrote of the Ten Wings as being either so profound or unclear "that they comprise great complicated thoughts and phenomena, and lead to different or even contradictory explanations."[15] But what a wonderful wisdom it is that it can hold and express meaning and furnish principles to the healing disciplines of four thousand years ago, and yet provoke the intense curiosity and interest in the medical research scientist of today.

To grasp an appreciation of the principle of yin and yang as applied to the medical arts in ancient China, one should read *The Yellow Emperor's Classic of Internal Medicine.* To see what timely interest it is to modern medical practice, one has only to read the reports of two distinguished American biologists, who with restrained enthusiasm tell of their witnessing the use of acupuncture in a large modern hospital in China today.

In a recent weekly news magazine, it is reported that Doctors Arthur Galston of Yale University and Ethan Signer of the Massachusetts Institute of Technology recently observed four surgical operations in China in which acupuncture was used as the anesthesia. Interest in the ancient tradition of acupuncture is not restricted to medical travelers abroad. This tradition, which envisions the forces of yin and yang at equilibrium within a healthy body, but which are in imbalance during periods of illness, is proving to be fascinating to many of our doctors of tomorrow. At the University of Washington, 130 students enrolled for a noncredit course entitled, "The Discipline of Acupuncture." A great number of those who enrolled were medical doctors.

Other doctors have witnessed acupuncture used as therapy and anaesthesia—Dr. Paul D. White, the New England cardiologist; Dr. E. G. Dimond, provost of the medical school at the University of Missouri; Doctors Rosen, White and Gutman; and Dr. Victor Sidel of Montefiore Hospital in New York City. The use of acupuncture as anaesthesia is still regarded by Chinese doctors as being in the experimental stage, although it has been used more than 500,000 times with patients, with a reported success of 90 percent.

Let me interrupt this collage to give a pattern supplied by *I Ching* for examining these many things. The "Eight Diagrams" [pa kua], are basic to the sixty-four kua of *I Ching*. The chart below gives their forms, names, relations and symbolic meanings:

Form	Name	Relation	Universe	Meaning
☰	Ch'ien	Father	Heaven	firmness
☷	K'un	Mother	Earth	yielding
☳	Chên	Elder Son	Thunder	to move
☴	Sun	Elder Daughter	Wind	to distribute
☵	K'an	Middle Son	Water	dark
☲	Li	Middle Daughter	Fire	bright
☶	Kên	Youngest Son	Mountain	stand still
☱	Tui	Youngest Daughter	Valley/Marsh	to collect

From this chart it becomes obvious that the "Eight Diagrams" are representations of four different natures and four different actions. Those defined as "firmness," "yielding," "dark" and "bright" are the four natures. Those meaning "to move," "to distribute," "stand still" and "to collect" are the four actions. They are of two classes, one opposing the other. "Firmness" reverses "yielding," "dark" reverses "bright," "to move" reverses "stand still," and "to distribute" reverses "to collect." This octet of trilinear images are representative of almost everything in the world, the universe and human society. Herein is the principle that supports the practice of acupuncture. An entire chapter could be written on the principles of yin and yang in ancient medicine, but this is not the place for it. A broad note will conclude this aspect. According to the ancient tradition, diseases relating to the yang principle go upward until they attain the crisis and then descend. Diseases relating to the yin principle go downward to the point of crisis then ascend. When air is injurious, it is the upper part of the body that is first affected. When water is the injurious element, it is the lower part of the system (as in dropsy) that is first affected. In these descriptions, the element of air or *feng,* wind, is most important. The ancient text of Su Wen has very much to say about both wind and water. Those who are interested in this feature should research it. There is an abundance of material to be studied.

We will turn our attention away from the healing arts to one of the arts of harmonics, namely that of music. A name of contemporary significance in the field of music is that of John Cage. The principles of mechanics built into *I Ching* were for a time interestingly experimented with by Cage in his work in creative musical composition. We mentioned above that the "Eight Diagrams" are representations of four different actions. In a chapter on composition in his book *Silence,* Cage writes of structuring music by means of the method established in *I Ching.*[16] After recounting the makeup of the pa kua, he writes:

> Where there are eight charts, four at any instant are mobile and four immobile (mobile means an element passes into history once used, giving place to a new one; immobile means an element, though used, remains to be used again).[17]

It calls for very little imagination to see that there is a very real notion of connection between the ancient's concept of the four natures and four actions, and Cage's four mobile and four immobile elements. The four immobile elements, "though used, remains to be used again," are equal to the four natures. The four mobile elements which pass "into history once used, giving place to" new ones, are equal to the four actions. It is through such acausal relationships as these that we begin to sense that there is a dynamic significance contained in and expressed through the wisdom of *I Ching*.

In developing his theme, Cage ingeniously adheres to the binary principle of *I Ching*. He presents his chart dealing with sound as consisting of thirty-two elements having a polarity relationship of yin and yang, in which he designates the even numbers as "silences." A further development made by Cage is that of carrying his charts to the subject of durations. Here there are sixty-four elements ("since silence also has length"). It is traditional among the Chinese sages to refer to the sixty-four kua as encompassing all that is in heaven and earth. About his charts for duration, Cage writes:

> Through use of fractions (e.g., 1/3; 1/3 + 3/5 + 1/2) measured following a standard scale (2-1/2 cm. equals a crotchet), these durations are, for the purposes of musical composition, practically infinite in number.[18]

The principle of the number sixty-four symbolizing a totality or an infinity is once again demonstrated. What an unimaginable dimension is embraced by the philosophical principles represented by the numerations, linear images and the verbal wisdom of *I Ching*! Its application is limited only by the imagination and initiative of man. As long as the imagination and initiative of man are on-stretching and limitless, so will be the adaptability of *I Ching* in making all phenomena not only understandable, but also possible. All things become possible because, with developed insight, one finds in the *I* a prescription for action.

Carl Gustav Jung, perhaps more than any other individual of the Occidental cultures, is most responsible for initiating the growing interest of the Western world in *I Ching*. As a practicing psychoanalyst, he involved and established *I Ching* as part of the historical experiments and experience of psychoanalytic research and practice. His elaborate thesis on synchronicity remains a challenging paper to fire the imagination and aspiration of those in whom there is even an ember of wanderlust for psychological adventure. Today, more and more, psychologists and psychiatrists are giving attention to *I Ching*, each in his own way finding an application for its principles in his particular practice.

Doctor Ralph Metzner, in his new book *Maps of Consciousness*, tells how he makes use of *I Ching* in working with certain of his cases:

> I myself have used it as an aid to the practice of psychotherapy, particularly in situations where neither patient nor therapist knew what was going on. Invariably the *I Ching* is like a ray of light from a higher source, pointing out the obvious facts and the nature of the obstacle.[19]

It may bewilder some that persons who have had the advantages of modern scientific training are being caught up in something as "hazy" and "confounding" as *I Ching*. A satisfactory explanation is furnished by Dr. Metzner:

> . . . a major value of the use of the *I Ching* in everyday life lies in its ability to shift the questioner's point of view and to lift him out of the personality-bound perception and enable him to look at the events from the point of view of ever transforming cycles of change. Conflicts, after all, can arise only where interpretations clash with the actual movement of events in space-time. . . . Lao-tse says: "To be proud with wealth and honor is to sow the seeds of one's downfall. To retire when your work is done is the Tao of heaven."[20]

Joseph L. Henderson, M.D., a distinguished analyst and author, tells of his recognition of *I Ching* as a useful avenue of expression and experience for certain of his patients:

> Perhaps I may have conveyed in these brief comments some reasons why the I Ching sounds less and less strange to modern ears since it embodies the kind of reasonable-

ness we associate with modern psychological insight. As a practitioner of analytical psychology I find the wisdom of this book is not only ancient but perennial, and therefore contemporary, and so I understand that when people use it practically to clarify their lives they are, for the most part, not indulging in wayward superstition but have found an authentic guide to a deeper knowledge of their motives.[21]

Of course there will be some protests to this professional medical understanding of *I Ching*. In rebuttal to such protests I can only join with Dr. Henderson in saying:

There are no psychological dangers that I know of in using the *I Ching*. People of unsound mind or emotion will misuse it, as they misuse other things, but there is too much common sense in its responses to set off autonomous psychic reactions, and there is no imagery that would exert an undue fascination.[22]

A still different area where *I Ching* is coming to exercise some influence is that of philosophy. Dr. José Argüelles has authored a brilliant article, "Compute and Evolve," that makes a fresh presentation of the current revolutionary events formulating throughout the world today. With his intellectual telescope trained on the scene in the United States, he observes:

If Mao is adding to the vigor and violence of this country's revolutionary spirit, the *I Ching* is operating to balance the scale by providing what may be described as a meta-revolutionary channel for action. Through this channel the very nature and function of the human psyche can be reviewed, not only in terms of the various specifics which guide "normal" special interest groups—oriented to economics, politics, education, ideology, or even race—but in terms of the totality of all these situations or relationships.[23]

The action of utilizing *I Ching* is a ceremonial acceptance of 'change', which rewards the actor with a code of instruction designed to be physically, emotionally, intellectually and spiritually implemented. When a man implements the coded instructions of the *I* on these levels, he will discover that his progress is aided and that he is moving through life in a state of pragmatic bliss. The actuality of life is not in being, but rather in the two states of becoming and 'begoning'. This is very much what Argüelles stresses, when he writes:

> . . . nothing and nobody exists except as a necessary function of karma, which represents a causality infinitely more extensive than ordinary, mechanical cause and effect.[24]

And elsewhere:

> Although modern cosmological theory is still fluid, most recent evidence seems to point toward a cyclic rhythm in the universe which may arise from a succession of numberless and almost inconceivably endless cycles of cosmic birth and death. In accepting such a view, even tentatively, modern science approaches agreement with the Indian theory of manvantaras and kalpas—enormous periods of activity and of rest—and also with the philosophy of the *I Ching*, which embodies the Chinese view of eternal change. This holds that the cosmos is a kind of perpetual interplay of two basic polarities, continually repeating the cycles of transformations that are the inescapable result of the primordial forces of the yin and the yang.[25]

These are sketchy illustrations of how *I Ching* has been, or is becoming, a part of the disciplines of medicine, music, psychiatry and philosophy. I shall conclude this section with only a brief word or two on some other areas which exemplify the influence of *I Ching*. Professor William Irwin Thompson, in an article appearing in the December 1971's issue of *Harper's* magazine, wrote: "All through evolution man has survived because he remained generalized and adaptable. He did not grow a claw on his arm; he held a tool and put it aside when he was finished with it."[26]

This, I believe, states the relationship that one should have with *I Ching*. One should not cling to it as a crutch, nor permit it to become like a growth upon the psyche. A most important lesson that *I Ching* teaches is that of remaining adaptable to other experiences. *I Ching* should be picked up and used as a tool to accomplish a given task—when necessary. He who keeps pouring after the cup has been filled wastes the tea. So with *I Ching;* once the desired development has been attained, put it aside. There is no nourishment in gluttony, no music in playing even the sweetest note over and over and over!

In the field of religion, *I Ching* is becoming a most respected and popular source of quotable texts. The Reverend Mr. William Bell Glenesk, a young and dynamic force in the Presbyterian church who handles two parishes (one in Brooklyn, the other in Manhattan) in New York City, has not only quoted from *I Ching,* but on several occasions delivered sermons on *I Ching* and the new spirituality. The well-known religious leader and author Dr. Erwin Seale uses *I Ching* as a sermon topic in addition to conducting seminars elucidating its meaning and uses for our time. Another minister, the Reverend Harvey Freeman, minister to the Center for Truth in Portland, Oregon, finds *I Ching* not only stimulating to his immediate congregation, but also to many persons in the community who are not parishioners. He now conducts a monthly workshop discussing the wisdom of *I Ching.* Dr. Joseph Murphy, author of many books on the science of mind, and who has a large and influential following in Los Angeles, has written a book that emphasizes parallels between the wisdom of *I Ching* and that of the Holy Bible, entitled *Secrets of the I Ching.*

It might be argued that the aura of mysticism is the principle connecting religious-minded persons to the confoundments of *I Ching.* Yet the interest in *I Ching* by both young and old is not restricted to the cloistered domains of religion. High school auditoriums and college campuses are peppered with small groups of students exchanging ideas about the meaning of the cryptic verses of *I Ching.* and many teachers and college professors have discovered through *I Ching* a new entrance into the confidence and affection of their students. A high school teacher who attended an *I Ching* seminar engaged my assistance in outlining his thesis, "Some Philosophical Applications of I Ching For Now," for his doctorate at the University of Southern California. Another student working for his masters

226 • The Eleventh Wing

degree did a paper on "Correspondences Between I Ching and Jung's Psychological Ideas." At the University of California in Los Angeles, at Davis and at Irvine, lectures, and programmed courses on *I Ching* have been scheduled. The academic world is most actively curious about *I Ching*.

One day there came to my office a young man who claimed to be an *I Ching* architect. I asked him, "In what way do you feel your *I Ching* architecture is different from any other?" He answered, "I design a house so that all the rooms have moving parts which are interchangeable. In this way there are endless possibilities of giving a fresh feeling to each room." He had brought no samples of his work to show me, although it remains a fascinating idea. I have no doubt that someone reading this book will pick up the idea and make good application of it.

I Ching is definitely exercising a subtle influence in American life. Not so long ago, a young artist visited our Taoist sanctuary. He noticed that a fountain had been broken. He offered to sculpt a fountain that would express the principles of *I Ching*. "How would you do that?" I queried. "I'll use metal—maybe copper—and sculpt a series of basins bearing the trigrams. I'll make them all movable by both the flow of water and the wafting air. That way as they keep moving around, they will form all the different hexagrams," was his retort. I do not know if he will ever produce his dream, or that we will ever enjoy it as a decoration. But at least I've experienced the excitement of enjoying his vision.

People in all walks of life are becoming aware of *I Ching*. Many now turning to it, unfortunately, do so with an over-zealous passion that will, in most instances, terminate in either painful disillusionment or zombielike enslavement. The average Westerner will not experience the full worth and potency of *I Ching* until, as Cary F. Baynes has so aptly put it, he is "drawn out of the accustomed framework of his thought to view the world in a new perspective, his imagination stimulated and his psychological insight deepened."[27]

I Ching—A Chance for a New Life

At this time in history it seems to many that the entire world is in revolt. Almost everywhere man is searching to supply himself with the things in which he has discovered himself to be deficient. To others, this pursuit for change and supplementation at a new and heightened pace is cause for alarm. There is a near frenzied furor to arrest the onward march. A frantic attempt by some, covertly and overtly, is being made to "return to the good old days." At the same time, others are blatantly or clandestinely seeking for the good old days by grasping after a kind of primeval simplicity and animalistic primitivism. Each camp summons supporters with the rallying slogan that they alone hold the key to the preservation of mankind and human society as it is meant to be. And there is the rub.

One group laments that we are deficient in moral purity. The other charges that we are overburdened with moral hypocrisy. One side calls for a return to individual freedom through an economy of uncontrolled capitalistic competition. The other side demands freedom from want, exploitation and ignorance for each individual through increased socialization and controls of the economy, business and labor. Of these two most articulate voices, one cries for a moratorium on change, while the other carols for easy acceptance. The situation is well described by Alvin Toffler:

> . . . there is danger that those who treasure the status quo may seize upon the concept of future shock as an excuse to argue for a moratorium on change. Not only would any such attempt to suppress change fail, triggering even bigger, bloodier and more unmanageable changes than any we have seen, it would be moral lunacy as well. By any set of human standards, certain radical social changes are already desperately overdue. The answer to future shock is not non-change, but a different kind of change.[28]

I Ching offers us one of the ways for making that different kind of change. Toffler writes that the only way to maintain a semblance of equilibrium during this period of turmoil is "to meet invention with invention—to design new personal and social change-regulators. . . . The individual needs new principles for pacing and planning his life along with a dramatically new kind of education." I believe that the philosophy and psychology of *I Ching* qualifies it as one of these "new kinds of education."[29] If this is so, then *I Ching* is truly a chance for a new life. Its wisdom offers modern man a new concept of his relationship with his environment. Psychologically, involvement with *I Ching* structures new personal behavior patterns which serve to regulate the individual's ability to mesh smoothly with the social changes of the times. While the principle of yin and yang is older than civilization, for this time it constitutes a new principle for man to use in "pacing and planning his life."

There is a great deal of merit to this recommendation. The statement will certainly mean different things to different people. One meaning, from an *I Ching* perspective, is to develop an ability that creatively meets every external technical and societally sys-

Tortoise shell with two of three coins showing: traditionally used by I Ching seers.

temic invention with a correspondingly equal inner invention of developed attitude, fresh emotional focus, a restructured intellectual evaluation and a new dimension of spiritual orientation. It will be by changing the inward structures to match the changed outward structures that we will successfully design the "new personal and social change-regulators" as harmonizing components of the "new kind of education" Toffler suggests.

The six lines, broken and unbroken, of any kua can serve as a key to discovering what the inner inventions should be and how they should be used in order to retain the total self in a harmonious balance with the environment without. Granted that the understanding of *I Ching* that will enable one to do this cannot be "instantized" verbally. It will take considerable time and much study to develop this depth of understanding. The excitements to be gained from studying *I Ching* are not for those who are satisfied with the flavor of instant coffee, or those who can relish the quality of a microwave-heated frozen dinner. But let us take a glimpse at what the potential is.

In the traditional literature, much is made of the fact that the sixty-four kua symbolically embrace the totality of the universe of beingness that is or can be known to the consciousness and experiencing of man. Yet nothing is mentioned of the fact that each kua contains within itself the possibility of every other kua in the system of *I Ching.* As we grasp an understanding of how the particulars of this possibility work, we shall strengthen our ability to change our inward structures to match and regulate the changing outward structures, which while external, are nevertheless attached to us.

Upon reviewing the ancient literature we learn that the Chinese, at one time, conceived of the universe as a cube. This does not mean that they visualized it as a gigantic die. It meant that the universe could be explained in terms of forces graphically related to each other by being assigned to the six sides of a cube. Some elementary exercises and diagrams will be found in a fascinating and secret-laden volume dealing with this and other correspondences of *I Ching,* entitled *The Symbols of Yi King,* by Z. D. Sung.[30]

In the following diagram, consider that the three surfaces constituting corners numbered 1 = Ch'ien, 2 = Tui, 3 = Li, 4 = Chên, 5 = Sun, 6 = K'an, 7 = Kên and 8 = K'un. Those assignments derived from the top left side and facing surfaces are yang, and the

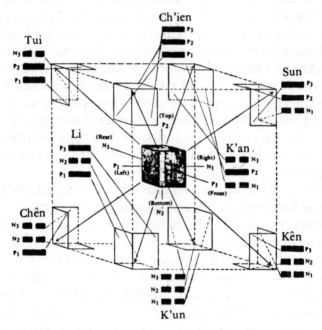

P = Positive (Yao, or Unbroken line)

N = Negative (Yao, or Broken line)

Yao = Line (or Elementary form of Yi Symbols)

1 = 1st (or Lower Yao position)

2 = 2nd (or Middle Yao position)

3 = 3rd (or Upper Yao position)

The Universal Expressed as a Cube of Eight Forces. (The original of this diagram appears in the book The Symbols of Yi King, *by D. Sung.)*

bottom, rear and right side surfaces are yin. The top gives the middle line, the left side gives the bottom line, the front face gives the top line for yang. The bottom gives the middle line, the right side gives the bottom line, the rear side gives the top line for yin. This illustrates how by taking any of the eight corners where three surfaces meet, and assigning it the proper linear image, all of the basic eight kua are contained on the cube.

In considering the individual six-line kua, visualize it as a cube. Study it. Begin by tossing three coins to build a kua with which to demonstrate some interesting points. More exciting discoveries await anyone who seriously turns to the study of the *I*. As an example for your independent study, I will now toss three coins and structure a kua-cube which we will study together. Here are the results of the tosses:

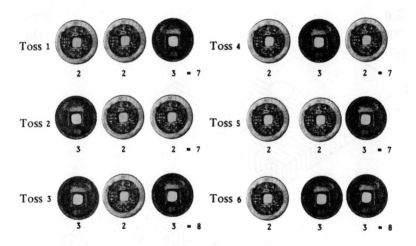

Toss 1   2   2   3 ▪ 7   Toss 4   2   3   2 ▪ 7

Toss 2   3   2   2 ▪ 7   Toss 5   2   2   3 ▪ 7

Toss 3   3   2   3 ▪ 8   Toss 6   2   3   3 ▪ 8

The kua thrown
is Tui—"The Joyous."

The results of the tossing is Tui over Tui, with no moving lines. In order to build a kua-cube, I have invented an *I Ching* study device. It consists of twenty-four wooden tiles, measuring two-and-one-quarter inches square, and three-sixteenths of an inch thick. In the center of each is an eighth-inch hole. There are three basic patterns, and there are six pieces of each pattern. A fifteen-thirty-second inch square of yellow is in the center of each of eighteen of the tiles. The remaining six are solid yellow. Of the eighteen tiles, six are solid black, six are solid red and six are one-half black and one-half red. Below are sketches of the three patterns:

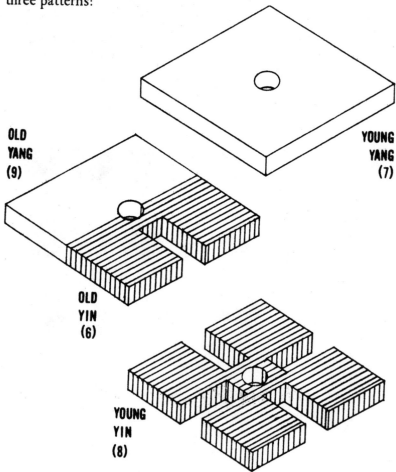

OLD YANG (9)

YOUNG YANG (7)

OLD YIN (6)

YOUNG YIN (8)

The solid red tile has the value of 7, solid black is 8, the red half of the bi-colored tile is 9, while the black half is 6. Keep this information in mind when building and studying a kua-cube, which looks like the following diagram.

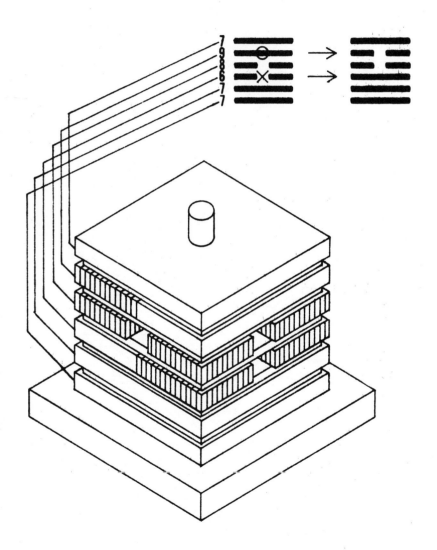

At the present we will be concerned only with observing that theoretically the linear structure of any kua has in itself the necessary potential for becoming any of the other sixty-three kua. By inverting, it becomes Sun over Sun. Changing the third and sixth lines it becomes Ch'ien over Ch'ien. A change of the first, second, fourth and fifth lines produces K'un over K'un. When all of the lines are changed into their opposite it results in Kên over Kên. By changing the first and fourth lines it becomes K'an over K'an. The changing of the second, third, fifth and sixth lines into their opposites gives us Li over Li. Then by a series of combinations of these changes all other kua can be structured. This is a simple graphic illustration of the principle of 'unity in diversity', and, incidentally, the significance of the term "religion," which means "to tie back to the one."

In addition to this very elementary example, there are avenues for studying these kua-cubes which awaken a deeper understanding. I will not here explore at any length any of these avenues. But when one goes in this direction one must at all times be mindful that the lines and the names symbolize a relationship of forces at play. These forces culminate in the actualization of the things being experienced. For example: each place in the kua has a number of references. The fifth place most often holds the ruling line. In those kua where this is so, the line represents the character of authority. As an example, the fourth place expresses the character of the minister. The second place symbolizes the makeup of the official. Remember, these are forces of intelligence and energy we are dealing with. I have already used the coins to set up the kua. In reading the value for each throw of the three coins (using Tui over Tui), we have the ruling line structured by 2+2+3=7. This may be interpreted that in the situation concerned, where authority must react or be exercised, it should do so gently at first, but it should be prepared when necessary to be harsh. The action, energywise, is yin, yin, yang.

Had the coins been arranged or read differently; e.g., 2+3+2=7, then the authoritative action in the situation should open gently, followed by a display of unquestioned ability to be harsh, then ease off to allow for reaction and compliance.

Another concept pictured by a kua, according to the traditions of *I Ching*, is that the lines in the first and second place represent the earth. The lines of the third and fourth place picture man. Those topmost lines in the fifth and sixth place represent heaven. Feeling these as symbolizing forces, another content is discovered.

It is in retraining our thinking, constantly observing our behavior and reactions to situations, discovering the motivation for these, and holding the results next to the image *I Ching* gives us of the same event, that we shall gradually find our way to a new and easier self-assurance. *I Ching* is an instrument that can be helpful to enable us to see ourselves as others see us. The study and application of the wisdom of *I Ching* will bring us closer to an objective understanding and recognition of ourselves. *I Ching* is a discipline that can effectively succeed in subjectively bringing us into an objective self-relationship.

Eleven
Postscript: Some Things I Meant to Write

Study Devices

To recognize the dialectics of the yin-yang philosophy operating in the world about us, make or invent several kinds of *I Ching* study devices. As an example, I will describe some original devices of my invention and explain how they can help to develop one's understanding of *I Ching* so it can be used as a very practical aid in coping with the variety of changes which seem to inundate us from day to day. As we work or play with different kinds of *I Ching* gadgets, we will come to recognize, through symbolic equation, techniques for exercising a more masterful control over our everyday affairs.

Here are a few of my patented *I Ching* study devices: the I Ching Universe-Cube; the Eight Houses Study Cubes and I Ching Oracle Disc. Since students and correspondents have most generously made me gifts of devices of their own making, I will include a couple of these in this presentation.

The I Ching Universe-Cube

One does not have to read *I Ching* for very long before it becomes apparent that the universe is always the deeper implication of all *I Ching* symbolism. "The *Book of Changes* contains the measure of heaven and earth; therefore it enables us to comprehend the Tao of heaven and earth and its order."[1] Another part of this section of Ta Chuan [The Great Treatise], as translated by James Legge, reads:

(Through the Yi), he comprehends as in a mould or enclosure the transformations of heaven and earth without any error; by an ever-varying adaptation he completes (the nature of) all things without exception; he penetrates to a knowledge of the course of day and night (and all other connected phenomena);—it is thus that his operation is spirit-like, unconditioned by place, while the changes which he produces are not restricted to any form.[2]

In the preface to one of his books Z. D. Sung writes:

The uses of Yi have been kept as esoteric secrets by philosophers mainly as a precaution against abuses, and therefore as yet remain a mystery . . . these symbols, when they are together cover one whole, and when separate, cover its parts, and when once assigned with a concept of our universe, they may be applied to entities such as, space, matter, force and time, as marks representing the Changes with which the said Yi King mainly treats as its principle philosophy.[3]

From these and corresponding paragraphs the idea was born to construct a cube model that would reflect the relationships and interrelationships of the symbols of *I Ching* within the universe. The cube form seemed to be the truest way to represent comprehension of the transformation of heaven and earth "as in a mould or enclosure. . . ." The device is structured as an open shell divided to hold four two-inch cubes on a lower level, and four identical cubes on an upper level, as shown in the photographs which follow.

I Ching Universe Cube with Kua Assignment.

1

2

3

Now visualize a cube with its corners numbered from 1 to 8, in such a way that 1 is diagonally opposite 8; 2 is diagonally opposite 7; 3 is diagonally opposite 6; and 4 is diagonally opposite 5. Corner 1 is Ch'ien; 2 is Tui; 3 is Li; 4 is Chên; 5 is Sun; 6 is K'an; 7 is Kên; and 8 is K'un. Paragraph two of chapter six of "The Material," reads:

> Looking upward, we contemplate with its help the signs in the heavens; [1 - Ch'ien], looking down, we examine the lines of the earth. [8 - K'un]. Thus we come to know the circumstances of the dark [6 - K'an], and the light. [3 - Li]. Going back to the beginnings of things [4 - Chên], and pursuing them to the end, [5 - Sun], we come to know the lessons of birth and of death. The union of seed and power produces all things; [7 - Kên], the escape of the soul brings about change. [2 - Tui]. Through this we come to know the conditions of outgoing and returning spirits.[4]

There are innumerable exercises that one can perform with this *I Ching* Universe-Cube. It can be used to get a visual picture of the mechanics of some philosophical or psychological principle, which may be difficult to grasp intellectually. It is also very helpful in interpreting meanings when one is consulting *I Ching* regarding a specific matter. The Universe-Cube is an interesting physio-mental exercise for relaxing, by seeing how many different combinations of changes you can create by turning the cubes about in the shell.

The Eight Houses Study Cubes

This study kit consist of 64 one-inch cubes in a compartmented box (interior measurement 8" x 11" x 1-1/4"). The box has right¹ and left² flaps, each 8" x 11". A top³ flap, 8" x 11" with a fold down lip 1-1/4" along the 11" length. A lower⁴ flap, 8" x 11" completes the box. Each of the 64 one-inch cubes is imprinted on all sides. Side 1 has the linear kua; 2 has the Chinese name; 3 has the English name; 4 has its number; 5 has the two nuclear kua; and 6 has the Chinese character for the kua. The interior of the box is divided into an 8" x 8" compartment, and a 3" x 8" compartment designed to hold a manual of explanation, instructions and suggestions. The 64 one-inch cubes fill the larger compartment, being arranged by houses or any other arrangement desired by the user. On the inner side of flap #4 there is the "Diagram of Cosmic Evolution." The outer side is imprinted with a chart of the calendrical arrangement of the kua. Flap #1 has the "Circular Arrangement" of the kua imprinted on the inner side, with markings indicating the monthly kua and the kua for the solstices and equinoxes. The outer side has a chart of correspondences between the Western astrological zodiac and the appropriate kua. Flap #2's inner side is imprinted with the Buddhist wheel of the "Eight-fold Path" and *I Ching* correspondences. The outer side pictures the eight immortals and the appropriate image of the pa kua. Flap #3's inner side has drawings of the head and hand with the pa kua assigned to the appointed areas of each, with a briefly printed legend explaining the meanings. The outer side is decorated with the name of the device: I Ching Eight Houses Study Cubes.

I Ching Oracle Disc and Interpretation Mandala

The Oracle Disc is a simple wheel upon a wheel device, the larger wheel being fixed and imprinted with the pa kua in the "Primal" arrangement credited to Fu-hsi, the smaller wheel having the pa kua in the "Sequential" or "Later Heaven" arrangement, plus small windows that spiral in toward the center of the wheel. When two kua are lined up so as to structure an image, the appropriate number identifying the combination can be read through the small window directly in line with the kua so aligned. On either side of the disc is printed the number of the kua, with its name, for easy reference.

The reverse side of the Oracle Disc is imprinted with the "*I Ching* Interpretation Mandala." This contains all of the information in the regular "*I Ching* Meditation Mandala" plus correspondences between the astrological signs, the Buddhist "Eight-fold Path" and the proper kua. This latter is truly an exciting and stimulating aid to anyone who must interpret an oracle for someone, or even for oneself.

I Ching-Dex

"I Ching-Dex" is a mechanical aid for use in conjunction with all occasions when an individual consults the wisdom of the *I.* The apparatus was invented at a time when *I Ching* was still comparatively unfamiliar to most Westerners. Errors in ritual and construction of the kua were quite commonly being made. "I Ching-Dex" was invented to furnish a mechanical means of preventing errors of execution by persons consulting *I Ching*.

It is basically a method and apparatus for determining and studying philosophical and oracle responses while simultaneously encompassing the commonly called element of chance, and bears a relationship to the phenomenon of tachyon energy impulses, as are found to be operative in a causalistic or acausalistic environment or both.

This apparatus is constructed so that when the instructions are followed it will visually indicate in order, individually, each of the six symbols that constitute a kua. This initial linear

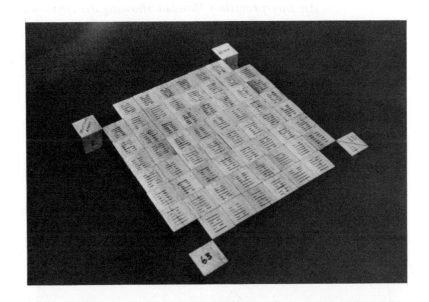

Eight-Houses Study Cubes.

An Interpretation Mandala showing the tie-in with the

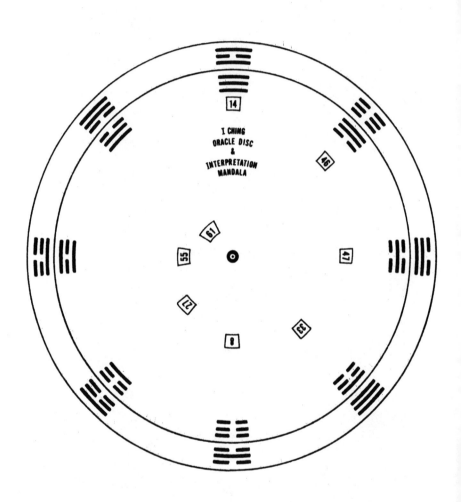

Buddhist Four Noble Truths and Eightfold Path.

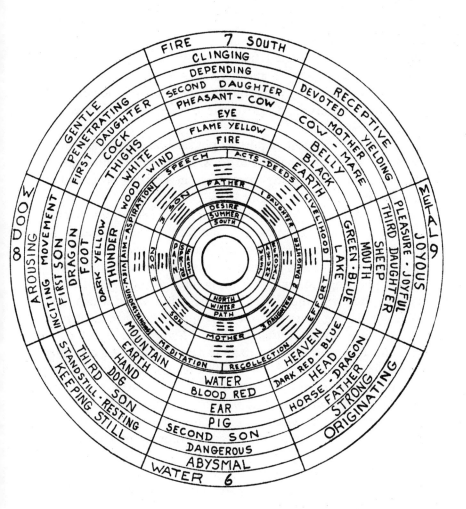

structure, known as the 'synchronic' kua, appears through six windows to the right of center on the face of the device. To the left of center of the device are six additional windows which, automatically, as the linear symbols appear in the right window, cause other symbols to appear in the left window. These left window symbols reproduce what is known as the two 'nuclear' kua, which are extracted from the 'synchronic' kua. On the back of the apparatus is another set of six windows. Through these, simultaneously, while the 'synchronic' and 'nuclear' kua are being structured, so also is the so-called 'transformed', or 'changed lines' kua.

Thus the three most important physical operations are safely executed by this mechanical process. There can be no marking the wrong line, no setting them down in a wrong order and no mistake in noting the changing lines.

When one has the 'synchronic' kua, it is dialed on the "Oracle Disc" device that is centered on the face of the apparatus. By turning the inner disc with the pa kua symbols so that a particular symbol lines up with another on the larger outer disc, thus duplicating the symbol showing through the right of center window, one will find through a small window (of which there are eight) in the inner disc the appropriate number identifying the kua. One now can use either the *I Ching* cards which come with the apparatus, or turn to a favorite text of one's choosing. On the back of the cards are the line readings for each kua. An advantage of the cards is that one is able to spread out before them all of the wisdom pertaining to their situation, so that it can comfortably be cross-studied. This, of course, is not possible when using a book, as it requires flipping pages back and forth to complete any cross-reference one may be intent upon.

In addition, this apparatus has a chart of the calendar assignments of the kua for the year. On the under side of the apparatus is a number and name index to the kua, and a mandala containing information about seven selected attributes indicating meaningful dimensions and aspects to a consultation. As a bonus offering there is secreted in the device a panel which holds a set of three finest quality reproductions of ancient

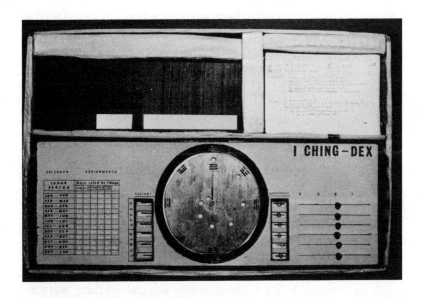

I Ching Dex.

Chinese coins. At present there are only a few "I Ching-Dex" in existence. Each was made manually to order, and was very expensive. It is possible that arrangements may soon be completed to have them manufactured in quantities sufficient to supply a mass market. This should greatly reduce the cost of "I Ching-Dex."

I Ching Cards

A deck of cards consisting of several of the classical diagrammatic arrangements of the pa kua, and sixty-four kua cards with Judgment and Image readings on the face, and line readings on the back were beautifully designed by Mrs. Helen Walker. She has had the initiative to organize her project so that "I Ching Cards" are now published by I Ching Productions in San Francisco, California.

There are any number of ways in which these cards may be used to develop one's understanding of and working with the principles of I Ching.

I Ching Cards.

I Ching Pyramid Kua

This study device was invented by Pharian D'Fucci. Its base is a diamond-shaped board upon which has been arranged sixty-four pegs, so spaced that each peg is able to accommodate a disc that is approximately one-and-a-quarter inch in diameter. Each disc is then surmounted with another slightly smaller disc, until there is a pyramid of six discs. Each disc (being either dark or light), represents a yin or yang line. By the studious rearrangement of the disc one develops a deep sense of forces at play. When one is able to observe the forces at play externally, it is a more simple matter, then, to begin to recognize these forces at play within one's self and the world about one. Mr. D'Fucci is a student of architecture, which is to say that he is fascinated with forms. Forms are the results of 'change'. It is through his interest in 'change' that we may yet hear from him architecturally. He is also responsible for most of the diagrams in this volume.

I Ching Pyramid Kua.

A Higher Teaching

By now it must be obvious that there has been no endeavor to pass on ultimatums, declare absolutes or pronounce the final dogma so that the reader can close the book comfortably certain that now, at last, he or she has a mastery of *I Ching*. Those who bravely attempt to spell out how a passage should be interpreted deserve either our admiration or our compassion. Any intent to wrap the *I* neatly in an explanation is like trying to package the full scent of a flower; or to seal in a can the total fragrance of a pine forest.

The higher teaching of *I Ching* cannot be verbalized. There is a teaching, but nowhere outside of yourself is there a teacher. Seminars, such as are sponsored by the International I Ching Studies Institute, are a compromise to accommodate Western emotional and intellectual impatience. The true teaching comes to the student when he is given problems to solve with *I Ching*. His solutions become the evidence of his success or failure in meeting the test that evaluates his learning accomplishment.

For what is *I Ching* if not a philosophy of life processes designed to develop within the student stronger powers of attention and concentration, and a harmonic rhythm that gives him control over all negative emotions? Control does not mean the elimination of negative emotions; but the constructive and productive use of them. When *I Ching* is mastered, one will experience a fuller awareness of one's environment, a sense of expanded peripheral vision, and heightened sensitivity through many other kinds of sensory clues.

This book does not claim to be the final revelation on *I Ching*. I've tried to present facts and views which might awaken and stimulate a sense of timely usefulness to be found in this amazingly long-enduring philosophy. It deals with 'change'. Surely the importance of being adaptable to 'change' can be recognized by all of us. As we stumble into a new age where the social structure is developing a repetitive computerized sameness (with promises of deep psychological monotony), we shall have to readjust not only to concepts of uni-sex, but to conditions of mono-dimensional experiences. This vision is not as fanciful as it may appear. We have only to consider that one of the primary concerns with the training programs of our astronauts is that of enabling them to adapt their consciousness to withstand extended periods of little or no change . . . that itself being the 'change'!

We have touched upon many facets and relationships of *I Ching* as a discoverable working phenomenon in a variety of social, scientific, physiological, musical, psychological and other areas of contemporary man's involvements. This *Eleventh Wing* will have successfully realized its intent, when the student comes to recognize that he or she has developed a sharpened competency in applying the basic principles of *I Ching* to his or her affairs. As one gains strength by deciding in situations of indecision; clarifying phases of confusion, and reenforcing resolutions with bold determination, one will awaken to a new concern: "How are kua evolved from one another?"

The study of this process is the next step in developing one's efficiency in utilizing the timely and enduring schemata of change. In none of the twenty or more books in English, dealing with *I Ching*, has an author dealt with this phase of usage.* To contemplate and practice the use of this wisdom as a blueprint for all evolutionary processes, signifies that the novitiate is preparing for a higher confirmation. In colleges and universities of China, where *I Ching* is taught as a meaningfully important foundation to most Chinese thought, the evolutionary process is emphasized. In order for this wisdom to serve a purpose other than fortune-telling, Westerners will have to probe into the binary expressed computeristics of the linear images depicting the infinite permutations of 'change'.

*A volume has just come to my attention authored by Wallace Andrew Sherril, which I hastily add to the bibliography. I haven't, as yet, given it more than a cursory perusal, which leads me to believe that Mr. Sherril may have treated the evolutionary process depicted in *I Ching*. If this is so, he is the first Western writer to carry an exposition of the *I* this further step.

Jung touched upon the thought when he wrote that knowing how a tree becomes a seed helps one to understand how a seed becomes a tree. This is but another way of expressing the forward and backward movements which are expressed inherently by the nature of yin and yang via the ever manifesting tao.

The evolutionary process is not a specific or rigidly defined condition or state of *I Ching*, but rather a method of usage. Those who are familiar with the Korean relish, *kim chee*, will understand this point. Many who are only partly initiated into the refinements of Korean cusine do not know that *kim chee* is a style of preparing many kinds of foods, and not just hot pickled cabbage. So it is with the evolutionary process of *I Ching*. There is the fifteen-phase cycle, the twelve-phase cycle, the nine- and eight-phase cycles. These may be identified as: 1. A Cosmic cycle (10, the number of earth plus, 5, the number of heaven), having fifteen phases to it. 2. The Horary cycle, consisting of twelve phases, and concerned with matters of time, like the twelve yin and twelve yang hours which make up a day; twelve months that make up the year, the twelve cycles of the sexegenary measure, etc. 3. The Completion cycle of nine phases, that is most useful in blueprinting a program of activity leading to some desired goal. 4. The Sequential cycle that is excellent for analysing a condition or the make-up of a particular situation or thing.

The mechanics for working with the evolutionary process of *I Ching* are considerably more complicated and will be examined and explained in a future work exploring other areas of more advanced studies into *I Ching*. Thus, *The Eleventh Wing* is merely a primer of *I Ching* studies. It only hopes to ready one for promotion from kindergarten into graded and more evolved studies which, once undertaken, may prove to be a reservoir of ever new and exciting discoveries for the rest of your life.

Notes

Preface

1. Shafica Karagulla, M.D., *Breakthrough to Creativity* (Los Angeles: De Vorss & Co., 1967), p. 17.
2. R. G. H. Siu, *The Man of Many Qualities: A Legacy of the I Ching* (Cambridge, Mass.: M.I.T. Press, 1968), p. vi.
3. *The Masters of the Secret Teachings.*

Chapter One

1. Hellmut Wilhelm, *Change: Eight Lectures on the I Ching* (New York: Harper Torchbooks, 1960), p. 3.
2. Donald F. Lach, *The Preface to Leibniz Novissima Sinica* (University of Hawaii Press, 1957), p. 35.
3. Bertrand Russell, *The Practice and Theory of Bolshevism* (London: George Allen & Unwin Ltd., 1920), pp. 117-118. (Taken from: *Dictionary of Mind, Matter and Morals,* edited by Lester E. Denonn, New York: Citadel Press, 1965, p. 216).

4. Richard Wilhelm, *I Ching: or Book of Changes*, translation by Cary F. Baynes. Foreword by C. G. Jung (New York: Bollingen Series XIX, Pantheon Books, 1962), Judgment to Kua 51, p. 210.

5. Bertrand Russell, "The Essence of Religion," in the *Hibbert Journal*, October, 1912, p. 59.

6. Hellmut Wilhelm, *Change: Eight Lectures*, op. cit., p. ix.

7. Ambrose Bierce, "Consult." *The Devil's Dictionary* (New York: Castle Books, 1967).

8. R. G. H. Siu, *The Tao of Science* (Cambridge, Mass.: M.I.T. Press, 1957), p. 69.

9. Ibid., p. 83.

Chapter Two

1. R. G. H. Siu, *The Man of Many Qualities*, op. cit., pp. 8-9.

2. Fung Yu-Lan, *A History of Chinese Philosophy*, Tr. by Dirk Bodde (Princeton: Princeton University Press, 1952), Vol. II, p. 459.

3. *Huai Nan Tzu (The Cosmology of Huai Nan Tzu)*, as quoted by Fung Yu-Lan, Vol. I, p. 395.

4. Ibid.

5. Ibid.

6. Ibid., p. 396

7. Ibid.

8. Ibid.

9. Ibid.

10. Ibid.

11. John Dewey, *A Dictionary of Education*, edited by Ralph. B. Winn (New York: Philosophical Library, 1959), p. 82.

12. Wilhelm/Baynes, *I Ching*, op. cit., Vol. II, p. 350.

13. John Dewey, *Dictionary of Education*, op. cit., p. 8.

14. Wing-Tsit Chan, *A Source Book in Chinese Philosophy* (Princeton, N.J.: Princeton University Press, 1963), p. 783.

15. Ibid.

16. There is a charming Zen anecdote that concludes with the caution: "Do not mistake the pointing finger for the moon."

17. Wing-Tsit Chan, op. cit., p. 784.

18. Ibid.

19. Ibid.

20. Fung Yu-Lan, op. cit., Vol. 1, p. 163.
21. Ibid., p. 166, (quoting Kuan-Tzu, Chapter 39).
22. Ibid., p. 166.
23. Ibid., p. 167.
24. Ibid., p. 167.
25. William Theodore de Bary, Wing-Tsit Chan and Burton Watson, *Sources of Chinese Traditions* (New York: Columbia University Press, 1960), Vol. I, p. 199.
26. Ibid.
27. Wing-Tsit Chan, *A Source Book in Chinese Philosophy*, op. cit., p. 248.
28. Wilhelm/Baynes, *I Ching*, op. cit., Book II, p. 283.
29. Ibid., p. 284-285.
30. Lao Tzu, *Tao Te Ching*, translated by Dr. John C. H. Wu, edited by Dr. Paul K. T. Sih (New York: St. John's University Press, 1961), Chapter 11, p. 15.
31. The Bible, Ecclesiastes 3:1-8.
32. The Bible, Genesis 1:5.
33. Fung Yu-Lan, *A History of Chinese Philosophy*, op. cit., Vol. 1, pp. 395-396.
34. Lecomte du Noüys, *Human Destiny* (New York, London, Toronto: Longmans, Green and Co., 1947), p. 10.
35. William Irwin Thompson, "Planetary Vistas," in *Harper's* magazine, December, 1971.
36. Ibid.
37. Lao Tzu, *Tao Te Ching*, translated by Ch'u Ta-Kao (London: George Allen & Unwin, 19   ), p. 57.
38. Lao Tzu, *Tao Te Ching*, Chapter 37. There are many translations using different words as equivalents. However the meaning of all of them is the same.
39. Ibid., Chapter 4, "Ch'u."
40. Paul Carus, *The Canon of Reason and Virtue* (Lasalle, Ill.: Open Court Publishing Co., 1913-1927), p. 103.
41. Ibid., p. 103 (end of Chapter 41.)
42. Lao Tzu, *Tao Te Ching*, p. 57., "Ch'u, F-1."
43. Ibid.
44. Lecomte du Noüys, *Human Destiny*, op. cit., p. 7.
45. Ibid., p. 19.
46. Lao Tzu, *Tao Te Ching*, Chapter 63.
47. Wilhelm/Baynes, *I Ching*, op. cit., Vol. I, p. 16.

48. Ibid.
49. Ibid.
50. Ibid.
51. C. G. Jung and W. Pauli, *The Interpretation of Nature and the Psyche* (New York: Bollingen Series 1955, Pantheon Books, 1955), pp. 134 and 137.
52. Joseph Needham, "Time and Knowledge in Ancient China," in *The Voices of Time* by Fraser (New York: George Braziller, 1966), p. 93, and n. 4, p. 608.
53. Wilhelm/Baynes, *I Ching,* op. cit., p. 285.
54. Ibid., p. 290.
55. Ibid., p. 289.
56. Ibid., p. 291.
57. Ibid., p. 290.
58. Ibid., p. 289.
59. Ibid., p. 287.
60. Ibid., p. 286.
61. Ibid., p. 286.
62. *Penguin Dictionary of English* (Baltimore: Penguin Books, 1965).
63. Fung Yu-Lan, op. cit., Vol. II, pp. 169-172, 174-175, 179-180, 180-189, 205, 207, 235 and 445. (See also Footnote 2, "Section on explaining the second appendix. See Chou Yi, 109-110. Ch'ien, the first hexagram, symbolizes masculinity, and therefore has firmness as its characteristic. K'us, the second hexagram, symbolizes femininity, and therefore has compliance as its characteristic. . . .")
64. Ibid., p. 184.
65. Ibid., p. 184.
66. Ibid., p. 184.
67. Wilhelm/Baynes, op. cit., p. xiv.
68. Ibid., p. xx.
69. There are a variety of ways to perform this experiment if one is interested in understanding the point of subtle differences. One may point to a second person with the index finger, making a comment about that person to a third person. Then point to yet another person with your little finger, making a comment again to the third person about the person you are now "pinky-pointing" at. Then ask the third person what their reaction or evaluation was of your statement, you, and the person you pointed to each time. See if they felt a difference when you pointed with your little finger. In this way you will get an idea how your pointing with a particular finger

not only changes your relationship to the subject, but how it can also effect the relationship between the subject and everyone you bring into relationship with it.

70. Wilhelm/Baynes, *I Ching*, op. cit., p. 235.
71. Robert O. Ballou, editor, *The Bible of the World* (New York: Viking Press, 1939-1959), "The Works of Chuang Tzu: Life is a Dream," p. 511.
72. Wilhelm/Baynes, *I Ching*, op. cit., p. 388.

Chapter Three

1. Raymond Van Over, *I Ching* (New York: New American Library, 1971), p. 14.
2. Charles Ponce, *The Nature of the I Ching* (New York: Award Books, 1970), p. 3.
3. Ibid.
4. Ibid.
5. Ibid., p. 17.
6. Wilhelm/Baynes, op. cit., p. ii.
7. Wing-Tsit Chan, *A Source Book in Chinese Philosophy*, op. cit., p. 265.
8. Ibid., p. 267.
9. A. Cornelius Benjamin, "Ideas of Time in the History of Philosophy," in *The Voices of Time*, edited by J. T. Fraser (New York: George Braziller, 1966), pp. 14-15, see also Note 28, p. 599.
10. Ibid., p. 599.
11. *Nan-Hua Chen-Ching*, Chapter 7 ("Pure Classic of Nan-Hua," another name for the *Chuang Tzu*), 3:35b-36a, as quoted by Wing-Tsit Chan in *A Source Book of Chinese Philosophy*, op. cit., p. 207.
12. Joseph Needham, "Time and Knowledge in China and the West," contribution to *The Voices of Time*, op. cit., p. 119.
13. Wilhelm/Baynes, *I Ching*, op. cit., p. 141.
14. William Russell White, *Leadership*, Vol. I (Boston, Mass.: Meador Publishing, 1951), p. 1018.
15. James Strong, S.T.D., LL.D., *Strong's Exhaustive Concordance of the Bible* (New York: Abingdon Press, 1890), research and statistics compiled from this reference.
16. R. G. H. Siu, *The Tao of Science*, op. cit., p. 29.

Chapter Four

1. Wilhelm/Baynes, *I Ching,* op. cit., p. ii.
2. Ibid., pp. ii-iii.
3. Pierre Teilhard de Chardin, *The Phenomenon of Man* (New York: Harper & Row, 1955), p. 149.
4. Ibid.
5. C. G. Jung, *The Archetypes and the Collective Unconscious,* Vol. 9, *Collected Works* (New York: Bollingen Series XX, Pentheon Books, 1959), p. 38.
6. "The Hunter's Quest," San Juan de la Cruz (Saint John of the Cross), 1542-1591. Original name: Juan de Yepis y Álvarez.
7. Wilhelm/Baynes, *I Ching,* op. cit., p. 302.

Chapter Five

1. Jordan Scher, ed., *Theories of the Mind: Mind as Memory and Creative Love* (New York: Free Press of Glencoe, 1962), pp. 440-463.
2. Charles Hartshorne, "Mind as Memory and Creative Love," contribution to *Theories of the Mind,* op. cit., p. 446.
3. Ibid., p. 458.
4. Ibid., p. 458.
5. Ibid., p. 452.
6. Ibid., p. 451.
7. Ibid., p. 451.
8. Matthew 12:30.
9. This is a free rendition from memory of Chapter 11 of the *Tao Te Ching.* A reference to any translation will very closely parallel this rendition as it does not deviate from the meaning of the passage.
10. Lao Tzu, *Tao Te Ching,* "Ch'u," p. 23.
11. Lao Tzu, *The Way of Life,* translated by R. B. Blakeney (New York: Mentor/New American Library, 1955), p. 63.
12. *The Book of Tao,* translated by Frank J. MacHovec (Mount Vernon, N.Y.: Peter Pauper Press, 1962), p. 42.
13. Lao Tzu, *Tao Teh King,* translated by Archie J. Bohm (New York: Frederick Ungar, 1958), pp. 18-19.
14. Lao Tzu, *Tao Te Ching* (op. cit., Wu/Sih translation), p. 15.
15. Juan-Eduardo Cirlot, *Dictionary of Symbols* New York: Philosophical Library, 1962), p. 221.

16. Marshall McLuhan, "Telecommunications: One World Mind," quoted in *Kaiser News*, No. 6 of The Market of Change series (Kaiser Aluminum and Chemical Corp. publication, 1971), p. 4.
17. Lawrence K. Frank, *The World as a Communications Network*.
18. Wilhelm/Baynes, *I Ching*, op. cit., p. 281.
19. Ibid., p. 315.
20. Ibid., p. 316.
21. Ibid., p. 317.
22. Ibid., p. 318.
23. Ibid., pp. 318-319.
24. John-Paul Sartre, *The Psychology of Imagination* (New York: Citadel Press/Philosophical Library, 1948), p. 133.
25. Quoted from *Kaiser News*, cited above, p. 33.

Chapter Six

1. Gustaf Stromberg, *Man, Mind and the Universe* (Los Angeles: Science of Mind Publications, 1966), p. 50.
2. Lao Tzu, *Tao Te Ching*, (op. cit., Wu/Sih translation), p. 53.
3. Stromberg, op. cit., p. 52.
4. Lao Tzu, *Tao Te Ching* (op. cit., Wu/Sih translation), p. 59.
5. Lao Tzu, *The Way of Life* (op. cit., Blakney translation), p. 93.
6. Lao Tzu, *Tao Te Ching* op. cit., p. 55, Chu translation.
7. *Science News*, Vol. 101, No. 7 (97-112), Feb. 12, 1972, p. 104.
8. Ibid.
9. Ibid.
10. This is a scene from Lewis Carroll's enduring classic.
11. Louis T. Culling, *I Ching—The Prophetic Book of Changes* (New York: Life Resources Institute, 1966), p. 8.
12. Fung Yu-Lan, *Chinese Philosophy*, Vol. II, p. 184.
13. Flora Davis, "Brain Training," in *Glamour*, Vol. 64, No. 2, October, 1970, p. 170.
14. Ibid.

Chapter Seven

1. John Caffrey and Charles J. Mosmann, *Computers on Campus*, American Council on Education, 1967 (excerpts).

2. Fung Yu-Lan, *Chinese Philosophy*, Vol. 1, p. 383, Appendix iii to the *I Ching* as quoted herein.
3. Ibid., p. 383.
4. Ibid., p. 388.
5. Ibid., p. 388.

Chapter Eight

1. Eva C. Hangen, *Symbols—Our Universal Language* (Wichita, Kan.: McCormick Armstrong Co., 1962), pp. 105-106 and p. 200.
2. Carl G. Jung, *Man and His Symbols* (New York: Doubleday, 1964), pp. 282-283.
3. Juan-Eduardo Cirlot, *Dictionary of Symbols*, p. 101.
4. Wilhelm/Baynes, *I Ching*, op. cit., p. 25.
5. Louis Pauwels and Jacques Bergier, *Morning of the Magicians* (New York: Stein & Day, 1960), p. 143.
6. Ibid., p. 139.
7. Arnold van Gennep, *The Rites of Passage* (Chicago: Phoenix Books/ University of Chicago Press, 1960), p. 3.
8. J. W. Dunne, *An Experiment with Time* (New York: Macmillan Co., 1938), pp. 7-8.
9. Joseph Needham, "Time and Knowledge in China and the West," in the *Voices of Time*, edited by J. T. Fraser (New York: George Braziller, 1960), p. 97.
10. J. W. Dunne, op. cit., pp. 32-33.
11. Ernest Cassirer, *Language and Myth* (New York: Dover Press, 1946), p. 9.
12. Edward Sapir, *Language*, (New York: Harcourt Brace, 1921), p. 15.
13. Rudolf Arnheim, *Visual Thinking* (London: Faber & Faber, 1969), p. 228.
14. Ibid., p. 157.
15. E. R. Hughes, "Epistemological Methods in Chinese Philosophy," paper in *The Chinese Mind*, edited by Charles A. Moore (Honolulu, Hawaii: East-West Center Press, 1967), p. 86.
16. Robert Keith Wallace and Herbert Benson, "The Psychology of Meditation," in *Scientific American*, Vol. 226, No. 2, February, 1972, pp. 85-90.
17. *Our Healing Auras*, (as told by Elaine Jacobs), Tampa, Fla., 1967.

18. Epistle to the Hebrews XI:4.
19. The Taming Power of the Small: (Kua 9) Hsiao Ch'u. By pulling the characters apart and analyzing them, one will discover a very deep and expansive content being indicated. The Chinese characters are •*J.* Hsiao 𣪠 Ch'u. (L. Wieger, in his classic *Chinese Characters—Their Origin, Etymology, History, Classification and Signification* (New York: Dover Press, 1965), [first published in 1915], comments as follows: " •*J.* Hsiao. Small, trifling, mean. This idea is represented by the partition of an object already small by its nature . . . it is the 42nd radical. It forms Chien. Point, sharp. A big object (L. 60) that becomes small on its top." The character Yao represents the idea of the "lightest thread, as it is obtained by the simultaneous winding of two cocoons." Wieger writes: "To put (L. 15) the thread in the dye; dyed thread; green color (later on the black one, on account of certain Taoist theories)." The bottom portion of the character Ch'u is 🔯 . Wieger describes it as: "T'ien. Field, country. It represents a furrowed field . . . this character being simple and easy to write is often used, as a symbol, for any object." Thus, what seems to be implied by "Hsiao Ch'u," is definitively expressed in Wilhelm's commentary for Kua 9.

Chapter Nine

1. E. R. Hughes, "Epistomological Methods in Chinese Philosophy," in *The Chinese Mind*, edited by Charles Moore, op. cit., p. 96.
2. Fung Yu-Lan, *Chinese Philosophy*, Vol. II, pp. 40-41.
3. Ibid., p. 26. "Diagram of Annual Revolution of the Yin and Yang as described in the Huai Nan Tzu." Here the diagram is righted (inverted and spun around) to conform with the Chinese principle of direction: south being placed at the top, north at the bottom, which necessarily switches east and west from their normal placements.
4. Ibid., p. 28. "Tung Chung-shu's Theory of Annual Movements of the Yin and Yang." Again the diagram has been switched and turned to have it conform to the visual concepts of the Chinese traditional compass.
5. Ibid., Vol. I, p. 391.
6. Ibid., Vol. I, pp. 388-389.

Chapter Ten

1. Lao-Tzu, *Tao Te Ching* (op. cit., Wu/Sih translation), pp. 59-60.
2. *Webster's Third New International Dictionary* (Chicago, London, etc.: Encyclopedia Britannica, 1954, 1955, 1956, 1958, 1959).
3. Wilhelm/Baynes, *I Ching*, op. cit., p. 246.
4. Ibid., p. 247.
5. Alfred Douglas, *How to Consult the I Ching* (New York: G. P. Putnam's Sons, 1971), p. 42.
6. Ibid., p. 43.
7. Ibid., pp. 43-44.
8. José Argüelles, "Compute and Evolve," in *Main Currents in Modern Thought*, Vol. 25, No. 3, January-February, 1969.
9. Joseph Edkins, "The Yi King, with Notes on the 64 Kua," *China Review*, Vol. 12., 1883-84, pp. 77-78. Also pp. 412-432. "The Yi King and its Appendices," *China Review*, Vol. 14, 1885-86, pp. 303-322. (Contains diagram of 64 Kua on the Horizon), p. 309.
10. F. Huberty James, "The History of I Ching," in *The Chinese Recorder*, July 1898.
11. Thomas McClatchie, "Confucian Cosmogony," *China Review*, Vol. 4, No. 2 (1875-76), pp. 84-95.
12. A Terrien De Lacouperie, *The Oldest Book of the Chinese, the Yh King and its Authors* (London: D. Nutt, 1892), pp. v-vi.
13. Ibid., pp. xvii-xviii.
14. Kiang Kang-Hu, "The Yi Ching or 'The Book of Changes,' " *China Journal of Science and Arts*, Vol. 3, 1925, pp. 259-264.
15. Ibid.
16. John Cage, *Silence* (Cambridge, Mass.: M.I.T. Press, 1969), p. 57.
17. Ibid., p. 58.
18. Ibid., p. 59.
19. Ralph Metzner, *Maps of Consciousness*, op. cit., p. 24.
20. Ibid., p. 25.
21. Joseph L. Henderson, M.D., "A Commentary on the Book of Changes," in *Psychic Magazine*, Vol. III, No. 2, September-October, 1971, published by Bolen Co., San Francisco., pp. 9-12.
22. Ibid.
23. José Argüelles, "Compute and Evolve," op. cit., pp. 1-5.
24. Ibid.
25. Ibid.

26. William Irwin Thompson, "Planetary Vistas," article in *Harper's* magazine, December, 1971, pp. 71-78.
27. Wilhelm/Baynes, *I Ching.*
28. Alvin Toffler, *Future Shock* (New York: Bantam Books, 1970), p. 373.
29. Ibid.
30. Z. D. Sung, *The Symbols of Yi King* (New York: Paragon Book Reprint Corp., 1969).

Chapter Eleven

1. Wilhelm/Baynes, *I Ching,* op. cit., p. 315.
2. James Legge, *The I Ching* (New York: Dover Publications), p. 354.
3. Z. D. Sung, *The Symbols of Yi King,* op. cit.
4. Wilhelm/Baynes, *I Ching,* op. cit., p. 316.

Bibliography

Albertson, E. *Complete I Ching For the Millions*. Los Angeles: Sherbourne Press, 1970.

Arnheim, Rudolf. *Visual Thinking*. London: Faber and Faber, 1969.

Bahm, Archie J. *Tao Teh King*. New York: Frederick Ungar Publishing, 1958.

Bary, William Theodore de; Chan, Wing Tsit; Watson, Burton. *Sources of Chinese Traditions*. (New York: Columbia University Press, 1960.)

Benoit, H. *The Supreme Doctrine*. New York: Viking Press, 1955-1959.

Blankney, R. B. *The Way of Life—Lao Tzu*. New York: Mentor Classics—New American Library, 1955.

Blofeld, J. *The Book of Change*. New York: E. P. Dutton & Co., 1965.

Bloodworth, D. *The Chinese Looking Glass*. New York: Delta Books—Dell Publishing Co., 1966.

Boyle, V. P. *Yi-King, Tao*. Chicago: Occult Publishing Co., 1929.

Brill, J. *The Chance Character of Human Existence*. New York: Philosophical Library, 1956.

Brown, B. *The Wisdom of the Chinese*. New York: David McKay Co., 1920.

Buber, M. *Ten Rungs.* New York: Schocken Books, 1947.

Bynner, Witter. *The Way of Life—According to Lao Tzu.* New York: Capricorn Books, 1944-1962.

Caffrey, John and Charles J. Mosman, *Computers on Campus,* American Council on Education.

Cage, J. *Silence.* Cambridge, Massachusetts: M.I.T. Press, 1939.

Carus, P. *The Canon of Reason and Virtue.* La Salle, Illinois: Open Court Publishing Co., 1913-1927.

Cassirer, E. *Language and Myth.* New York: Dover Press, 1946.

Chai, C., and Chai, W. *The Humanist Way in Ancient China.* New York: Bantam Books, 1965.

Chan, W-T. *A Source Book in Chinese Philosophy.* Princeton, New Jersey: Princeton University Press, 1963.

Chang, C. *The Development of Neo-Confucian Thought.* New York: Bookman Association, 1957.

Chang, C-Y. *Original Teachings of Chan Buddhism.* New York: Pantheon, 1969.

———. *Creativity and Taoism.* New York: Harper Colophon Books, Harper & Row, 1963.

de Chardin, P. T. *Man's Place in Nature.* New York: Harper & Row, 1956.

———. *The Phenomenon of Man.* New York: Harper & Row, 1955.

Chen, L-F. *Philosophy of Life.* New York: Philosophical Library, 1948.

Ch'u, Ta-Kao. *Tao Te Ching.* London: George Allen & Unwin Ltd., 1937.

Christie, A. *Chinese Mythology.* Middlesex, England: Hamlyn Publishing Group, 1968.

Cirlot, J.-E. *A Dictionary of Symbols.* New York: Philosophical Library, 1962.

Creel, H. G. *Chinese Thought—from Confucius to Mao Tse-tung.* New York: Mentor Books, 1953.

Culling, L. T. *The Incredible I Ching.* Cheltenham, Glostershire: Helios Book Service Ltd., 1965.

———. *I Ching—the Prophetic Book of Changes.* New York: Life Resources Institute, 1966.

Dawson, R. *The Legacy of China.* Oxford, England: Oxford-Clorendon Press, 1964.

De Bary, William T., ed., *Sources of Chinese Tradition.* (Compiled by de Bary, Chan, & Watson), New York: Columbia University Press, 1960.

De Bono, E. *The Mechanism of Mind.* New York: Simon & Schuster, 1969.

Dewey, J. *Dictionary of Education.* Edited by Ralph B. Winn. New York: Philosophical Library, 1959.

Do Dinh, P. *Confucius and Chinese Humanism.* Translated by C. L. Markmann. New York: Funk & Wagnall, 1969.

Douglas, A. *How to Consult the I Ching.* New York: G. P. Putnam's Sons, 1971.

Dunne, J. W. *An Experiment with Time.* New York: Macmillan Co., 1938.

———. *The Serial Universe.* London: Faber & Faber, 1934.

Eranos Year Books. *Spirit and Nature.* Bollingen Series XXX-1, Pantheon.

———. *The Mysteries.* Bollingen Series XXX-2, Pantheon, 1955.

———. *Spiritual Disciplines.* Bollingen Series XXX-4, Pantheon, 1960.

———. *The Mystic Vision.* Bollingen Series XXX-6, Princeton, New Jersey: Princeton University Press, 1968.

———. *Man and Time.* Bollingen Series XXX-3, New York: Pantheon, 1957.

Fitzgerald, C. P. *China—A Short Cultural History.* New York: Frederick A. Proega, 1935.

Fraser, J. T. *The Voices of Time.* New York: George Braziller, 1966.

Fuller, R. B. *Nine Chains to the Moon.* London: Southern Illinois University Press, 1938-1963.

Fung, Y-L. *The Spirit of Chinese Philosophy.* Translated by E. R. Hughes. Boston, Massachusetts: Beacon Press, 1947.

———. *History of Chinese Philosophy.* Translated by Dirk Bodde. 2 Vols. Princeton, New Jersey: Princeton University Press, 1952.

Gennep, A. van. *The Rites of Passage.* Chicago, Illinois: University of Chicago Press, 1960.

de Givry, G. *Witchcraft, Magic & Alchemy.* Translated by J. C. Locke. Frederick Publishers, 1954.

Glessner, N. *Confucius, the Man and the Myths.*

Goodman, M. *Modern Numerology.* New York: Paperback Library, 1968.

Guiman, Gerold. *Taoist Ideas of Prolongevitism.* Transactions of the American Philosophical Society. Vol. 56, Part 9. Philadelphia, 1966.

Gutheil, E. A. *The Handbook of Dream Analysis.* New York: Washington Square Press-Liverwright, 1951.

Hangen, E. C. *Symbols—Our Universal Language.* Wichita, Kansas: McCormick-Armstrong Co., 1962.

Hartshorne, C. "Mind as Memory and Creative Love." *Theories of the Mind.* Edited by Jordan Sher. New York: Free Press of Glercoe, 1962.

Hashimoto, M. *Japanese Acupuncture.* New York: Liverwright, 1966.

Hawkes, D. *Ch'u Tz'u—The Songs of the South.* Boston Massachusetts: Beacon Press, 1959.

Hellerman, L. and Stein, R. L. *China—Readings on the Middle Kingdom.* New York: Washington Square Press, 1971.

Herbert, E. *A Taoist Notebook.* Wisdom of the East Series. London: John Murray, 1955.

Hoffer, E. *The Ordeal of Change.* New York: Harper & Row, 1963.

Huard, P. and Wong, M. *Chinese Medicine.* New York: World University Library—McGraw-Hill Book Co., 1968.

Hughes, E. R. *The Art of Letters—Lu Chi's "Wen Fu" A.D. 302.* Bollingen Series XXIX, Pantheon, 1951.

Ishihara, A. and Levy, H. S. *The Tao of Sex.* New York: Harper & Row, 1968.

Jayasuriya, W. F. *The Psychology and Philosophy of Buddism.* Colombo, Young Men's Buddhist Association Press, 1963.

Johnson, Willard. *I Ching—An Introduction to the Book of Changes.* Berkeley, California: Shambolu Publications, 1970.

Jung, C. G. *Alchemical Studies.* Bollingen Series XXX. Princeton, New Jersey: Princeton University Press, 1967.

———. *The Spirit in Man, Art and Literature.* Bollingen Series XX. Pantheon, 1966.

———. *The Archetypes and the Collective Unconscious.* Bollingen Series XX. New York: Pantheon, 1959.

———. *Man and His Symbols.* Garden City, New York: Doubleday & Co., 1964.

——— and Pauli, W. *The Interpretation of Nature and the Psyche.* Bollingen Series LI. New York: Pantheon, 1955.

Kaltenmark, M. *Lao Tzu and Taoism.* Stanford, California: Stanford University Press, 1969.

Karagulla, S. *Breakthrough to Creativity.* Los Angeles, California: DeVorss & Co., 1967.

Kwan, K-G. *Chinese Cavalcade.* London: Herbert Jenkins, 1963.

Lao Tsze, *Tao.* Wheaton, Illinois: Theosophical Publishing House, 1926.

Lau, D. C. *Lao Tzu—Tao Te Ching.* Baltimore, Maryland: Penguin Books, 1963-1967.

Lee, Chu, and Wong, K. *I Ching Book of Change.* Tujunga, California: K. King Co., 1971.

Lee, Joy. *Understanding the I Ching.* New Hyde Park, New York: University Books, 1971.

Legge, J. *The I Ching—(1899)*. New York: Dover Publications, 1963.

Legge, J. *The Text of Taoism*. 2 vols. *The T'ao Shong Tractate*, and *The Writings of Chuang Tzu*. New York: Dover Publications, 1962.

Lehner, E. *The Picture Book of Symbols*. New York: William Penn Publishers, 1956.

Leibniz, G. *Novissima Sinica*. Translated by D. F. Lach. Honolulu, Hawaii: University of Hawaii Press, 1957.

Leon-Portilla, M. *Aztec Thought and Culture*. Translated by J. E. Davis. Norman, Oklahoma: University of Oklahoma Press, 1963.

Lessa, W. A. *Chinese Body Divination*. Los Angeles: United World, 1968.

Levenson, J. R. *Liang Ch'i—Ch'ao and the Mind of Modern China*. Berkeley, California: University of California Press, 1967.

Lidstone, R. A. *Studies in Symbology*. London: Theosophical Publishing House, 1926.

Lu, K-Y. *Taoist Yoga, Alchemy and Immortality*. New York: Samuel Weisen, 1970.

MacHouec, F. J. *I Ching—The Book of Changes*. Mt. Vernon, New York: Peter Pauper Press, 1971.

——. *The Book of Tao*. Mt. Vernon, New York: Peter Pauper Press, 1962.

MacKenzie, F. *Chinese Art*. Middlesex, England: Spring Books, 1961.

Mann, F. *The Treatment of Disease by Acupuncture*. London: William Heineman Medical Books Ltd., 1963.

——. *Acupuncture—the Ancient Chinese Art of Healing*. New York: Random House, 1962.

Mears, I. *Tao Teh King*. London: Theosophical Publishing House, 1922.

Medley, M. *A Handbook of Chinese Art*. London: G. Bell & Sons Ltd., 1964.

Metzner, R. *Maps of Consciousness*. New York: Collier Books, 1971.

Moore, C. A. *The Chinese Mind*. Honolulu, Hawaii: East-West Center Press—University of Hawaii Press, 1967.

Morgan, W. P. *Triad Societies In Hong Kong*. Hong Kong: Government Press, 1960.

Moss, H. M. *Chinese Snuff Bottles—A Catalog*. Sussex, England: Hugh Moss Ltd., 1969.

Murphy, G. and Murphy, L. B. *Asian Psychology*. New York: Basic Books, 1968.

Needham, J. *Science and Civilization in Ancient China*. 6 vols. Oxford, England: Oxford Press.

Neumann, E. *The Origins and History of Consciousness*. New York: Harper Torchbooks, Harper & Brothers, 1954.

Osawa, G. *Acupuncture and the Philosophy of the Far East.* Boston, Massachusetts: Order of the Universe Publications.

Palos, S. *The Chinese Art of Healing.* New York. Herder & Herder, 1971.

Paracelsus. *Selected Writings.* Edited by Jolandi Jacobi. New York: Bollingen Series XXVIII, 1951.

Pauwels, L. and Bergier, J. *The Morning of the Magicians.* Translated by Rollo Myers. New York: Stein & Day, 1964.

Ponce, C. *The Nature of the I Ching: Its Usage and Interpretation.* New York: Award Books, 1970.

Rawcliffe, D. H. *The Psychology of the Occult.* London: Derricke Ridgway, 1952.

Rice, T. T. *Ancient Arts of Central Asia.* New York: Frederick Praeger, 1965.

Rudhyar, D. *The Astrology of Personality.* New York: Doubleday, 1936.

Russell, B. *Dictionary of Mind Matter, and Morals.* Edited by L. E. Denonn. New York: Citadel Press, 1965.

Russell, C. F. *Book Chameleon Yi King.* Los Angeles, California, 1967.

Sartre, J-P. *The Psychology of Imagination.* New York: Citadel Press, 1948.

Schafer, E. H. *Ancient China.* New York: Time-Life Books, 1967.

Schilling, H. K. *Science and Religion.* London: George Allen & Unwin Ltd., 1963.

Shah, S. I. *Oriental Magic.* New York: Philosophical Library, 1957.

Shimano, J. *Oriental Fortune-Telling.* Rutland, Vermont: Charles E. Tuttle Co., 1956.

Siu, R. G. H. *The Man of Many Qualities: A Legacy of the I Ching.* Cambridge, Massachusetts: M.I.T. Press, 1968; paperback, *The Portable Dragon.*

——. *The Tao of Science.* Cambridge, Massachusetts: M.I.T. Press, 1957.

Sivin, N. *Chinese Alchemy: Preliminary Studies.* Cambridge, Massachusetts: Harvard University Press, 1968.

Smith, D. H. *Chinese Religions.* New York: Holt, Rinehart & Winston, 1968.

Smith, R. W. *Pa-Kua—Chinese Boxing.* Tokyo, Japan: Kodansha International Ltd., 1967.

Stromberg, G. *Man, Mind, and the Universe.* Los Angeles, California: Science of Mind Publication, 1966.

Sung, Z. D. *The Text of Yi King and Its Appendices—The Symbols of Yi King.* New York: Paragon Book Reprint Corp., 1969.

Swann, P. *Art of China, Korea and Japan.* New York: Frederick A. Praeger, 1967.

Sze, M-M. *The Way of Chinese Painting.* New York: Vintage Books—Random House, 1956-1959.

Tart, C. *Altered States of Consciousness.* Edited Collection. New York: John Wiley & Sons, Inc., 1969.

Toffler, A. *Future Shock.* New York: Bantam Book—Random House, 1970.

Tulku, T. *Kalachakra.* (Tibetan Astrological Chart.)

Van Over, R. *I Ching.* New York: Mentor Book, New American Library, 1971.

Veith, I. *Huang Ti Nei Ching Su Wen—The Yellow Emperor's Classic of Internal Medicine.* Berkeley, California: University of California Press, 1966.

Waley, A. *The Way and Its Power.* New York: Evergreen, Grove Press, 1958.

——. *The Travels of an Alchemist.* (The journey of the Taoist Ch'ang Chun as recorded by his disciple Li Chih-Ch'ang.) London: Routledge & Kegan Paul, Ltd., 1931.

Wallnofer, H. and Von Rottauscher, A. *Chinese Folk Medicine.* New York: Crown Publishers, 1965.

Waltham, C. *I Ching—The Chinese Book of Changes.* New York: Ace Publishing Corp., 1969.

——. *Chuang Tzu—Genius of the Absurd.* New York: Ace Publishing Corp., 1971.

Watson, B. *Chuang Tzu—Basic Writings.* New York: Columbia University Press, 1964.

Weber, M. *The Religion of China.* New York: Tree Press, Macmillan, 1951.

Wei, W. W. *The Tenth Man.* Hong Kong University Press, 1966.

Welch, M. *Taoism—The Parting of the Way.* Boston, Massachusetts: Beacon Press, 1957.

Werner, E. T. C. *A Dictionary of Chinese Mythology.* New York: Julian Press, Inc., 1961.

——. *Myths and Legends of China.* New York: Brentano's, 1922.

Whitlock, H. P. and Ehrman, M. L. *The Story of Jade.* New York: Sheridan House, 1949.

Wilhelm H. *Change: Eight Lectures on the I Ching.* New York: Torch Book, Harper, 1960.

Wilhelm, Richard. *I Ching—Or Book of Changes.* Bollingen Series XIX. Princeton, New Jersey: Princeton University Press, 1950.

—— and C. G. Jung. *The Secret of the Golden Flower.* New York: Harcourt, Brace & World, Inc., 1931.

——. *A Short History of Chinese Civilization.* Translated by J. Joshus. Viking Press, 1929.

Wright, A. F. *Studies In Chinese Thought.* Chicago: University of Chicago Press, 1953.

——. *Confucian Personalities.* Stanford, California: Stanford University Press, 1962.

——. *The Confucian Persuasion.* Stanford, California: Stanford University Press, 1960.

—— and Nivison, D. S. *Confucianism in Action.* Stanford, California: Stanford University Press.

Wu, J. C. H. *Lao Tzu—Tao teh Ching.* Edited by P. K. T. Sih. New York: St. Johns University Press, 1961.

Yang, C. K. *Religion In Chinese Society.* Los Angeles, California: University of California Press, 1961.

Yee, C. *Chinese Calligraphy.* London: Methuen & Co. Ltd., 1938.

Zahorchak, M. G. "Yin and Yang—a Four-Thousand-Year-Old Formula for Long Term Investing." Talk delivered to the Society for the Investigation of Recurring Events of the New York Academy of Sciences. July 17, 1968.

Journals and Articles Appearing in Journals Relating to I Ching

The Academy (an English publication—issue of August 12th—year unknown.)

Affinity of the Ten Stems of the Chinese Cycle with the Akkadian Numerals by A. Terrien De Lacouperie—*The Academy*—Sept. 1, 1883.

The *Athenaeum,* #2862.

Biblioteca Sinica, Henri Cordier, Vol. I coll. 645-647.

Catalogue of Chinese Coins including those in the British Museum, p. viii 7 p. 582.

China Review, 1883 vol. xii (July and August) p. 59-60.

Chinese and Akkadian Affinities by A. Terrien De Lacouperie, *The Academy,* Jan. 20, 1883.

Chinese Mythical Kings and The Babylonian Canon by A. Terrien De Lacouperie, *The Academy,* Oct. 6, 1883.

From Ancient Chaldea and Elam to Early China Vol. V 1891 (B & O.R) Believe this to be the *Biblical and Oriental Review.*

Journal Asiatique, 1887 pp. 155. 1889 p. 164-170 Jan.-Feb. 1891.

Journal of the Royal Asiatic Society, 1884, Vol. XVI, p. 371-372.

The New Accadian, Rev. C. J. Ball. (P.B.A.) 1889-1890.

Notes and Queries on China and Japan, by Rob Swinhoe Vol. I, p. 131, Oct. 1867.

Notes Critiques pour entrer dans l'intélligènce de l' Y-King by P. de Premare, *Bibl. Nat. Fonds. Chinois,* #2720.

Old Babylonian Characters and Their Chinese Derivates by A. Terrien de Lacouperie *(B & O. R.* vol. II) 1888.

Progress of Chinese Linguistic Discovery, *The Times* (England), Apr. 20, 1880.

Zodiac and Cycles of Babylonia and Their Chinese Derivatives by A. Terrien de Lacouperie *The Academy,* October 1880.

Yi King with notes on the 64 Kwa by James Edkins, *China Review,* Vol. 12, p. 77-86 (2nd part), Vol. 12, p. 412-432 (1st. part). 1883-84.

Yi King and Its Appendices, by James Edkins *China Review,* Vol. 14, p. 303-322.

The When of I Ching, a study of the I Ching calendar by K. A. Dhiegh.

Taoist Breathing Charts by Ch'ao-Li Chi, published by Intern'l. I Ching Studies Institute.

T'ai Chi Ch'uan and I Ching or the Book of Changes, by Wen-shan Huang, *Chinese Culture,* Vol. X, #1 March 1969.

Synchronicity and I Ching by Wayne McEvilly in *East-West Philosophy magazine,* Hawaii University Press.

The Sacred Books of China by James Legge (a review by Thos. W. Kingswell) *China Review,* 1882-83.

Relationship of the Persian and Chinese Calendars by Joseph Edkins, *China Review,* 1888 Vol. 16, p. 95-98.

Phallic Worship, Rev. Thos. McClatchie, *China Review,* 1875-76, Vol. 4 #4 p. 257-261.

On Chance and Change in I Ching, Douglas Low (Private publication).

New Time Religion—*New York Times Magazine* Section.

Mathesis—Mathematical Analysis of Qualities by James Churchyard (Private publication).

Letters, by James Edkins in *China Review,* Vol. 17.

Leibniz Introduction and Approach to China, by David E. Mungello, *East-West Philosophy.*

I Ching and Social Crisis by Wei Tat in *Chinese Culture* magazine.

The I Ching, by Wei Tat (a talk at Spiritual summit conference, Calcutta, India, Oct. 22-26, 1968.

The I Ching (the most mysterious book in the world) P. Manly Hall, PRS, 1967.

Geomancers Compass, by De Groot in *Religious Systems of China*, Vol. III, p. 959-982.

Dragon in the Field, by Joseph McCaffree (Private publication).

Divination and Historical Allegorical Sources of I Ching, Joseph McCaffree (Priv. printing).

Did Confucius Study the Book of Changes? by Homer H. Dubs, *T'oung Pas*, Vol. 25, 1928, p. 82-90.

Confucius and the I Ching by Wei Tat, in *Chinese Culture*.

Confucian Cosmogony by Thomas McClatchie, *China Review*, 1875-76, Vol. 4, #2 p. 84-95.

Circulation of Events as Depicted in The Chinese Book of Changes, Richard Wilhelm, Spring 1961.

Sources with Publisher Information Missing

Biographies of Words by Max Muller, p. 116.

Black Heads of Babylonia and Ancient China, A Terrien De Lacouperie, 1892.

Chips of Babylonian and Chinese Palocography, A Terrien De Lacouperie, 1888.

Chinese Researches, by Thomas Fergusson (Part One: Chinese Chronology and Cycles), Shanghai, 1880, 12 mo.

Deluge Tradition and Its Remains in Ancient China (Monograph), by A. Terrien De Lacouperie.

Early History of Chinese Civilization, by A. Terrien De Lacouperie, 1880, p. 25.

Guide to the Tablets in a Temple of Confucius by T. Watters, Shanghai, 1879, 8 vols.

Journeys in North China, A. Williamson, Vol. I, p. 380. 1870.

Kwoh Tze Kien—An Old Chinese University, W. A. P. Martin, 1871, p. 86.

Notes on Chinese Literature, Wylie, p. 24.

The Oldest Book of the Chinese, by A. Terrien De Lacouperie, London, 1892.

On The Astronomy of the Ancient Chinese, J. Chalmers, 1875.

Origin of the Early Chinese Civilization, by A. Terrien De Lacouperie, Ch. viii, p. 141-145.

Prehistoric Antiquities, by O. Schrader, p. 262.

Syllabic Dictionary of the Chinese Language, Dr. Wells Williams, p. 434.

Traite de la Chronologie Chinoise, P. Gaubil, p. 81.

Uranographie Chinoise, C. Schlegel, p. 528.

Books Published in China, Hong Kong, and Taipei

A Commentary on the "I" Study of pre-Chin, Han, and Wei, Chueh Wan L. (An authoritative study of the developmental studies of I Ching by different authors in the last 2000 years.) Published by Students Book Store, Taipei, Taiwan: 1969.

Concerning I, Tai Chun-Yin (an authoritative study of the developmental studies of I Ching, with deep understanding.) Published by Keiming Book Co., Taipei, Taiwan: 1949.

A Comprehensive Bibliography for the Study of I Ching." See, Li Chin-Kang.

"A Comprehensive Explanation of I Ching." See, Wang Shu-Sen.

Fang Tung-Mei, *Reference Books on the Meaning of the "I".* (A supplement to the list of Li Chin-Kang. pp. 167-177, appended to the same "Essays".)

Five Books on I Ching. See, Wang Chin.

A General Explanation of the Ancient Classics-Chou I. (unknown). (Emphasis on the period when the kua were initiated.) Published by Chung Hwa Book Co., Hong Kong: 1968.

Hang Hsin Chy, *A Series Study on I Ching.* (A series of monographs written from the modern point of view on different phases of the *I Ching.*) Published in Canton, China, date unknown, c. 1914.

Heritage of Change: A Background to Chinese Culture and Thinking, Wallace Andrew Sherrill (Taipei, Taiwan: East-West Eclectic Society, 1972).

I Ching—A New Explanation Based on Mathematical Sciences. (A study of *I Ching* in the light of modern mathematical sciences. Recently it led to a great deal of controversy with modern Chinese mathematicians and scientists in Taipei.) Published Shanghai: 1930; now obtainable.

I Ching and the Bible, Chung Chun Fu. (In Chinese with Synoptic Text in English.) Published by Chinese Religious Culture Research Society, Christian, Hong Kong.

I Ching in Plain English, Shih Ta-Fang. Published by Far Eastern Book Co., Section 1, 64 Chung King Road S., Taipei, Taiwan: 1969. (The classical language in the original texts is explained in present-day Mandarin. A good guide.)

Li Chin-Kang, "a comprehensive Bibliography for the Study of I Ching." Lists over 1000 books concerning *I Ching.* The most exhaustive list on the subject. In, *Essays on the Discussion of the I Ching,* Published by Truth, Goodness, and Beauty Book Co., Taipei: 1964 (pp. 147-166).

The Meaning of the Symbols of the Chou I. See Wang Chin.

A New Treatise on I Ching, Yin Ling-Fan. (Concerning the philosophical principles and method of I Ching. It leads to the study of the structure and foibles of the appendices.) Published by Chin Chung Book Store, Taipei, Taiwan: 1969.

On The Reason Of "I," Wu Pien-Li. (A study emphasizing the mathematics of the *I Ching.* It points out the Ideal of Great Harmony as the main theme of this book.) Published by Eastern Publisher, Lane 258, No. 22 Kim Hua St., Taipei, Taiwan: 1966.

On The Secrets Of Chou I, Hsu Shih-Ta. Publisher unknown; date unknown.

Reference Books on the Meaning of the I. See Fang Tung-Mei.

A Series Study on the I Ching. See Hang Hsin Chy.

Simple Explanation of the Meaning of "I," Ho Chin-Chuen. (An orthodox explanation, believing that Confucius is the author of the Ten Wings. No new discovery.) Published by Life Publisher, Kowloon: 1950.

A Special Collection From The Exhibit Of The Diagrams And Symbols Of I Ching. See Yu Tzu-Chai.

Sun Yat-Senism and the Philosophical Thought of Chou I, Chao Chi-Tzu. (A study of this classic from the standpoint of archaeology and philosophy. The political thought of Chou I is compared with that of Sun Yat-Sen.) Published by Lion Book Co.: 1967.

Wang Chin, *The Meaning of the Symbols of the Chou I.* (Written in Chinese calligraphy by the author with annotations.) Published by the author, 312 Min Kang Rd., 3rd Floor, Kowloon, Hong Kong.

Wang Chin, *Five Books On I Ching.* (Consists of a series of books by the ancients, including Sho Kang Chi and Wang Chi Chin Shih; with good explanations.) Published by the author, address same as above: 1965.

Wang Shu-Sen, "A Comprehensive Explanation Of I Ching." (Good for beginners.) Published by the author, Peitao 5, Wen Hua, 4th Route, Taipei, Taiwan: 1969.

Yu Yzu-Chai, *A Special Collection from the Exhibit of the Diagrams and Symbols of the I Ching.* Published by Min Sang Book Co., 70 Hollywood Rd., Hong Kong.

Early Western Investigators Into I Ching

Some twenty or more persons have recently written about or offered translations of *I Ching* into English. The material has, for the most part, been restricted to rephrasing what has quite beautifully been expressed by both James Legge and Richard Wilhelm. What has not been included in the recent writings on *I Ching* is some of the exciting philological and lexicological studies made by Western sinologists of the later eighteenth and the nineteenth centuries. This class of scholastic endeavor is seldom engaged in today. Yet, it is valuable beyond measure. In the various publications listed in the bibliography of journals, the following persons have contributed valuable, exciting or provocative papers on *I Ching*. Often the full name is not (at present) known. I therefore list these contributers mostly by family name. The serious student who will extend his researches and go to these old journals will discover new and even more precious treasures in *I Ching*.

P. Amiot
C. J. Ball
J. Bretschneider
Dr. Bushell
J. Chalmers
Henri Cordier
De Guignes
De Mailla
F. Delitzsch
R. K. Douglas
Du Tartre
J. Edkins
Thomas Fergusson

A. Helfferich (1868)
F. Hommel
F. Huberty James
R. A. Jamieson
J. Klaproth
A. T. de Lacouperie
James Legge
G. W. von Leibnitz
F. Lenormant
W. A. P. Martin (1871)
Martini
Matwanlin
W. F. Mayers

J. H. Plath
Dame U. Pope-Hennessy
P. Premare
P. Regis
A. Remusat
F. von Richthofen
Saint Martin
A. H. Sayce
G. Schlegel
W. Schott
O. Schrader
J. P. Schumacher (1763)
Seyffarth

G. Van der Gabelentz

P. Gaubil (1770)

H. A. Giles

J. Haas

J. Halevy

C. de Harlez

P. Haupt

G. W. F. Hegel

Medhurst

T. McClatchie

Nevmann

J. Oppert

G. Pauthier

M. P. Philastre

T. C. Pinches

O. Piper

Rob Swinhoe

M. Claude Visdelou

A. Waley

T. Watters

Wells Williams

A. Williamson

Wylie

P. A. Zottoli

Below is Appended a Partial List of Contemporary Contributors to the Literature of I Ching in English

Albertson

José Arguelles

Cary F. Baynes

John Blofeld

E. P. Boyle

John Cage

Winberg Chai

Wing-Tsit Chan

Chen Huan Chang

Chung-Yuan Chang

Ch'ao-Li Chi

Louis Culling

Wm. Theo. de Bary

Alfred Douglas

Homer Dubs

Gia-fu Feng

Yu-Lan Fung

Hermann Hesse

Aldous Huxley

Willard Johnson

Carl G. Jung

Young Lee Jung

Kang-Hu Kiang

Kirk, Jerome

Chin Lee

William A. Lessa

Douglas Low

Frank J. MacHovec

Joe McCaffree

Wayne McEvily

Ralph Metzner

Donald W. Mitchel

Joseph Murphy

Joseph Needham

Charles Ponce

C. F. Russell

Jimmei Shimano

R. G. H. Siu

Z. D. Sung

Raymond Van Over

Helen Walker

Clae Waltham

Burton Watson

Helmut Wilhelm

Richard Wilhelm

Kay Wong

Index